The Tourist-Historic City

THE TOURIST-HISTORIC CITY

G. J. Ashworth
and
J. E. Tunbridge

Belhaven Press
(a division of Pinter Publishers)
London and New York.

First published in Great Britain in 1990 by Belhaven Press (a division of Pinter Publishers), 25 Floral Street, London WC2E 9DS and PO Box 197, Irvington, NY 10533

British Library Cataloguing in Publication Data A CIP catalogue for this book is available from the British Library

ISBN 85293 022 5

Library of Congress Cataloging-in-Publication Data
Ashworth, G.J. (Gregory John)
    The tourist-historic city / G.J. Ashworth and J.E. Tunbridge.
       p.   cm.
    Includes bibliographical references and indexes.
    ISBN 1-85293-022-5
    1. Tourist trade. 2. Historic sites. I. Tunbridge, J.E.
  II. Title.
G155.A1A75   1990   90-37103
338.4'791091732--dc20   CIP

Typeset by Selectmove Ltd, London
Printed and bound by Biddles Ltd, Guildford and Kings Lynn

Contents

List of figures

List of plates

List of tables

Preface

A preface should answer the reader's curiosity about how and why a book came to be written.

The origins and background to this book are as diverse as those of its authors. One works in North America; the other in continental Europe. One lives in a seventeenth-century monument, in an historic inner city of a multifunctional provincial market town that is celebrating 950 years of evolution; the other in a contemporary house in a twentieth-century suburb of a planned national capital, founded in the nineteenth century. From early seeds of collaboration at Portsmouth a decade ago, we have been led to the tourist-historic city along substantially different routes. One was led from a concern with conservation of the urban historic environment to its impact upon the city's economy and society; the other from an interest in urban tourism to the resources that attracted visitors and the motives that brought them to cities. Each independently and from different directions came to the realisation, through both their research and teaching, that the city at the end of the twentieth century was increasingly exploiting historicity as a contemporary resource, particularly in response to a growing demand in society for the phenomenon we call the tourist-historic city. We believe that this has already set a course for the city in the twenty-first century.

We do not apologise for a conclusion that raises more new questions than it provides answers. In no sense is this book a last word on this subject from us or indeed, we hope, from others. If we have outlined an approach to the city which provokes others to apply it in different contexts, to modify it in the light of different experience, or even to refute it on the basis of a different logic, then we have achieved our primary purpose.

A collaborative book incurs the strengths and weaknesses of dual production, trading off the advantages of a coverage of areas and topics wider than any individual could hope to achieve, against the difficulties of weaving a seamless garment. We have reconciled our differences of perspective to our mutual profit; we do not claim that no nuances of difference remain and that the garment is entirely seamless, but we do believe it has been worth the weaving.

All books depend on others but the theme of this one has encouraged the use of particularly diverse expertise and a world-wide spread of experience. We have tried to acknowledge adequately the work of others in the text but inevitably we are indebted to many more for a host of stimulating ideas, critical observations and just supportive encouragements whose origins remain unrecognised and in some cases extend back many years to mentors long departed. To those who recognise 'their' contribution, perhaps in an unexpected context, we can only offer our general thanks.

We are grateful to those who by their help made so profitable our expeditions of academic looting and informational pillaging around the world over many years. We are specifically indebted to the following for assistance and source materials which are not otherwise referenced: Ann Breen (Waterfront Center, Washington D.C.), Stephanie Churchill (Historic Savannah Foundation), Gordon Goodwin (formerly of the Planning Office, City of Harare), Rob Haswell (deputy mayor of the City of Pietermaritzburg), A.R. Jones (Pietermaritzburg Publicity Association), Stuart Lazear (City of Ottawa), Felicity McMurray (City of Durban), William Moss (City of Quebec), John Murche (Weekend Australian), Oskar Schubert (former mayor of Rothenburg), Michael Turner (Jerusalem), Evelyn Wakaruk (Parks Canada), Barbara Zydenbos (Sydney Cove Redevelopment Authority) and the staff of the Boston Redevelopment Authority, National Trust for Historic Preservation (Boston), the Boston Preservation Alliance, Office of Culture and Foreign Tourism, Rothenburg, the National Parks service of Boston and Lowell and the Department of Tourism of Martinique.

We would like to single out our colleagues, Yvonne Court (formerly Portsmouth Polytechnic), Patrick de Groote (University of Limburg), Myriam Jansen-Verbeke (University of Nijmegen), Chris Law (University of Salford), Doug Pearce (University of Canterbury), Ray Riley (Portsmouth Polytechnic), Morgan Sant (University of New South Wales), Dietrich Soyez (University of the Saarland), Yu Qingkang (Chinese Academy of Sciences), Geoff Wall (University of Waterloo), Trevor Wills (University of Natal), Sioux Harvey (University of Zimbabwe) and, closer to home, David Fitch, Wayne Adam and John Souter at Carleton, and Theo de Haan and Henk Voogd at Groningen. The cartographic and photo-reproductive craftsmanship of Chris Earl, Alan Pendlington, Eric Runau, Johann Zwart and Theo Smid speaks for itself in the illustrations, and the varied administrative help of Pete Stanley and Elsie Clement was invaluable. Without the sympathetic support of Dave Bennett at Carleton the deadline would never have been met. Finally, the initial encouragement and subsequent patience of Iain Stevenson of Belhaven Press has not passed unappreciated.

An activity even more testing than writing a book is living with someone who is. Angela and Elaine, our companions through many tourist-historic cities, know this more than most.

The most appropriate dedication is to our students, past (at Portsmouth), present (at Ottawa and Groningen) and future; for it is they who have borne the brunt of our teaching on, and relentless field excursions around, so many tourist-historic cities; it is also for them that the book was ultimately written and it is they who have also, albeit often unknowingly, contributed so much to its writing.

December 1989

G.J. Ashworth
J.E. Tunbridge

1 Introduction

The city between two futures

In 1958 Ian Nairn published an impassioned polemic in the architectural press, appropriately entitled *Outrage*, which pilloried contemporary practices of urban development and design, and, striking a chord of popular unease, this tract reached a wide non-professional readership. The simple, impressively illustrated and inevitably overstated case was that the post-war years had witnessed an unprecedented physical change in the urban landscape of Britain. The damage done by wartime destruction had been more than equalled in extent by a ruthless post-war reconstruction. A generation's concentration of effort on the almost overwhelming needs for new housing, new industry and new infrastructure had led to an abrupt break in the centuries-long evolution of the physical fabric of cities. The past and its values had been rejected in favour of a 'brave new world' whose creation threatened to destroy all trace of preceding architectural achievement. This was to be a last warning of impending disaster and a call to a last-stand rescue action of concerned citizens.

Around 30 years later, a number of equally impassioned, popular polemics have appeared issuing equally dire warnings of an imminent catastrophe and calling for popular action before it is too late. Hewison's *The Heritage Industry* (1987) and Lumley's *The Museum Time Machine* (1988), among others on the same campaign, sketch a Britain so obsessed with its past as to be incapable of confronting the problems of the present or challenges of the future. The form of cities has become so preserved as to be largely incapable of change, and they increasingly function as large open-air museums housing a comforting re-creation of a sanitised reassuring past.

Both sets of warnings were drawn from British experience but in each case the British city was seen as only a more advanced case of a wider problem of Western urban societies.

This book occupies the ground between these positions in a number of different ways. In terms of time it explains how within a single generation fears *for* the survival of an urban past could become fear *of* the consequences of its conservation. History has become heritage, heritage has become an urban resource, and this resource supplies a major 'history industry', which shapes not merely the form but the functioning and purpose of the 'commodified' city. Since the principal task is description and explanation of what has occurred in and to cities, this book does not need to begin by either adopting or confronting the assumptions, underlying values or political positions of any of these propagandists. Admittedly, once the consequences of these processes are outlined and the resulting issues thereby emerge from the first part of this book, then it becomes necessary in the second part to pose the questions, 'who has so changed our cities, by which methods and for what reasons?' From here it is a very short step to the question 'what sort of cities therefore do we want?'; when this question is posed, we are back to supporting or rejecting either or both polemical positions.

The dimensions of the tourist-historic city

The focus of this book is encapsulated in the phrase 'the tourist-historic city'.

A fundamental point needs to be made immediately and as unambiguously as possible. This is a book about cities: the two adjectives in the title should not detract from the focus on the noun. This is neither a history of cities nor an account of urban tourism. It is a book about the modern city: the urban situation in the last years of the twentieth century. Both the past and the future are intrinsic characteristics in the modern city: the present is frequently explained in terms of an evolution through time and much of the shape of the future is already apparent in current trends. However the focus remains on the modern city: its nature, functioning, problems, opportunities and management. This is neither an urban historical geography nor a set of predictions for a future to be striven for or to be avoided. Neither Utopia nor Armageddon appear as case studies.

The two adjectives in the book's title can help to set the boundary markers around our chosen terrain.

The term 'historic' does not imply that this is an account of the history of urban development although episodes and aspects of that development are critical determinants in the creation of our modern cities. Still less is this book intended to be a panegyric for old buildings or a plea for their preservation in the fabric of the conserved urban form, although without such passions in others and the success of just such pleading, much of the content of this book would not exist.

Similarly, our use of the term 'tourist' does not mean that there follows an account of the rise of the tourism industry, the 'golden horde', whether this is to be welcomed or feared. This is not a plea for tourism development in cities nor a warning of its consequences, although the tourist is a central actor in the developments related, and the tourism industry is frequently the motive powering such developments.

The heart of our concern is in the conjunction of tourist, historic and city. Of course not all tourism is concerned with historic resources, nor are such resources inevitably or invariably concerned with tourism, and both can be located in rural as well as urban situations. However the justification for this book rests upon three axioms, namely that tourism in its various forms has played, and continues to exercise, a critical role in the development of such resources, while conversely that historical resources form an equally critical part of a growing tourism industry and that the symbiosis of the two has become a major activity of cities and a major force in the design and structure of the modern city.

The demarcation of the tourist-historic city can be made clearer not only by means of the disclaimers above but more positively through a series of tensions between a number of its dimensions that will form the leitmotifs through much of what follows. The tourist-historic city is, or can be viewed as:

1.   both a form and a function. It is a particular sort of urban morphology but also, and increasingly, an urban activity.
2.   both a particular type of city and a specialised morphological–functional region within a city.
3.   both a particular use of history as a tourism resource and a use of tourism as a means of supporting the maintenance of the artefacts of the past and justifying attention to the historicity of cities.

The account of the tourist-historic city that follows is intended at least initially to be:

1.   descriptive of what has occurred and is occurring rather than prescriptive of what should, or should not, occur.
2.   an account of what is happening rather than a manual of instructions about how to make it happen.
3.   an account of a *phenomenon of cities in general* rather than of specific special areas within a particular category of cities: the book addresses urban geography as a whole.
4.   a monitoring and explanation of similarities and differences between cities, countries and continents, rather than a search for a recommended 'best practice' of universal application to cities in all circumstances.

All of these statements require extensive definition, exemplification and justification and the intentions held at the outset will be more difficult to sustain and necessarily modified in the course of this amplification.

Conceptual scope and structure

There can be few introductions that do not claim that the subject to be embarked upon is an intellectual *terra incognita*, in need of delimiting and mapping. This is no exception, but the authors are under no illusion that most of the originality lies in the ordering of existing knowledge into new juxtapositions, so that new perspectives are possible.

The fields of tourism development, urban conservation and urban development have each generated substantial, and rapidly growing, literatures which have been drawn upon extensively wherever relevant. A fundamental problem, however, is that each of these bodies of knowledge and accumulated experience has been created without reference to the others. Urban conservation had developed from the investigative and custodial concerns and skills of historians, archaeologists and architects, working on the basis of professional norms, evaluated according to some criteria of public interest, usually within collectively responsible organisations. Tourism on the other hand is rooted in the techniques and justifications of commercial management, even when such management is undertaken by public organisations, and its academic study has adopted this industrial bias by concentrating upon attempts to isolate, and thus define and delimit, its demand and supply components. If conservation has had difficulty shifting its focus of attention from the building to the wider impacts of its preservation, so tourism has faced a similar difficulty in relating the tourist, the tourism facility and the tourism industry to the multimotivated consumer of the multi-used product in the multifunctional city. Thus studies of specifically urban conservation and urban tourism have usually involved little more than the acknowledgement that building preservation or tourism activities can occur in cities, rather than investigations of the specific urban dimension in either tourism or conservation.

Even the enormous quantity of literature produced by the related disciplines of urban geography, urban planning and development, which might fulfil a co-ordinating role in this respect, has tended to neglect the tourism function of cities, as either so ubiquitous to all cities as to be almost invisible and thus unworthy of attention, or conversely so important within a few specialised resorts as to be discounted as atypical.

Thus we are faced with more or less self-contained groups of specialists, each of which has only a partial view of our central topic, and each of which has evolved its own working practices and terminology, sets of concepts and methods of analysis, institutional allegiances and professional justifications. The most fundamental task, therefore, has been to find ways of bridging these gaps so as to confront the activity of tourism, with the conservational philosophy of management, within the city, which is itself more than a stage upon which these processes occur and actively contributes a distinctly urban set of characteristics, active variables and management objectives and constraints to the tourist-historic city.

The book is divided into two parts. The first attempts to define and explain the composite concept of the tourist-historic city, and to outline the processes which have created and maintain it, while the second concentrates on the planning and management of such cities. The first necessarily therefore focuses upon general trends and processes and seeks to develop general descriptive and explanatory models, while the second pays more attention to the details of the creation of particular tourist-historic cities.

The subject of the book does not in fact appear until Chapter 4, because an understanding of the composite concept is dependent upon a prior understanding of its two components. The task of Chapter 2, therefore, is to chronicle and explain the rise of the urban conservation movement as a climate of informed opinion and as a set of legislative and planning instruments, and to trace the processes through which aspects of the past have become 'heritage'. The end product is the 'historic city', which is paralleled in Chapter 3 by a definition of the concept of the 'tourist city' and an account of its development. Only then is it possible to combine the two to produce the 'tourist-historic city'. This 'city' does not exist in isolation but in a series of associations, whether functional or spatial, with other urban activities, thus the tourist-historic city must be occupied and populated by its uses and users in Chapter 5.

The focus on planning and management in the second part of the book requires a taxonomy of tourist-historic cities. This can be attempted using a number of different dimensions. Chapter 6 examines the types of planning and management, broadly defined, found in practice, in terms of organisational structures, objectives, available instruments and management philosophies. The application of a variety of these techniques and practices of intervention follows in the next three chapters. Chapter 7 considers those cases where either the historic or the tourist elements are so relatively important as to be categorised as 'monofunctional' historic 'gems' or tourist resorts. Chapters 8 and 9 both survey examples of multifunctional cities, where tourist-historic elements coexist with other urban functions. In both the major world metropolises of Chapter 8 and the medium-sized multifunctional cities of Chapter 9, the role of tourist-historic elements in urban revitalisation programmes will receive particular attention in various spatial and organisational contexts.

Global scope and selection

No claim to a comprehensive coverage of the history of urban development has been made, but a similar claim to global cover is asserted, in the sense that the tourist-historic city is approached as a world-wide phenomenon needing general, universally applicable, explanation. There are thus no regional or continental qualifiers in the title: the book is not intended to be a study of the West European, or North American, city in particular. This intention is modified by the content in which large parts of the world are cursorily treated, while others receive lavish attention as sources of examples and illustration of general points. In part this reflects the accident of an uneven distribution of world knowledge that the authors share with most of the academic world. There is in addition, however, the justification that the tourist-historic city as conceived and developed was principally if not a European then a Western phenomenon, and although it has had an increasing significance in other parts of the world, its study is likely to be rooted in the experiences of Europe, and those parts of the world where European influence, whether through settlement, colonial government or, more recently, tourism demands and investments, has been most marked. Therefore the trends and conclusions investigated in the cities of Europe, the Eastern Mediterranean, North America, the Caribbean, Australia and Southern Africa are intended, and likely to have, a global relevance.

The selection of particular illustrative cases from within these areas of the world was influenced by two convictions: first that detailed studies in depth of a limited number of cities would be more revealing than superficial reference to a large number, and secondly that long-term, firsthand experience was needed to supplement secondary information if reliable comparable conclusions on what was occurring were to be drawn. These intentions, which would not always be fulfilled, result necessarily in some repetition of examples in different illustrative contexts.

Several more specific geographical constraints need to be clarified. First, little particular reference is made to many of the best known tourist-historic cities. Cities like Florence, York and Salzburg are implicitly rather than explicitly present. Others such as Norwich or Quebec are discussed at length because in the authors' experience they manifest important principles of wider relevance. We reiterate that our primary concern is to alert the reader to a much more comprehensive urban phenomenon in which the famous gems are only glamorous centre-pieces and stimulating catalysts.

Secondly, we make limited reference to the global giants of tourism, such as London, Rome or Paris, where tourist-historic resources make a major contribution to *national* economies. These cities are the extreme manifestations of the significance of our theme. They cannot, however, be comprehensively addressed in this book but will be referred to where they illustrate particular more widely applicable dimensions of the tourist-historic city.

Thirdly, the socialist world receives little explicit attention despite the impressive historic conservation and restoration of cities such as Leningrad, Warsaw and Prague. The spatial organisation of socialist cities has hitherto followed quite different principles and they have not as yet been exposed to the full force of free-market tourism. Nevertheless, the economic and political liberalisation, evident during the late 1980s, has made it likely that the cities of Eastern Europe and the Soviet Union will increasingly be regarded as a variant in detail of the more general models we shall be discussing.

Finally, although the less developed world is discussed, space does not permit justice to be done to the tantalising urban diversity it contains. Cases drawn primarily from Southern Africa and the Caribbean broach questions of much wider significance, especially the various dilemmas of whose heritage is, or should be, preserved, and promoted to whom, in post-colonial and other culturally pluralist societies. It is our intent to raise these issues tentatively and thereby place them firmly on the agenda for future studies of the tourist-historic city. To this future agenda, and the interdisciplinary perspectives that it requires, the substance of this book as a whole is, of course, more generally dedicated.

2 The historic city

The 'historic city' is a concept that must be defined and delineated. The raw material of which it is composed is principally the preserved urban forms that have survived in the contemporary city. The concept has been endowed with different meanings at different spatial scales and contains elements derived from the intrinsic characteristics of the built environment but also the values and attitudes held about it and the planning and management designations ascribed to it. This chapter, therefore, must first relate the history of concern about the preservation of aspects of the past urban-built environment. This account provides an explanation of how various public and private initiatives, for a variety of motives, have led to the current legislation and management practice and to current choices about what is to be preserved. The following step is to examine how the historic city concept is formed and how it can be delineated in actual cities. The progression in the analysis is from a focus on the preservation of artefacts, through a concern for the conservation of areas and the development of conservational philosophies of urban management, to finally a functional view of commodified cities as marketable heritage. Thus the historic city originates from architectural forms and morphological patterns, as well as the historic associations they contain, but ultimately is resolved in economic and social priorities.

The rise of the urban conservation movement

From amateur enthusiasm to official policies

Instances can be found in many different countries, through much of recorded history, of governments or individuals intervening to prevent the destruction of old buildings because of their historic or symbolic value. Nevertheless, conservation as an officially sponsored and organised systematic attempt to preserve past built environments is a recent phenomenon, as is the public consensus that motivates it. The architects and builders who created most of the structures, whose antiquity is now valued, had themselves few qualms about obliterating the work of their predecessors. It is ironic that current conservation planning controls would have frustrated the creation of most of the historic buildings they now protect.

The renaissance of the sixteenth century had rediscovered the Mediterranean Classical world and the eighteenth-century Enlightenment made it fashionable, among the better educated classes in Northern Europe, to value, visit and support the preservation of its surviving architectural relics. It is notable for the focus of this book that the origins of both modern conservation and an important aspect of modern tourism were closely linked through the concern for classical monuments and the 'Grand Tour'. Many themes that will persistently recur are discernable from these beginnings. Interest in the artefacts of the past was the preoccupation of a small, but influential, group who were motivated by a sufficiently crusading vision to allow this aspect of planning to be labelled a 'movement', whose driving force was the enthusiasm of amateurs rather than the technical expertise of professionals. There was from the beginning a spatial discrepancy between a dominantly North European demand and a largely South European supply, resulting in both an early internationalisation of conservation and a consequent flow of historic-city tourists. Finally there was an enormous selectivity about what could be considered worth preserving, explicable only in terms of shifts in fashionable tastes. The Enlightenment dismissed the products of the medieval world as 'gothic', leaving them to be reinstated by the 'romanticism' of the nineteenth century.

The history of this conservation movement through much of the eighteenth and nineteenth centuries is dominantly a chronicle of artistic, literary, historical and scientific societies in such centres as London, Berlin and Paris. Composed of enthusiastic individuals that a later age would label a 'passionate minority', with the occasional support of royal patronage, these societies stimulated an interest in antiquity as such, which led to the shaping of a new attitude towards the relics of the past. Conservation of the built environment represented one facet of the wider conservation ethic. The nostalgic romanticism for a vanished or fast receding rustic idyll, a nineteenth-century reaction to rapid urbanisation and industrialisation, led to parallel pressures for the conservation of natural environments and rural landscapes. The establishment of the National Parks movement in the United States, Australia and Canada, and, in 1895, the National Trust in Britain, all of which subsequently acquired responsibilities also in the built environment, were symptoms of this concern.

The period was punctuated by occasional pieces of protective legislation, such as those of the Napoleonic regimes in Belgium (1809), and the Netherlands (1814), which were usually neither enforced nor enforceable. The ruling consensus in most countries endorsed Dutch Prime Minister Thorbeke's statement in the middle of the nineteenth century that 'art is not the business of government', and such matters should be left to the initiative and charity of private organisations and individuals.

Strong urban growth in much of Europe during the second half of the nineteenth century, including the dismantling of town walls, created, in many cities for the first time, a demolition versus conservation dilemma (Hall, 1986).

A first step in government involvement was the establishment, often in reaction to pressure from the amateur societies, of an office of the national administration charged with creating an inventory of national historical architectural resources. Revolutionary France had such a 'Commission for Art and Monuments' as early as 1790 although serious inventorisation did not begin until 1889. Belgium established a 'Committee for Art and Monuments' in 1835 and the Netherlands formed a department for the care of monuments (later *Rijkscommissie voor het Monumentenzorg*) in 1875. The titles and responsibilities of such departments changed frequently throughout the nineteenth century. Such offices were usually small, and lacked both financial resources and legal powers to initiate much restoration on their own account, or even to prevent demolition. They were, however, in a position to draw up lists, which in turn needs the establishment of criteria for allocating the status of 'monument', and thus to initiate some national inspection system. The task was clearly defined, namely the protection of buildings from harm, the cost to the public purse was small and the motivation was dominantly aesthetic and historicist.

It is a short logical step from the passive recording of what exists and the establishment of standards, to active intervention to protect such monuments and to impose such standards. Although both logical and inevitable – why create a list if inclusion on it has no effect on the building concerned? – there was a long gap in time, a century in some countries, before such enabling legislation was enacted.

The inventories themselves often took 30 years to be drawn up. In the Netherlands the first national list was 'complete' in 1908, and contemporary opinion thought in terms of the compiling of a once-for ever 'complete' list. More fundamentally the civil servants' interest in intervention, prompted by the pressure groups, was opposed by a strongly held principle of the liberal state, namely that of individual property rights. Some intellectuals may have endorsed Victor Hugo's observation that 'the use of a monument is the owner's but the beauty belongs to us all' (Naeyer, 1975); few of the property-owning classes, however, would have been prepared to restrict their 'use' if it conflicted with such 'beauty'. It was just not acceptable either in terms of law or popular consensus to interfere in an owner's use of property to the extent that effective conservation demanded, until well into the post-Second World War period when attitudes towards the relative roles of the state and the individual had drastically altered. Even in the Netherlands, where the acceptability of modifications of land ownership rights in the public interest was more widespread than in most countries, attempts to introduce a comprehensive Monument Conservation Act failed in 1910, 1921 and 1955. Effective monument preservation had to wait until a more general land-use planning was politically acceptable. Resistance on these grounds to the use of general planning controls for conservation continued longer in North America than in most countries of Western Europe; there such use had to await state and provincial enabling legislation largely in the 1970s, although specific monument preservation was undertaken earlier through federal national parks agencies.

Many countries had enacted some legislation in the course of the first half of the twentieth century, conferring some protection on the highest grades of monuments which, if not preventing damage, at least made it a more bureaucratically involved procedure. In the UK, for example, the prompting from, amongst others, Morris' Society for the Protection of Ancient Monuments, led to the Ancient Monuments Act of 1882 which initiated a listing and protection procedure, although specifically excluding either churches or occupied houses. The French 1913 Law on Historic Monuments even included a compulsory purchase option (Sutcliffe, 1970). Belgium's 1931 Act for the Protection of Landscapes and Monuments, for example, could be and frequently was circumvented by determined developers, but it did demarcate clearly the claims and responsibilities of the state in this field; it just lacked the powers to enforce them. In most countries much depended upon interpretations, and much could be achieved if local opinion was favourable. Conversely, if local opinion was not supportive little could be achieved despite the existence of national legislation; Italy's 1939 Act, for example, was rarely implemented.

The role of amateur enthusiasm in creating a climate of opinion that makes legislation possible has been equally important in North America, but has generally occurred later; here the urban conservation movement is essentially a twentieth-century phenomenon and in particular has exerted a substantial influence on planning only in the last 20 years. In the United States, where individual freedom to exercise property rights is enshrined in both the constitution and national attitudes, the City of Charleston was able in 1931 to enact the country's first Historic Area Zoning Ordinance covering 130 acres of the central area (see Chapter 9). Successful efforts by voluntary philanthropic organisations, as in Charleston or in Williamsburg, Virginia (see Chapter 7), were the exception before the Second World War; from these beginnings, however, over 500 historic districts had been created in the USA by the 1980s (Tournier, 1980).

The creation of the US National Trust for Historic Preservation in 1949 (Hosmer, 1981) provided a unified national voice which instigated various urban initiatives, such as the 'Main Street' programme, to assist small communities to revitalise historic central areas. Similarly in Canada, the Heritage Canada Foundation was founded in 1973, with federal seed funding, as a national pressure group, in response to unease about rapid urban change; its initiatives have largely mirrored those of its southern counterpart. Both of these organisations are accepted as national co-ordinators by loose confederations of state/provincial and local voluntary conservation organisations, some older than the national 'head office'; there are also numerous state/provincial conservation organisations funded by their respective jurisdictions. The national organisations act as clearing-houses for evolving conservation policy, and are usually the instigators of a developing conservation philosophy which, by design, fosters supportive opinion and influences relevant public policy; this influence has become the more effective as they have mastered the techniques of political lobbying, often in coalition with other interests over specific issues. The evolution of the 'area conservation policy' discussed below, and the promotion of cultural tourism in the North American city, cannot be understood without reference to the voluntary conservation sector.

In the New World context generally (i.e. the areas of overseas European settlement), centennial milestones play a disproportionate role in fostering a receptive climate of public opinion for conservation. The 1976 bicentennial in the USA served this purpose, notably with respect to regenerating interest in urban waterfront revitalisation (Lowenthal, 1977; Newcomb, 1983). The 1967 Canadian centennial and the 1988 bicentennial of Australian white settlement are even more fundamental landmarks in the establishment of national cultural, thus necessarily historical, identity. The celebration of centennials in individual cities has proved a particular boost to the promotion of the tourist-historic city and thus of conservation; noteworthy examples are Victoria (British Columbia) where the Centennial Square project was begun in 1962, Vancouver's 1986 'Expo'-related activities, and Johannesburg's 1986 replica development of its original frontier town.

The establishment of national legislative frameworks

The degree of similarity among the various legislative measures imple-mented during the 1960s and 1970s by different countries in Europe, and even beyond, is notable. It is another symptom of the intrinsic international element in the conservation of the built environment that this aspect of planning, in particular, should result in such broadly similar pieces of legislation, designed to resolve similarly defined problems, even in countries where other planning traditions and practices were markedly different. A country-by-country description of this legislation would be unnecessarily repetitive (see Kain, 1981; Dale, 1982). The most significant difference is in the importance placed on different levels in the hierarchy of spatial planning authorities, which generally reflects deep-seated national traditions in the balance of central and local powers. These range from the French centralised tradition where the selection of conserved buildings and areas, and what can be termed 'stimulational leadership', was largely undertaken by a central Ministry of Culture (Kain, 1975); through the delegation of both legislation and implementation to the regional level in West Germany (*Land*), Austria (*Land*), Belgium (*Cultuurgemeenschap*) and Switzerland (*Canton*); to the British reliance upon local initiatives and implementation of the national legislation.

In the New World jurisdiction decentralisation is typically carried further still, as a result of federal government structures in which land-use and related issues are generally controlled by the second tier of government, the states of the United States and Australia and provinces of Canada. Thus conservation legislation primarily emanates from the state/province level; but the pattern of government influence is complicated by federal initiatives such as national inventorisation, voluntary funding programmes and other incentives. In addition, the federally run National Parks Services of the USA and Canada exert absolute control over their extensive land holdings, including urban parks, sites, canals and other features, and they exert a wider influence both statutory and advisory.

Despite these differences, a number of common strands can be detected running through the legislation. It is worth stressing immediately however, that the most notable aspect of this pile of legislation is that it occurred at all. It involved the acceptance of both a major role for the collective sector in general, and the assumption of a leading role for national governments in particular, in establishing a single framework for inventorisation, protection, maintenance and rehabilitation. The assumption of this hegemony occurred in a field of urban affairs with a long tradition of private initiatives and local civic, rather than national, concern. It occurred in addition not only in the East European republics and China (McQuillan, 1985), where centralised planning was the norm, but also in the democracies of Western and Southern Europe and North America. It included not only those countries with a social democratic interventionist tradition such as in Scandinavia (Skovgaard, 1979) and the Netherlands (Nelissen, 1975), but also those with a strong tradition of private property rights, such as Belgium. It even included those with little experience from elsewhere in their planning systems of stringent controls over individual freedoms in favour of collective social goals, such as Portugal, Ireland, Turkey and the United States.

The similarity in the timing, as well as in the content, of the key pieces of national legislation is remarkable. Within just over a decade very similar administrative structures and executive measures were established in countries with otherwise distinctly different traditions of planning (Burtenshaw *et al.*, 1981). The degree of congruence between for example the Dutch *Monumentenwet* 1961, French *Loi Malraux* 1962, British Civic Amenities Act 1967, Italian Urban Planning Act 1967 and even Turkish Monument and Historic Buildings Act of 1973 suggests both the same continent-wide reaction and also an active interchange of ideas amongst those framing the legislation.

Significantly the US National Historic Preservation Act (1966) which, *inter alia*, provided federal funding for the states and the National Trust, dates from the same period (Datel, 1985).

In most countries the national legislation was both a consolidation and continuation of previous official involvement as well as the introduction of two new elements. The existing national inventorisation systems were reorganised, enlarged and often renamed and the proportion of the national financial contribution to the costs of renovation increased. The two new elements were the shift in emphasis from the individual building to ensembles and areas, and the clearly consequent development of conservation as a general philosophy of urban planning rather than a special reaction to exceptional cases.

The broadening of the definition of monument led to a rapid inflation of the monument lists with newer, smaller and less spectacular examples. There has been a long-standing widespread tendency for the chronological criteria to creep forward: Britain's 1882 Act, for example, was framed initially for prehistoric artefacts; protection was extended in 1900 up to the arbitrary date of 1714, and under successive pressure from the Georgian Society (founded 1937) and Victorian Society (founded 1958) to buildings from well into the twentieth century (Kain, 1984). There has even been some national competition detectable, with the strength of national conviction being measured by the number of protected buildings (Vlaeminck, 1987). Such inflation in turn demanded a scaling of the qualitative merit of the building and thus its level of entitlement to protection and subsidy. This could be as in Britain a simple numerical grade or, as in the Netherlands, the introduction of the distinction between a *monument* whose essential importance was intrinsic and a *beeldbepalend pand* ('streetscape-determining building') whose significance lay in its contribution to the wider scene.

The idea of considering the broader morphological context in which a building was set, and seeking to protect both building and setting, was not new: the French had some protection for the *champs de visibilité*, 100m around major monuments, since 1913, and this was extended to a *zone protégé* of 500m in 1962 (Moindrot, 1984). The stress on areas as the object to be preserved, however, was new. The terminology of their consequent designation, whether *secteurs sauvegardes, conservation areas, heritage areas* or *beschermde stadsgezichten* (conserved urban scene) differs, but the evolution of the idea has even been traced in China (McQuillan, 1985). This stress on area conservation *per se* was closely related to the novel concept that vernacular heritage – the homes and workplaces of the ordinary people and all that they imply for cultural identity – was as worthy of conservation as the heritage of the social élite which major monuments frequently reflect.

The adoption of the historical townscape in place of the monument brought the town planner to centre stage in place of the architect and art historian. The designated areas were assessed in terms of the contribution to the townscape of buildings, streets and spaces, as an ensemble regardless of their individual merit. From this area 'façadism' (Slater and Shaw, 1988), it is a short and necessary step, through area conservation, to local land-use planning. If the townscape or cadastral unit as a whole is the object of concern then this has implications for the functioning of such areas which were not so obvious when monuments could be treated as isolated islands. Current and future land-uses, traffic circulation and not least the demographic and social composition in such areas become involved in conservation issues.

This can be viewed as either the introduction of planning into conservation, or more broadly the introduction of conservation into urban planning (Anderson, 1987). Most countries legally required the devising of a local land-use plan for conserved areas. One of the most stringent, at least in theory, is the Dutch *bestemmingsplan* ('ultimate land-use plan'), which is a mixture of permitted morphological and land-use characteristics, including building heights, plot densities and types of permissible use at the scale of the individual building block.

No longer is it sufficient to preserve monuments; areas must be planned for conservation (in the germanic languages the clear distinction between the process of *Denkmalschutz* or *Monumentenzorg* and *Stadtsbewahrung* or *Stadsbescherming*). The shift in terminology reflecting a real shift in working practices and philosophies of urban management. In Burke's (1976) well-known phrase, conservation is 'preserving purposefully', which introduces function to the conservation process. This change of emphasis, together with the broadening of the definitions of what was to be conserved, led to the conservation of larger and larger proportions of more and more towns, until it became exceptional, in most Western European countries, for a town not to have most of at least its central area under some form of conservational designation. Such planning therefore became not so much a special sort of planning reserved for a few unique instances in a special category of cities, but a way of planning for cities in general. There is a recognition of the continuity of the built environment and the endeavour to 'manage the rate of change' (Ford, 1978). This also implies in practical terms that 'we must accept not only that the measurement is a continuing process but also that the basis of control will have to be varied' (Ward, 1968). There is thus a new permanent and general form of urban management discernable in Western Europe. This has yet to be attained in North America, although the progression from area conservation to more general management of the built environment is the well publicised objective of leading voices in the conservation movement (Williams *et al.*, 1983). Given the high degree of local government autonomy typical of North America, however, the attainment of this objective is sought through social consensus rather than through state/provincial legislation.

The operation of the legislation

The legislation of the period created the legal and executive framework for the implementation of conservation policies in those countries over the past 20 years or so. The experience of such implementation led to the development of a body of interpretive practice as a result of confrontation with practical difficulties. The main problem, aside from the inevitable local development conflicts, has always been that of access to financial resources commensurate with the responsibilities imposed by the Acts. This situation is neither unique to this facet of public planning nor particularly new, although central government budgetary policies in some North-west European countries exacerbated it in the 1980s. The financing problem has, moreover, a number of aspects peculiar to conservation planning.

The conferring of statutory protection upon buildings or areas, as allowed and implicitly encouraged by the legislation, incurs in itself no direct public costs. Even the implied responsibility for public investment in those parts of conservation areas owned by public agencies, and expenditures on common spaces and associated street furniture, may not be unduly onerous. The problem is that the conferring of such status contains an open-ended permanent commitment to the maintenance, renovation and rehabilitation of the area as a whole. The result has frequently been an overambitious designation of areas within which little in practice can be done, and even if local policies are successful in renovating large areas this very success creates a future financial commitment for maintenance.

Almost all the legislation includes assumptions about an active role for private investment. Governments may list and designate, while local planning authorities may express intent through local plans and symbolic public investments, but ultimately most financing for the renovation of individual buildings is assumed to come from private sources. Mixed public–private development organisations were one solution, used especially in France, and a reliance on investment from individual building owners became more pronounced as the wider definition of conservation areas led to the inclusion of larger numbers of domestic buildings. This in turn created two problems. First it made the implementation of public policies almost totally dependent upon the economic behaviour of individual owners and, however generous the subsidies on offer, the pace of renovation (the *reconquête progressive* described by Roussel, 1987, in Nancy), and the selection of areas in which it will occur, rely upon the take-up rate of subsidies, which in turn is controlled as much by the prevailing housing and financial markets as by public policy. Secondly, private investment, whether by individual householders or companies, was necessarily motivated by expectations of profit, which in turn often led to unexpected or, from the collective viewpoint, undesirable demographic or social changes. Such 'speculative' behaviour might be deplored by public authorities on social grounds but was actually needed if the required private investment was to be obtained. In North America acceptance of the existence of a profit motive has been fundamental to most conservation activity; government and voluntary sector policy has concentrated on stimulating private investment through partnerships, key infrastructural investments and financial incentives, such as tax concessions.

The legislation of the 1960s and 1970s was enacted during a period of steady economic growth in most countries, and it was reasonable to assume that the task of conservation planners was to control and channel the various competing demands for space in the city. It has generally proved in practice far easier for planners to prevent an undesirable use occupying a conserved building or area than to attract a desirable one. Very little attention was given, especially in Europe, to the problem of positively stimulating the location of desirable users of the increasing quantity of conserved space, especially if the overall demands for space in the city slackened off. In North America, on the other hand, the newly perceived heritage resource is generally in short supply and the planning problem typically becomes that of restraining over-commercialisation, after active encouragement of the profit motive.

Finally, the balance of responsibilities between the different levels in the planning hierarchy shifted in the course of 20 years' practical experience. In general a trend towards greater local responsibility for the selection and development of conservation areas can be detected, even in countries such as France where central governments had played a leading role. In Belgium the regional communities (*Cultuurgemeenschapen*) assumed many of the previous functions of the national government after 1972, but most often, as in the UK, it was the cities that increasingly took more responsibility. This was in part a consequence of the continuing success of the conservation movement in being accepted at the local level by municipal authorities and including more buildings of local, rather than national, significance. It was also in some countries, such as the Netherlands (Kamerling, 1987), a thinly disguised economy measure, and extension of a political ideology committed to reducing the role of central governments in favour of local and private initiatives. In North America decentralisation has been the norm as a result of the strong tradition of local autonomy. The most relevant higher level is the state or provincial government, and even in Canada, where provinces hold ultimate power over land-use, the leading province, Ontario, leaves compliance with the Ontario Heritage Act provisions primarily to local initiative (Ministry of Citizenship and Culture, Ontario, 1987). A consequence of decentralisation is a measure of destandardisation, which in turn leads to large differences between cities in the amount, and direction, of the conservation effort. Some of the implications of this for users of the historic city will be considered later in this chapter.

Thus 20 years' experience in operating the national legislation resulted in distinct changes in emphasis within the framework. It is significant that despite many of the difficulties, mentioned above, that emerged from practice, there is little call in most countries for drastic revision of the fundamental legislation. There is a realisation that the short-term future at least rests with decentralised, destandardised and largely *ad hoc* planning and management at the local scale rather than the more Olympian visions that motivated central government actions in the 1960s and 1970s. It is clear that there was an idea implicit in the legislation that the urban architectural heritage existed in a fixed quantity and that the task of governments was to define it against some abstract norms, locate it and preserve it. Practice has demonstrated that this was a misconception and no such immutable quantity exists. The conservation movement in that sense creates what it wishes to conserve and the more successful the movement, the more is created to preserve. Designation of protected status proved to be the beginning, not the culmination, of public responsibility as the planning implications of conservation became evident. Thus local urban management practice has assumed a greater importance than centralised criteria and inventories stemming from national legislation.

The internationalisation of urban conservation

The above brief account of the history of the urban conservation movement contains a strong element of internationalism, expressed through tourism and through the concerns of enlightened opinion which developed the concept of a common international architectural heritage. Architecture has the advantages of being on free, permanent display and needing no linguistic translation. It is thus understandable that formal institutional recognition of the international dimension often predates national legislation. An international congress of professional architects was held in Athens as early as 1931 on the topic of monument conservation. The private associations of enthusiasts had established a continental forum, *Europa Nostra* (under the auspices of the Council of Europe), in 1963. Governmental international agencies such as UNESCO were similarly active, summoning a world conference, appropriately in Venice, in 1964.

It was however the catastrophic floods of 1966 in Venice and Florence that galvanised international public opinion by their revelation of the vulnerability of this international heritage. The result was a flow of funds and concern. UNESCO's declaration that 'Venice is a moral obligation on the international community' was answered by a wave of aid agencies whose very names ('Save Venice', 'Venice in Peril', 'Venezia Nostra', 'Arbeitskreis Venedig', 'Comité pour la Sauvegarde de Venice') demonstrate the depth and breadth of international concern. A series of international conferences were held in this crusading spirit between 1971 and 1976 at Split, Edinburgh, Budapest, Krems and Amsterdam and the Council of Europe declared 1975 'European Architectural Heritage Year'.

Events since 1966 have demonstrated both the strengths and inherent weaknesses of the international movement. An international community of concern proved to be an effective medium for the pooling of technical skills and expert personnel, a method of transferring funds and a useful means of putting pressure upon countries lagging in their development of national policies. The Council of Europe's promotion of 'best practice' examples, such as their 58 'town schemes' (Kain, 1981), as a means of 'rounding-up' is typical. International action has been at its most effective in reaction to a clearly recognised and preferably spectacular crisis, such as UNESCO's emergency 'operations' of which the 'rescue' of Abu Simbel was among the best publicised. The Council of Europe has pleaded that 'European conservation policies have only emerged when the problem has reached a crisis' (Matthew *et al.*, 1972, p.13). Hopes that 'there should exist a European list of those sites and monuments which deserve, from a European point of view, full preservation, full rehabilitation, through European means and with European money' (Matthew *et al.*, 1972, p.14) are a long way from being fulfilled.

If Venice illustrates the strength of international feeling in reaction to a threat to international heritage, it also made evident its limits. The flow of international sympathy, money and volunteers can only be effective within the framework of national and local plans. International efforts to 'Save Venice' could renovate individual buildings but could do little to remove the threats to the lagoon city as a whole (Fay and Knightly, 1976). This can only be done by the governments of Italy, the Veneto region and the commune of Venice. If the will or the ability does not exist then the inviolable sovereignty of the nation-state imposes distinct limits on the effective meaning of the concept of an international architectural heritage. At the international level there is no dilemma: Venice is heritage that must be preserved by limiting the atmospheric pollution from the neighbouring petrochemical complex at Marghera/Mestre and controlling the water level in the lagoon. At the national and local levels Venice is also a place to live and work that needs to remain open to shipping and attractive to industrial enterprise. It is not surprising therefore that a combination of administrative and political obfuscation and confusion resulting from the different interests of the four levels of government (national, regional, provincial and commune) and various political parties delayed the creation of an agreed plan to counteract the fundamental causes of the threats to the city.

The difficulties and frustrations of bringing international concern to bear upon Italian cities are multiplied when the cultural gap between donor and recipient is greater. It is dangerous to allow the assumptions and experience of the conservation 'front runners' in Western Europe and North America to determine urban conservational practice in societies with quite different attitudes towards the built environment (Zetter, 1982). There always was a hint of cultural colonialism in the Grand Tour, as there can be in modern historic-city tourism, and the limits of international conservational concern may in practice be drawn by their concordance with local priorities. Some of the implications of this will be considered later.

The consequences of success

The story that began with small groups of amateur enthusiasts culminates with large-scale international efforts supported by major international organisations. A rearguard action to save some of the most important urban monuments from imminent destruction has become a planning designation for large areas of the city. A reaction to the chance survival from the past of a few special cities, such as Florence or Bath, is now an all-pervading philosophy of urban management also relevant in Sheffield or Duisburg.

The obsession of a few eccentrics has become a popular consensus and part of 'the collective psyche' (Lowenthal, 1985). The objects of history are now part of popular entertainment. The Council of Europe has viewed urban conservation as an integral part of broader cultural programmes (Mennell, 1976) and thus part of what it regards as increasingly 'popular' culture. The implications of this to tourism are discussed later but it is noteworthy here that the concerns of the 'passionate minority' are now also those of many, if not a majority, of citizens in many countries. In Britain, for example, many impressive figures for visits to historic sites were produced in the 1970s (such as more than 20 million annual visits to historic cathedrals; 15 million to the ancient monuments of the Department of the Environment: Binney and Hanna, 1978), but the important point was that these figures, and those for the membership of national and local associations and trusts, grew between two and fivefold during the decade. A national survey in France (Busson and Evrard, 1987) revealed that one-third of the total population visited museums annually. If historic buildings alone are considered, in the Netherlands almost two-thirds of Dutchmen (61 per cent) 'felt involved in the protection of monuments', while 30 per cent would personally react to a threat to a monument in their immediate environment (Kamerling, 1987).

Such a wide-reaching series of outcomes was not foreseen by the prophets of the conservation movement nor were its consequences for the city consciously intended. Over the longer span of history this whole episode may be considered to have been an aberration. The reasons why this has occurred will be discussed later but the success of the conservation movement has had a fundamental effect upon the way cities are viewed. Instead of a city being composed of a few special protected buildings or 'islands' set in a 'sea' of the 'real' city where normal urban life continues, the contemporary city, particularly but not only in Europe, now consists of areas that are conserved, that could be conserved and that may be conserved by later generations.

All threats to the architectural inheritance have not been removed and monuments will still be demolished. The story related above is drawn primarily from a small, if articulate, corner of the world and the ideas outlined are chiefly those of a small group of the world's citizens who have mobilised public consensus in their support. Even within this restricted area, between 2 and 5 per cent of protected buildings are lost annually. Buildings have a physical life-span that cannot be extended indefinitely, suffer natural and man-made misfortunes and still fall victim to the greed or short-sightedness of public or private developers. However a more important threat stems from the very success of the conservation movement itself which has determined that, paradoxically, demolition is an integral part of conservation. The logic of preserving the total built environment leads ultimately to a complete halt to development and change; it fossilises the physical fabric and structure of the city. The closer conservation came to that situation, the more evident it became that the capacity to change must itself be preserved.

Accommodating evolution within a conservation policy is illustrated in Figure 2.1 (NIROV, 1986). In this Dutch example both buildings and their morphological settings are scaled according to their intrinsic worth, so producing nine possible categories of physical structures to which can be applied four broad urban policies, ranging on a spectrum from preservation to reconstruction. Although structures of the highest quality are afforded strong protection, many compromises and sacrifices are called for in the middle ground, if sufficient space for change is to be created.

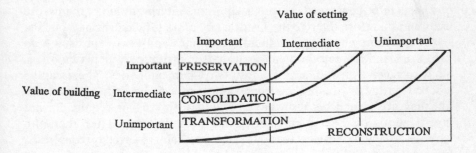

Figure 2.1 *Conservation policies and development*

The North American conservation experience has much in common with that of Europe but has not as yet achieved the same degree of success, outside a few show-piece examples. In addition, a different balance has generally been struck in the series of compromises between the roles of the public and private sectors in conservation activity, reflecting a difference in the acceptance of individual and collective rights and responsibilities.

These differences are most visible in the nature of adaptive reuse and the extent of the acceptance of market forces in remodelling structures to suit the demands of their users. Many examples of this will be examined in Chapters 8 and 9. None the less, there are tentative signs of a convergence of viewpoints between development and conservation interests, aided by mutual education, such as the work of the Heritage Canada Foundation towards the goal of the management of change through-consensus rather than confrontation.

We arrive at a position where urban conservation practice has resulted from a complex set of conditions, evolving through time, and deriving from the nature of the society in which it occurs. The reasons why it has occurred, and the continuing justifications for it, must now be outlined. Only then can a link be made between the physical structure and its users, and thus relate urban conservation to the wider concept of the historic city and to the wider functioning of cities in general.

Motivations and justifications

The simple question of why buildings should be conserved has received a number of far from simple answers. An examination of all the many varied motives of individuals and governments that have powered the conservation movement would fill a book in itself (see Newcomb, 1979). All that is needed here is sufficient understanding of motivation to explain the origins and nature of the historic city. In particular the sort of motive will be a determining influence upon the establishment of criteria and thus selection of what is to be conserved, as well as upon the interpretation of the past to users and therefore the role the historic city plays for citizens and tourists.

The question why people value old buildings and towns sufficiently to live, work and recreate in them, as well as contribute to their support, is likely to receive answers that fall into two main categories. These can be labelled 'aesthetic' i.e. they are valued as intrinsically beautiful; or 'antique' i.e. they are valued because they are old. Both reasons require further investigations, on the one hand into what is beautiful and, on the other, into why age is valued. Answers to the first are generally resolved by consensus, but a consensus of the taste-forming élite, which will vary over time and space. Thus the historic city is essentially a product of the time and place of those who shape it, which in turn has implications for both international comparisons and for the management of such cities in the longer term. A particular problem is presented by those styles and periods for which no such consensus has yet emerged, often because insufficient time has elapsed. The first 50 to 100 years in the life of a building are probably the most hazardous, until the line between modern commonplace and historic masterpiece is crossed. Good Victorian and Art Nouveau styles for example are now acceptable in Europe and highly valued in North America, but the jury is still out on Bauhaus industrial buildings, and much residential estate architecture of the inter-war period (see Ford, 1986).

Answers to the antiquity question are interesting because it is not necessarily age itself that is valued, although this increases a building's rarity value on the principle of the older the fewer, which is why age criteria exist in most of the legislation. There is also the representative function of architecture in providing a link between past and present. Buildings are used to evoke a period from the past or an association of a place with an historical personality (termed in the United States the 'Washington slept here' phenomenon, while other countries would substitute Queen Elizabeth I, Napoleon, Bolivar or Ghandi as appropriate). A further stage in the explanation is to ask why one should wish to evoke a past and indulge in nostalgia, a word originally meaning not merely the recall of pleasant memories but literally the pain experienced through the unattainable longing to return to the past. A number of answers will now be examined.

Authenticity and heritage

Explorations of motivation must come to terms with two freely used, but loosely defined, expressions which embody distinctly different approaches to historic artefacts and thus the historic city. *Authenticity* and *heritage* are terms often used in adjectival relationship to each other. They are also often used separately as self-explanatory justifications for the selection and presentation of artefacts, yet neither provides a set of clear guiding principles nor is there necessarily unanimity between them.

It is useful to maintain a distinction between the two: authenticity derives from the object being conserved, while heritage derives from its user. Authenticity appeals to the intrinsic aesthetic or historic qualities of the building or place and thus appears to offer 'pure', rather than 'applied', justifications that can be implemented with objectivity. The enthusiasts campaigning in defence of historic buildings took it largely for granted that the intrinsic qualities of the buildings were self-evident once these had been brought to the attention of the decision-makers and the public. Similarly the national inventories and status designations assumed that the intrinsic qualities of monuments were recognisable and could form the basis for the assigning of degree of protection or subsidy. Factors such as chronological age, and artistic or historical significance, are used in most such national inventories as a means of establishing priorities, as if these were agreed measurable quantities. While urban conservation was largely an emergency rescue operation, salvaging a few universally acclaimed buildings from development, then any questioning of such intrinsic criteria would have seemed an irrelevant distraction. However, once conservation has succeeded in becoming a broad pervasive philosophy of planning, or is viewed as a resource to be packaged for consumers, then such questioning becomes not only possible but essential. The idea of the existence of an objective, universal and measurable set of intrinsic criteria can be shown to be untenable; and authenticity in the sense of an accurate revelation, through its architecture, of the past as a fixed truth must be replaced by a more flexible concept.

The existing stock of old buildings is a result of survival over time. Apart from the large random element involved, the chances of survival are higher for particular building types, materials, districts and towns. What is left to preserve is a result of such diverse factors as the frequency of earthquakes and fires, the obtainability of stone, the prevalence of particular building traditions, the history of economic pressures for urban change, fortunes of war, or social conservatism. A range of fundamental biases exists which distorts the authenticity of conservation as an accurate revelation of the past, before it has begun.

The deliberate actions of protection, maintenance, repair, restoration and reconstruction all involve choice as to what is to be treated, as well as in what quantity and where. It is likely, especially in the early stages of the conservation process, that the spectacular will be preferred over the mundane, large over small and unusual over commonplace. In spatial terms the differences in degree of protection offered between countries, regions and cities is enormous and explicable more in terms of the financial resources and political will to conserve, rather than the intrinsic importance of the artefacts themselves, and still less does it reflect any 'authentic' representative collection of the world history of urban architecture and development.

Similarly, protection implies repair and restoration of what cannot be repaired. There is no clear distinction between repair and reconstruction and even between reconstruction and facsimile building. If authenticity is the accurate reflection of a past through its architecture, then skilful reconstruction may be more authentic than scattered remnant relics. Most old urban structures are the result of much adaptive reuse. Restoration therefore faces the problem of choosing which past from many should be restored. In practice the solution to this problem has generally depended on little more than prevailing architectural taste.

All these arguments derive from an approach to conservation in which the object itself provides the justification and criteria for selection and management. Even so authenticity has little absolute meaning. Once the focus of attention shifts from the object to the user, then a further, and quite different, set of contexts must be considered.

The concept that provides the link between the preservation of the past for its intrinsic value and as a resource for a modern community or commercial activity is *heritage*. The word, although sometimes rather loosely used as a synonym for historic relics, does encompass a meaning, equally present in its French (*patrimoine*), German (*Erbschaft*) or Dutch (*erfgoed*) forms, that adds a significantly different dimension to both 'preservation' and 'conservation'. Heritage necessarily contains both the idea of some modern value inherited from the past as well as a legatee for whom this inheritance is intended.

The inescapable implication is the existence of a market. Preservation or even conservation can seek criteria for its justification from the intrinsic values of the object itself, whose continued existence is sufficient goal. Heritage not only automatically poses the question, 'whose heritage?' but, even more fundamentally, can only logically be defined in terms of that market. Heritage is brought into being and maintained for a legatee. Authenticity justifications will result in 'supply-oriented' preservation and any subsequent use will be incidental and secondary. Heritage, however, implies a 'demand-orientation' with the nature, location and use of what is preserved being determined ultimately by those whose heritage is being presented.

The increasing popularity of the use of the term heritage in association with conserved urban morphology implies, in itself, some shift in approach to the historic city but it is still necessary to recognise a distinction in meaning. Terms such as 'heritage planning', 'heritage conservation', or 'heritage tourism', are descriptive of a presentation and interpretation of history and its relics to an implied consumer, while preservation or conservation has no such direct implication and focuses upon the artefact or area itself. Such a terminological distinction has consequences in the management approaches to the historic city considered later.

MacCannell (1976) has explored the basic relationship between the conserved physical artefact and the user. An attraction is a combination of *site*, that is the intrinsic qualities of a place such as its beauty, antiquity or associations, and *marker*, which is the deliberate indication of selected qualities for the appreciation of the consumer. This marker may be an on-site notice or printed information or previously acquired information. The result is the 'sacralisation' of space, where a site whose physical characteristics may be unremarkable, or even indistinguishable from others, is endowed with value by the process of *enshrinement*. The process becomes cumulative as such initial site marking is reinforced by use. The consumer's interest in the site is reinforced by the presence of others and by the accumulating ancillary support services, which all underline the importance of the site. Thus, MacCannell argues, no 'naturalist definition of a site is possible', i.e. from the intrinsic nature of the site itself, and visitors make a ritualistic collection of 'sights' that have been appropriately marked rather than 'sites' defined by intrinsic criteria.

Thus sites can be defined by the expectations of users who may not distinguish history from mythology. The 'marking' of urban artefacts as part of the historic city becomes as much a matter for creative imagination as for historical scholarship. Bath, as an historic city, becomes inextricably linked with characters from the novels of Jane Austen, Florence with Dante and Haworth with the Brontës. The controversy between a number of

English cities about who 'owns' Robin Hood is sharpened by its reported value of around £100m annually in tourist receipts; Coventry is profitably secure in its ownership of Lady Godiva, even if it must contest the Shakespeare country, while in Australia the 'Jolly Swagman' has been successfully captured by Winton, Queensland. The distinction between history and literature can become extremely blurred. At least Cavendish, Prince Edward Island, was well known to the author of *Anne of Green Gables* (Squire, 1988). But the Grand Pre National Historic Park in Nova Scotia commemorates the 1755 expulsion of the Arcadian settlers, through the medium of memorials to 'Evangeline', the completely mythical heroine of a poem by Longfellow who never visited the place. The extreme case of such hijacking of literature by places must be the selling of Western Romania to tourists through the central character of an Irish novel, as 'the Dracula country'. On a local level, a glance through a selection of 'heritage trails' produced by tourist authorities in historic cities reveals a mixture of popular literary, mythological and historical occurrences used to mark sites within the historic city.

Marking can occur when nothing remains of the site apart from its location, and much urban heritage is marked historical or literary place associations rather than physical structures. 'London Wall' is a marked and interpreted route along the line of the long-demolished city wall. The ultimate use of markers is where no site in a strict sense actually existed, but this leads to the awkward question of the construction rather than conservation of historic artefacts which will be considered later. Marking, including that of no longer, or never, existing relics, is particularly well developed in North America (as in the case of Boston's 'Freedom Trail' discussed in Chapter 8).

The point to be stressed here is not that there is something dishonest in this process, but only that the historic city is not the totality of preserved artefacts from the past. It is a contemporarily created phenomenon which, like the study of history itself, can be re-created anew by each generation according to the prevailing attitudes towards the past. Cohen (1979b) has related the authentic nature of the scene to the impression of it gained by tourists (see Table 2.1). This line of thought, however, assumes that 'real' and 'contrived' are recognisable qualities. Authenticity defined as the accurate presentation of the past through the conservation of its relict features has little relevance to the definition of the historic city. Conservation is the 'necessary myth' (Goodey and Ophir, 1982). A closer analogy would be to regard the relics and events of the past as a raw material which can be selectively quarried and used in accordance with contemporary attitudes or in support of contemporary notions. Such use is limited only by the very elastic constraints of the availability of the resource and the creativity in exploiting it.

A series of small steps links selected preservation, repair and reconstruction, facsimile building and new building in the spirit of the old.

Table 2.1 Variety of experiences of authenticity

Nature of scene	Tourist's impression of scene	
	Real	Staged
Real	Authentic	Doubted authenticity
Staged	Failure to recognise	Recognised as contrived

Source: After Cohen, 1979b

The distinction between 'resource-based' and 'demand-based' historic sites is frequently not clear-cut. Conserved buildings can be moved and reassembled in more 'desirable' locations, as is the practice in many open-air museums. Venetian *palazzi* have been moved to, amongst other places, Bochum, Disneyworld Florida, and Sydney Harbour. Replicas of what once existed can be built, as in Den Gamle By at Aarhus, or Turin's 'Old City'; or what ought, or could have, existed but by chance did not, can be created, and ultimately fantasy is made concrete. Many examples will be considered in detail in Chapter 7 and it is only noted here that between the archaeological site and Disneyland there are many intermediate points which in practice are where most of the world's historic cities are to be found.

The city of Norwich, for example, sells itself to visitors as a medieval urban experience, with its most popular attractions being the castle, town walls, cathedral and Elm Hill conservation area. The castle and town walls are Victorian reconstructions of what such medieval structures should have been, while Elm Hill, with its cobbled street surface and 'period' light fittings, is an early-1960s renovation of a variety of building façades dating from the fifteenth to the twentieth centuries. The result is more a film set within which visitors can enjoy the medieval experience they expect, than a museum of authentic relics. This is a denigration neither of Norwich, which possesses many well-preserved historic buildings, nor of the consumer, whose experience in the city reinforces the preconditioned expectations. Ultimately the historic city, and monument, is what and where we say it is, and although the 'we' in these contexts is worth investigating, authenticity rarely is.

Social and psychological justifications

The paradox encountered in investigations of this category of motivations is that, although widely expressed, it is extremely difficult to be specific.

There is a long historical record from many different countries of bland non-controversial statements about the importance of conserving the built environment to the well-being of the individual or society (Lowenthal and Binney, 1981). The historic city is a link between the past, the present and the future. 'Our cities should provide visible clues to where we have been and where we are going' (Ford, 1978). The reasons why they 'should' are usually less clearly stated. Place familiarity is valuable in maintaining the individual's psychological stability and an over-abrupt change in the physical environment must be modified by conservational policies, so that the 'excitement of the future should be anchored in the security of the past' (Lynch, 1960). A related argument asserts that places are also 'centres of individually felt values and meanings' (Pred, 1984, p. 79) and that society as a whole endows places with symbolic values (Firey, 1945; Lowenthal, 1975) whose loss would be damaging. Taking the argument further, places have been shown to be important in the socialisation process and as part of the legitimation function in the reproduction of the principles of a society (Pred, 1984). Thus places are converted by a process of 'sacralisation' (MacCannell, 1976) from mere locations to social assets, and the conservation of selected places is a social as well as psychological necessity.

However, although such assertions are in themselves attractive, and provide copious emotional ammunition for conservationists in planning conflicts, they are difficult to elaborate, or illustrate in practice. Although there are clinical experiments on the disorientating effects on individuals of a loss of memory, there are no examples of a society without any consciousness of its past nor comparative studies of the state of social or psychological well-being in cities with and without conservation policies. Therefore these approaches provide no usable guide for urban conservation planning and historic city management. They may make a contribution to the answers to the question 'why?', but not to the more generally encountered questions of 'what, how much and where?'

Political ideology and heritage

Ideology, as a coherent set of political ideas, plays an important role in the selection and interpretation of urban structures and thus the nature of the historic city. Education is often included among the many justifications for conservation and thus it is hardly radical to suggest that the historic city has a socialisation function in reproducing the dominant political ideas of the community. Equally cities and artefacts which portray the 'wrong' history, or interpretations contributing to the 'wrong' ideology, will tend to be ignored. Not all conservation programmes are deliberately executed by government officials for explicit political purposes, but conservation ostensibly motivated by non-ideological, technical approaches in search of historical accuracy, aesthetic beauty or even just entertainment, can contribute to popular political opinion. The issue has been reviewed by Ley and Olds (1988) with respect to theme parks, discussed in Chapter 7.

Elements of many different ideologies can be traced in most historic cities and it is difficult to link a particular ideology with any particular city; not least because individual consumers may react quite differently to the same historic stimulus. Therefore although a summary can be made of some ideological dimensions commonly encountered, this is followed by case studies of individual cities in which more than one approach can be identified.

Nationalism v. internationalism Nationalism, the modern world's most widespread state-forming philosophy, is a powerful force behind much conservation, with the historic city being used to bolster the nation-state idea. The 'national memory' (Zywiecka, 1985) was used as the basis for a consensus for the conservation of 'national values' in Polish towns. New nationalisms in particular require the celebration of selected aspects of the national character, national values, and preferably a founding mythology of national emergence. The conserved historic city can contribute through its symbolic architecture, its 'marked' historic associations and as the show-case for national cultural productivity. This is abundantly manifested in the United States, where, for example, the Williamsburg 'Historic Triangle' (Chapter 7) and Boston (Chapter 8) exude the values of revolutionary resistance to Imperial tyranny; while much of the Canadian heritage described in Chapter 7 and 9 is presented as opposition to American tyranny. However, emergent nationalisms in former colonies have difficulty in relating to a conserved urban heritage that recalls former colonial administrations or settler minorities, until these are no longer perceived as a threat (Western, 1985). This discordance has provoked a variety of responses which will be considered in Chapter 8 and 9.

A variant on the nationalism theme is escapism, when attention is directed to past glories as a distraction from present problems and future uncertainties. Countries with a distinguished past historical role and a reservoir of past cultural achievements are particularly prone to fall back upon a selective nostalgia, taking refuge from painful change in an obsession with tradition and what Davies (1987) has called 'cultural necrophilia'.

Conversely, a stress on the international aspects of heritage is generally little more than a vague recognition that architectural ideas and historical events operate on a wider stage than the nation-state. The international dimension of the conservation movement, discussed earlier, and its reflection through the work of the international agencies and international tourism has, however, encouraged a world or continental perspective which may contradict purely national interpretations. A few historic cities do project themselves as symbols of international interaction, often stressing their 'cockpit' locations. The 'European capitals' of Brussels, Luxembourg City and Strasbourg have an obvious strong vested interest; the three neighbouring cities of Aachen (FRG), Maastricht (Netherlands) and Liège (Belgium) engage in joint promotion of this border triangle, and this is also being encouraged for the Saar-Lorraine-Luxembourg urban–industrial region (Quasten and Soyez, 1987). Much internationalism in response to tourism, however, is more a sort of transported nationalism which presents the contribution of the heritage of the host country to the national identity of the visitors or vice versa. The potential conflict between interpretations of heritage drawn from the national mythologies of residents and those intended for foreign consumption will be considered later. It is worth noting however that the coveted UNESCO designation of *World Heritage Site* is used for national aggrandisement and commercial advantage within the international competition for tourists, more often than in celebration of an international identity.

Regionalism v. centralism Regionalism, a local variant of nationalism, may use interpretations of urban heritage to stress distinctive local identities. This can be little more than the local colour much used by tourist boards, or the assertion of political separatism. In opposition to this is centralism, or even imperialism, which stresses the region's place in a wider political system or contribution to a wider supra-regional culture. This polarity has clear implications for answers to the question 'whose heritage?'. Conservation policies based upon the local self-image may not be equally suitable for marketing to visitors, and the regional image, saleable to tourists, may not be equally acceptable to locals. The problems arising from this discrepancy will recur in different guises in the later discussion of management.

Socialism v. capitalism This dimension contrasts the conservation of the major buildings, and the stress upon the famous people engaged in important events who inhabited them, with the conservation of the less spectacular, domestic buildings and the presentation of the mundane lives of the common people. The distinction is between a view of history as being determined by notable individuals or as an anonymous society driven by abstract forces. The lessons for contemporary society, drawn from such diverse interpretations of the past, may be, explicitly or not, used to reinforce an individualist or collectivist political ideology.

There are a number of practical developments which tend to favour a shift towards a 'common people' rather than 'heroic individual' approach; although there is rarely a stated ideological intention, such approaches can be harnessed to notions of class struggle rather than individual enterprise.

First, early conservation concerned itself necessarily with the spectacular and the unique, if only because such buildings were an obvious popular starting-point. Later conservation planning is equally necessarily likely to be concerned with smaller, less spectacular structures, often as 'setting' for the 'gems' conserved in the first wave. Secondly, the shift already noted from central to local government involvement is likely to favour the choice of vernacular buildings and the selection of locally rather than nationally relevant themes. Thirdly, the development of heritage theme parks has encouraged both the use of the commonplace as a ready means of identification for the visitor with the historical artefact and the peopling of exhibits with live participants, which almost inevitably stresses a common humanity rather than an uncommon heroism. The extent to which this can be attempted is illustrated in the restored fortress town of Louisbourg (Nova Scotia) where the reconstructed architecture is peopled by a 'French garrison' whose unkempt state of dress and unruly behaviour (but not unsavoury smell!) is supposed to convey the poor living conditions and demoralisation of the ordinary soldier.

Other dimensions There are many other possible dimensions that can be identified in heritage interpretations that are more nuances of approach than coherent ideologies. The art–technology dichotomy stresses either aesthetic beauty or the industrial archaeology of technique. The physical robustness of much military architecture, and thus its high chance of survival, together with the emotional attraction of war, has led to a strong emphasis in the historic city on military buildings and events. These in turn may be interpreted either through what amounts to militarism, the glorification of war, or through pacifism, by means of 'the horrors of war' approach (Ashworth, 1988). Many of these dichotomies will re-emerge, explicitly or not, in the later consideration of the marketing of the historic city.

Ideological interpretation in practice The above listing of ideological dimensions gives an impression of simplicity rarely encountered in practice. Even the painstaking reconstruction of the devastated historic towns of Eastern Europe after 1945 by Communist governments is presented with a mixture of nationalist, aesthetic and pacifist themes as well as state socialism (Carter, 1981).

On the national scale there can be differences of ideological approach that can amount to tension. In Canada, the National Capital Commission is charged with the projection of a national identity through promoting the twin cities of Ottawa and Hull as a national symbol. However the provincial (Ontario and Quebec) and local administrations who have most of the legal responsibility for conservation reflect sectional and regional identities, as do most of the designated conservation bodies, whether voluntary or government promoted, which are also organised on a provincial basis. Quebec City is presented as an architectural symbol of the history, values and contemporary political aspirations of francophone Canada, while the towns of Newfoundland, the Maritimes, Ontario, the Prairies and Pacific tend to promote these regional identities rather than a 'nation-state'. A further complication is the paradox that Canadian national identity was defined historically through the maintenance rather than rejection of an imperial connection. Thus the assertion of a national distinctiveness, especially in relation to the United States, depends very largely upon Canada's role in an imperial heritage. In the examples of Halifax (Nova Scotia), Fredericton (New Brunswick), Upper Canada Village (Ontario) and Victoria (British Columbia), all considered in more detail later, aspects of imperial, national, language group and regional ideologies can usually be identified in the presentations.

Some of the problems arising from a discrepancy between ideological requirements and existing urban resources can be seen on the Celtic periphery of the British Isles. Traditional Welsh society was rural rather than urban in character and thus the towns of Wales represent various 'foreign' influences (Carter, 1965), which presents problems in using an urban heritage deriving from medieval Marcher barons, Tudor plantations or nineteenth-century industrialists to support distinctively Welsh ideologies. Similarly in Ireland, the Georgian heritage of Dublin has suffered neglect since the establishment of the state of which it is the capital, because it is seen as representing a British rather than Irish political dimension (Kearns, 1982). The Scottish kingdom, more fortunately in this respect, did produce an urban heritage before its absorption into the British state, allowing Edinburgh to be projected as a national cultural capital. However, the rivalry between Scotland's two largest cities is fuelled by the difference between Edinburgh's Scottish national nuance and Glasgow's more Scots-Irish, cosmopolitan-industrial, projected image.

Even in a single city different ideological dimensions can be discerned. As a former dockyard town, Portsmouth (UK) is promoting itself as 'Flagship of Maritime England' on the basis of a collection of maritime museums, renovated historic ships and its historical associations with Royal Naval personalities and events. The choice of exhibits and presentation reflects a number of ideological strands. The unremitting account of the success of British arms can be seen as 'nationalist', its ostensible glorification of force 'militarist' and its verdicts on the impacts of Britain on a wider world have been described as 'romantic imperialist' (Bradbeer and Moon, 1987). It is also claimed that the stress on the central role of the actions of the individual historic hero, and the encouragement of individual enterprise and the reward of initiative, can be related to the political philosophy of 'Thatcherism'. Although it is possible to identify such strands in Portsmouth's heritage, those engaged in these promotions argue that they use the historic resources that are extant, and these in such a town are necessarily dominantly military. Also the consumer, in search of entertainment rather than historical or political education, is best served by a concentration on exciting historical episodes and personalities. Finally, quite different dimensions can also be identified in the heritage promotion of the city, including the 'technical/industrial' ('warship design through the ages'), and 'the common people' ('the daily life of the seaman'), both strongly represented in the allegedly nationalistic *Mary Rose* exhibition.

Economic justifications

The first observation that should be made about economic justifications for the historic city is that it is felt necessary to seek them at all. Through most of the history of the conservation movement, especially in Europe, economic arguments are conspicuous by their absence from the reasons for the necessity of preserving past architecture; the national legislation in most countries fails to use economic justifications or criteria for selection; and in almost all cases conservation policy is administered by ministries or departments of culture or planning rather than economic affairs.

The contemporary imperative to find a motive for conservation in the economic use of conserved buildings, or through the indirect economic benefits accruing to public or private sectors as a result of treating historic cities as a commercial resource, is usually a *post-hoc* justification of an already existing policy. The increasing importance of economic factors can be seen to be a consequence of a success attributable to other reasons. Those West European countries with a long-standing widespread acceptance of conservation planning are now faced with a growing stock of protected buildings which need purposeful occupation. Additionally the maintenance costs, inescapably implied by the act of preservation, have proved an increasing burden on public finances during a period of retrenchment in public expenditure in a number of North-west European countries. Therefore economic solutions have been sought to growing economic problems. Meanwhile countries with less developed conservation planning have seized upon apparently successful economic exploitation of historic resources elsewhere as a convincing argument in support of their own policies.

Two types of economic argument are used, direct and indirect. The former stresses that demolition and rebuilding may cost more than preservation, renovation and subsequent maintenance. Although often used such arguments require estimates of building life expectancy, future maintenance costs and predicted potential economic returns to investment through the entire life cycle of a building. However difficult to quantify, such arguments made in defence of conservation correctly establish in the popular and political imagination the idea that new does not automatically imply cheaper. The second type of argument is that the historic city is a resource which repays investment by returns to the wider urban economy. The most usually considered aspect of that economy is tourism, whose relation to the historic city is discussed in Chapter 3. However, it has become apparent to many city governments that much modern commercial and industrial enterprise is 'footloose' and thus selects suitable locations on the basis of the quality of the working and residential environment: a major contributor to this quality is conservation. The promotion of cities to potential investors, residents and visitors through such 'amenity' factors as historic heritage is a rapidly expanding preoccupation of many public urban authorities (see Ashworth and Voogd, 1986a; 1986b; 1988).

Conflicts between the motives to conserve

The justifications for urban conservation rarely begin or end with the tourist-historic city. As noted above, the perception of heritage as contributing 'amenity' to residential environments has been quite as important, and generated more academic literature. The 'amateur enthusiasts', whose energies were so important in awakening public concern for the inherited built environment, themselves frequently inhabit it. The process of conserving the inner city as a high-amenity residential area inevitably confuses public and private interests (see Ley, 1986, on Toronto). The technical and social justice issues raised by the question 'in whose interest is the city conserved?'will be considered later in terms of the coexistence of functions in the tourist-historic city (Chapter 6), as well as underlying many of the examples of management in Chapters 7 to 9.

In the context of this chapter it is important to note that the various motives for conservation may contradict, as much as reinforce, each other. Not only is the 'sellable heritage package' for each group of users likely to be different but so also are the various justifications. Equally there is no clear-cut distinction between purely economic arguments in favour of conservation for tourism, social arguments justifying a different sort of conservation for local amenity, and even political arguments stressing conservation as a vehicle for presenting ideologies. The relationship between the motivations discussed in this chapter, the tourist function (Chapter 3), and the various other coexisting urban functions within the tourist-historic city (Chapter 5), is more complicated. Tourism, and other uses of the historic city, provide a wide selection of justifications for conservation chosen from the range presented above, with no one function being linked exclusively to one type of motive.

The concept of the historic city

Thus various individuals and institutions, for a variety of motives, have conserved urban artefacts and shaped attitudes towards them that have led to the creation of the historic city. This concept must now be defined more closely and the different elements that in practice are combined in such definitions must be made clear, as well as the various ways in which the concept is being used.

There is a double meaning inherent in the phrase 'the historic city' that has become so deeply entrenched through usage as to be inescapable. On the one hand it can refer to the city as a whole, in the sense that a city is thought of as historic rather than modern, with the added implication that this is a functional as much as an age designation. The dominant ethos of the city is 'historic' regardless of the proportion of its building stock that is conserved, in the same sense that a 'steel town', or a 'textile town', can derive its ethos from a particular function whether or not such a function is the sole, or largest, employer. On the other hand the phrase can be used in the distinctly different sense of a particular district within the town, known as 'the historic city' so as to distinguish it from other more modern districts. Although the two meanings are related, in that the ethos of the former is dependent upon the existence of the latter locations, they should not be merged. The historic city as a physical area of the city is delimitable and cartographically reproduceable and has a traceable extent which could be as large as the city as a whole or, at least theoretically, as small as a single building. It is possible for an historic city in this second and regional sense to exist without the parallel existence of an historic city in the first, and holistic, sense. Few would describe Ottawa, Canada's federal administrative centre, for example, as an historic city, although it would not be unreasonable to refer to the Byward Market district within it, where a conservation effort has been concentrated, as an historic city in the regional sense (Tunbridge, 1987a). The reverse, however, is more difficult to imagine.

Therefore the concept of the historic city as a distinctive zone within the city, definable in terms of the mix of morphological and functional characteristics described above, can be applied in particular cities as an exercise in regionalisation. Such empirical information then forms the basis for generalisation into models of the location and development of such historic cities.

For these purposes it is necessary to isolate, collect and describe sets of variables indicative of the elements that compose the historic city and thereby reveal its functional-morphological zoning. In both senses of the term, however, there are at least three quite different sets of criteria that contribute towards its conceptualisation.

The qualities of the forms

First and most obvious are the characteristics of the urban artefacts themselves. The age, aesthetic beauty, architectural significance and associations with historical events and personalities are the elements which are related to individual buildings, clusters of buildings and spaces, or to the cadastral forms of the town plan as a whole. Listing such characteristics does not in itself create selection criteria, despite the existence in much of the legislation described above of just such lists, which present a spurious sense of objectivity. The choice of combinations of such characteristics and the significance attached to any one of them is a subjective judgement based upon the prevailing consensus among decision-makers as to what is beautiful, significant, or even old. Such judgements on individual artefacts are based ultimately upon collective decisions, whether stated or not, about the purposes of the past, as discussed earlier. Therefore the historic city is defined by, and must equally conform to, the chosen images of the past. Thus what appear to be objective selection criteria are rarely so in practice. Architectural beauty is as prone to fashion as any art. The current popularity in Dutch historic cities of dominantly mid-seventeenth century architectural forms, or of early eighteeth-century forms in 'Georgian' cities such as Bath, would not have been so readily appreciated a century ago, while late Victorian architectural forms that dominate many European cities still await a general revival in popular taste.

Even chronological age is capable of quite different valuations in different societies or cities and is rarely in itself sufficient to justify the title 'historic'. The city of Atlanta in Georgia has an historic district, the Martin Luther King Conservation Area, in which the oldest building, a Baptist chapel, dates from the 1920s. The Dutch monument preservation law of 1961 on the other hand expressly prevents buildings less than 50 years old being listed as national monuments, which has led to considerable controversy about the protected status of the so-called 'young art' of the inter-war period (Werkgroep Jongere Bouwkunst, 1983). There is finally the problem of determining not only the age of a building, but deciding which of the frequently many periods that have contributed to the contemporary form of any particular building or ensemble should take precedence in conservation. Ruskin's tirades against Victorian restoration, and the current fashion in a number of Dutch cities (such as Deventer) for the removal of eighteenth-century façades to reveal fifteenth-century brickwork, both show that quite different historic cities can be created from the same buildings. Thus although these characteristics inherent in the artefacts themselves are important determinants of the historic city, they are neither as objective, nor as easy to inventorise and map, as is implied in much of the planning legislation and working practices.

Information on the age of individual buildings is generally readily available from official sources or from observation. The main problem is the assignment of particular buildings to a single age category, and the patchwork that results is too detailed to be used to delimit and regionalise the historic city. Figure 2.2, for example, shows some generalisations derived from such information for building age in central Colmar (France). These include a calculation of dominant age category, or combination of categories, within 100m grid squares calculated using land-use combination techniques, as well as perceived 'historic appearance' and officially designated conservation areas (Ashworth and de Vries, 1984). It is clear that the regionalisation conclusions that can be drawn about the central area by the age of surviving buildings are very general, and similar conclusions would result in the central areas of most historic cities.

Planning designations

It is undoubtedly very convenient for the investigator to accept the formal designations of urban planning authorities as important criteria. The historic city in these terms is quite simply those cities, parts of cities or buildings, so designated by those responsible for doing so. International bodies have on occasion singled out particular cities, such as UNESCO with its *Cities of Outstanding Universal Value*, or the Council of Europe with its *European Heritage Cities*. Individual countries as varied as Poland (Zywiecka, 1985) and China (Yu Quingkang, 1987) have produced lists of officially designated historic cities. Similarly at the intra-urban scale listings of selected areas or buildings as historic are an integral part of the conservation legislation in many countries, as described earlier.

The use of such formal ascribed status as a definitional criterion not only removes the responsibility for subjective choice from the researcher but can also be amply justified on practical grounds. Such designations imply at the very least some protection from arbitrary physical damage and in many cases permit access to a range of financial and technical assistance for maintenance, restoration and rehabilitation. Thus designated sites are likely to become popularly accepted as part of the historic city, even if they are not already in that position, through the circular argument that conservation status will be awarded to sites considered of historic value by the decision-makers, who represent some consensus of existing national or local opinion in this respect. Thus it can easily be argued that planning designations are both reflections and determinants of the historic city. If a monument or heritage area is either so designated because it is already recognised as part of the historic city, or will become such as a result of the designation, then the question remains as to whether this is in itself a sufficient criterion for defining and regionalising the historic city.

There are a number of reasons for doubting that this is the case. Official designations vary enormously in their criteria, comprehensiveness and even intent between countries, cities, and even urban districts. The list of 62

(a) The central area (major historic monuments in black)

35	1	1	15	1234	235			
14	12	2	123	123	23	35	13	234
		23	12	124	124	12	13	24
		145	145	1	1	14	12	13
		15	25	15	14	12	1	1234
		15	1	1	1	4	125	
		12	1	12	1	124		
		12	15	1	124			

(b) Dominant building age
(1 = before 1871 2 = 1871–1919 3 = 1920–1945 4 = 1945–1970 5 = after 1970)

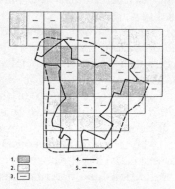

(c) Historical appearance
(1 = Historical 2 = Non-historical 3 = Uncertain = Secteur Sauvegarde (1966) 5 = Extension (1972)

Figure 2.2   *Building age in the central area of Colmar (France) (Ashworth and de Vries, 1984)*

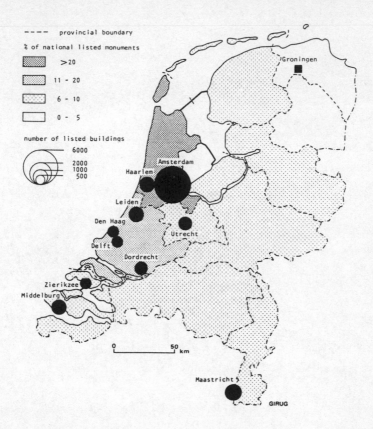

Figure 2.3   *National listed buildings in the Netherlands*

Chinese historic cities mentioned above, for example, is derived on the basis of 'absolute values', i.e. the national importance of the architectural artefacts in each city, and the list is therefore headed by all the major Chinese urban agglomerations. In contrast, the Council of Europe list is based on 'proportional values', i.e. the relative physical significance of historic artefacts within the total built environment, and thus ignores cities like London, Paris or Vienna in favour of Bath, Florence and Salzburg. Similarly, international comparison based upon different national monument designations is rendered meaningless by national differences in the inclusion criteria and the liberality of their application. For example, a comparison of conservational policies among near neighbours in North–west Europe (Dobby, 1978) reveals that there are five times as many British *listed buildings* as French *monuments inscrits*. The conclusion is not that Britain possesses five times as much architectural heritage as France, nor is that much more concerned with architectural conservation, but merely operates a more generous decentralised set of inclusion criteria.

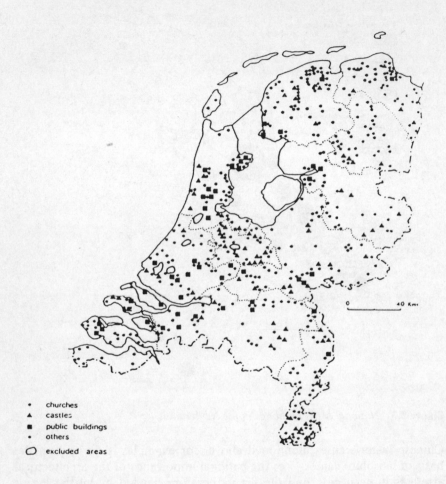

- • churches
- ▲ castles
- ■ public buildings
- · others
- ⬭ excluded areas

Figure 2.4   *Buildings of historical or architectural value in the Netherlands (Ashworth, 1983)*

Even between cities in one country, or within a single city, there is frequently a distinct clustering effect in that monumental status is more likely to be awarded to sites in cities, or districts, which are already recognised as historic and contain existing monuments than in areas without this neighbourhood effect. This is not mere subconscious prejudice on the part of officials but a necessary recognition that monuments exist within a wider morphological context and their value is enhanced, or not, by the status of their neighbours. Thus it cannot be assumed that planning

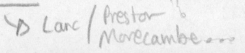

designations, whether of historic cities, conservation areas, or individual monuments, are sufficiently equal in value to serve as the sole criteria for delimiting the historic city.

The distribution of officially designated monuments, even in a small, administratively centralised and socially homogeneous country, illustrates this problem. Figure 2.3 shows the distribution of national listed monuments in the Netherlands. The concentration in the two Holland provinces is striking and all but Maastricht of the top ten cities are in the west. Such a skewed distribution does not accurately reflect either the distribution of modern or historic populations, wealth and economic activity or even the concentration of historical associations, personalities and artistic talent in the core area around which the Dutch state was formed. Figure 2.4 maps the Council for Archaeology's list of buildings of more than average intrinsic historical or architectural value and, although the major western cities are excluded, a comparison of the more even spread of historical architectural resources with the listings of Figure 2.3 raises questions of regional bias in listing procedures.

Two further pieces of evidence increase these doubts about spatial equity. The composition of the monument lists as well as their length varies from province to province. In particular, the lists for the western provinces include a much higher percentage of small domestic buildings. In Noord-Holland, the top-spending province, 88 per cent of all protected buildings are domestic houses, compared with 48 per cent in the peripheral province of Groningen, which suggests a qualitative difference in the ascribing of monument status. Secondly, only a small proportion of individual local authorities (66 of the 875) had published policies for conservation, and an even smaller number (27 of the 875) were, at that time (1982), busy constructing their own supplementary local monument list, although local authorities had long possessed the legal power to award such 'local' monument status (NIROV, 1981). In fact, 35 authorities had each designated more than 200 monuments, while 571 had less than 50 (Kamerling, 1987). This small minority of local authorities with active conservation policies and local lists were, in almost every case, the cities, and most especially the western cities. Thus it can be concluded that what could be termed a 'conservation consciousness' is to be found concentrated in the western urban municipalities for a variety of reasons, which may include their social class composition, proximity to the centres of national decision-making, national show-case function or just the contagious example of neighbouring authorities.

Two lessons emerge from this Dutch national-scale case study, which could be replicated for other European countries (Vlaeminck, 1987, for example on Belgium). The first is that it cannot be assumed that planning designations have equal weight: thus Amsterdam, with almost 7,000 state monuments, is not twelve times as much an historic city as

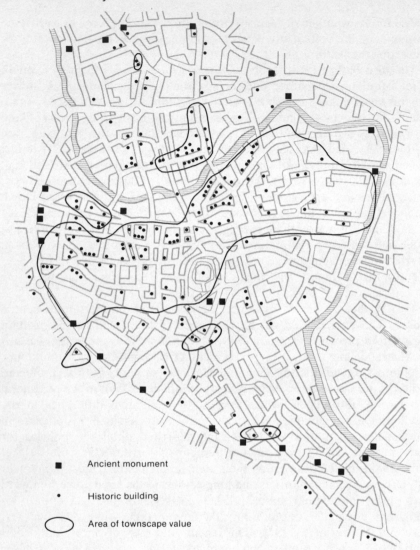

Figure 2.5   *Distribution of listed buildings: Norwich (UK)*

Groningen, with 500. Secondly, conservation planning depends upon a pervading consciousness, manifested in a philosophy of management by the public authorities, and the status designations are thus mere symptoms of the extent of such an urban management approach. The historic city therefore becomes a town or district whose planning and management is rooted in the idea of controlling the pace of morphological change.

The collection of information on buildings enjoying conservation status in some form or other, being legally defined, is relatively straightforward. Figure 2.5 shows the distribution of historic buildings, variously defined, in Norwich (UK). It indicates the spatial distribution of official attention, but is not entirely satisfactory as a delimitation of the tourist-historic city. The listing of buildings relates only to the character and quality of the individual building, without a direct regard for its contribution to the overall scene. The area designation, on the other hand, confers a measure of protection from change on areas whose constituent buildings may or may not individually be worthy of preservation. All these designations are in the first instance only protective, and represent a statement of intent that more active conservation measures by either the local authority or private interests will occur. The result is a wide scatter of individual buildings through the central area of the city, with a concentration of interest in an east–west belt across the centre with numerous outlying clusters.

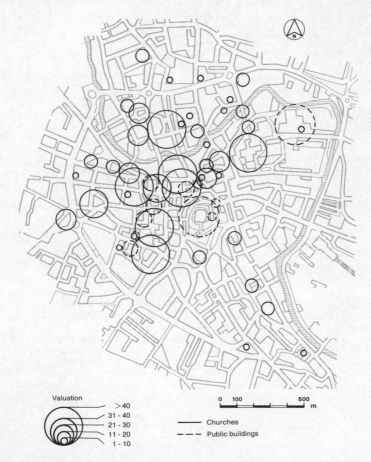

Valuation
> 40
31 - 40
21 - 30
11 - 20
1 - 10

0   100   500
|___|___|___|___| m

—— Churches
- - - Public buildings

Figure 2.6   *An establishment view of the historic architectural resources of Norwich*

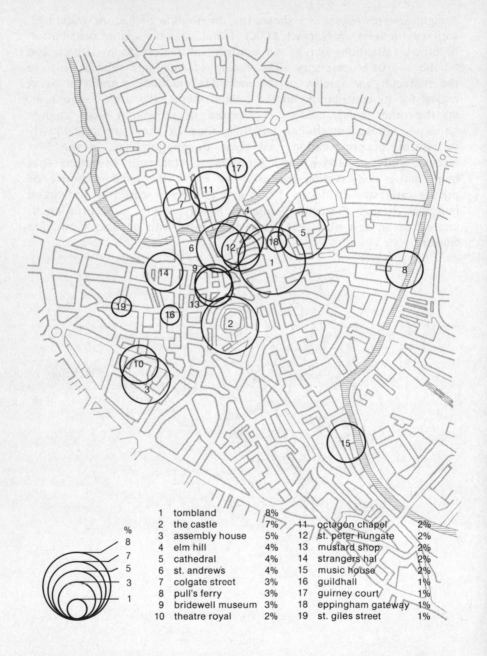

1	tombland	8%
2	the castle	7%
3	assembly house	5%
4	elm hill	4%
5	cathedral	4%
6	st. andrews	4%
7	colgate street	3%
8	pull's ferry	3%
9	bridewell museum	3%
10	theatre royal	2%

11	octagon chapel	2%
12	st. peter hungate	2%
13	mustard shop	2%
14	strangers hal	2%
15	music house	2%
16	guildhall	1%
17	guirney court	1%
18	eppingham gateway	1%
19	st. giles street	1%

Figure 2.7   *Tourist office view of the historic resources of Norwich*

Ascribed values and attitudes

In the development of the conservation movement there was frequently a distinct time-lag between public appreciation of historic values, even if this 'public' was a small minority, and the legislative recognition of such opinions. Certainly much of the North–west European and North American experience was that 'passionate minorities' shaped an acceptable climate for subsequent legislation and the endowment of conservational status. Indeed it can be argued that area conservational policies were usually dependent upon the pre-existence of such a climate for the private financial resources needed for their detailed execution. Planning designations did not determine the location of the historic city but merely recognised its existence.

A slightly different case in this respect has been the valuation of historicity by those outside the city or even country, whose concern eventually prompts local action. This was clearly the case in the Italian cities of Venice and Florence after 1966, and remains a feature of much conservation in less developed countries, in which architectural conservation may be accorded lower priority by inhabitants than by foreigners, either because other needs are perceived to be more pressing, or because of cultural differences in attitudes towards the built environment (Zetter, 1982).

It is possible that official designations can precede popular valuations, with governments forming rather than following the climate of opinion. Some of the best examples of this occur in newly designated national 'show-case' cities such as Ottawa, where the National Capital Commission, a federal agency engaged uniquely in local planning, has long been busy in such 'top-down' designations. In either event it can be argued that the historic city cannot be defined in terms of official planning designations alone but must take into account the way cities or parts of cities are valued and treated.

This does not necessarily imply that the concept has been reduced to a totally subjective set of attitudes that can be sought only in the psychology of individuals. The argument that the historic city is what is thought of as such can be extended logically to claim that it is what in practice is treated as an historic city. Thus the historic city is the city or district that functions as an historic city for the various groups of users: not only the justification but also the definition of the historic city must ultimately depend on its users (Solesbury, 1975). Behavioural characteristics are easier to observe and measure than the attitudes and values they reflect. If visitors, residents or commercial users are using premises or districts because of their historic values then the resulting patterns of occupancy, land values or visitor flows act as valid surrogate measures of the location of the historic city.

The difficulty of collecting information on the values placed upon buildings and areas of the city lies not so much in the mechanics of data collection as determining what information to collect. Inevitably

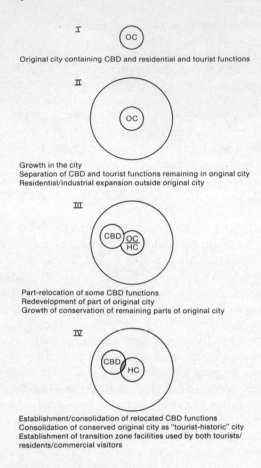

I

OC

Original city containing CBD and residential and tourist functions

II

OC

Growth in the city
Separation of CBD and tourist functions remaining in original city
Residential/industrial expansion outside original city

III

CBD OC HC

Part-relocation of some CBD functions
Redevelopment of part of original city
Growth of conservation of remaining parts of original city

IV

CBD HC

Establishment/consolidation of relocated CBD functions
Consolidation of conserved original city as "tourist-historic" city
Establishment of transition zone facilities used by both tourists/
residents/commercial visitors

Figure 2.8   *Evolutionary model of the historic city*

the attitudes of actual or potential users of the city can only be approached through various surrogate variables that reflect such attitudes. In the Norwich case, two examples of the sort of information and the resulting spatial pattern can be seen in Figure 2.6. The first reflects the views of the 'expert architectural establishment'. Pevsner's *Buildings of England* series is an encyclopaedic description of buildings deemed worthy of attention, through their aesthetic or historical significance. An indication of the strength of the valuation is given by the length of the entry.

The resulting pattern differs from that of conservational status in two respects. First, fewer buildings are chosen for description, and these are concentrated more distinctly than the official designations in a broad NE–SW swathe of the central area. Sites outside this belt are relatively neglected. Secondly, attention among those selected is focused more strongly on a few favoured sites, in particular the cathedral, which accounts for half of the entire city entry.

The Pevsner information, although aiming to reflect intrinsic values, is intended to serve as a guide for the informed visitor as well as an exhaustive source of reference. Factors external to the building, such as accessibility and proximity to other buildings of similar interest, a sort of 'neighbourhood effect', cannot be excluded. The second source used in Figure 2.7 is the valuation of the Norwich Tourist Office. The city consciously promotes itself as an historic city and supports this claim in publicity material that features particular buildings and areas.

The places recommended in the most popular guide to the city provide a quantitative measure of the values placed on each site by tourism. The resulting spatial pattern is even more restricted than that revealed by the experts or the planning designations. A site has a better chance of being mentioned if it lies in the heart of the central area, i.e. within the triangle formed by the cathedral, castle and market, and thus on the recommended tourist routes, than if it is more peripherally located. Intrinsic antiquity or beauty is insufficient qualification for inclusion. Secondly, the quantity of attention devoted to particular buildings varies dramatically; a handful of key buildings receive the lion's share of prominence in the guides. Here is a clear demonstration of 'marking', with a small number of sites being selected as symbols of historic Norwich, allowing instant identification and collectability. The other buildings, despite their intrinsic characteristics or their official status, are reduced to a supporting cast that provides at best a setting, with the amount of attention they receive being related principally to their location relative to the star performers.

The historic city therefore is composed of elements from the description of the characteristics of urban form, the designated planning status with its underlying philosophy of urban management and the way the city is viewed and functions for resident and non-resident users. The three elements are not competing alternatives as there is considerable obvious mutual interdependence. The ascribed values depend on both the intrinsic characteristics and the planning status, while planning designations in turn reflect the attitudes towards the characteristics. The three do however provide distinctly different methods of approaching the definition and delimitation of the historic city, and their application can produce considerable discrepancies in the resulting patterns. The results of such applications of the concept to particular cities must now be considered.

A development model

The various elements described above can be summarised in the form of a simple evolutionary model (see Figure 2.8). In the first phase the 'original city' is assumed to encompass all urban functions, whether commercial, administrative or residential. In phase II growth is assumed to have occurred outwards in all directions and thus logically the centre will be the oldest part of the city. If this is not the case, because of either the redevelopment of the central area or because of an historical accident that has caused old buildings to be scattered through the city, then the chances of the city becoming historic, in our sense, is less and the exceptions become irrelevant.

The 'birth of the historic city' occurs during phase III as a result of two processes. The first is the revaluation of the historic-architectural heritage leading to the introduction of conservational attitudes and policies. These will be applied in a selected, probably contiguous, part of the original city which inertia or chance has preserved from development. The proportion of the original city chosen for this treatment depends upon the strength of the conservation movement, the extent and condition of the relict structures and the pressures for redevelopment within it.

The second process concerns the relationship between the historic city and the central functions of the town. The introduction of conservation policies for the physical fabric of the area places constraints upon the ability of some commercial enterprises to realise the profit potential of their city-centre sites. They may be unable to increase the density of site occupancy or to modify existing buildings in response to changes in demand or technology. In addition, the accessibility that makes the central area attractive as a commercial location may be reduced by the inability of the old, and now preserved, street and cadastral patterns to adapt to meet new transport demands. In short it is likely that there will be commercial pressures to migrate out of the area, even without any conscious encouragement to do so from planners eager to eject land-uses considered to be non-conforming with the newly created historic image of the area.

A number of North American commentators on this process (Ford, 1979; Tunbridge, e.g. 1987a) have related the location of conservation areas quite specifically to the 'zone of discard' of a Central Business District (CBD) in process of migration. In most of these cases, however, the sequence of events is more likely to be the reverse of that hypothesised from Western European experience. The outmigration of commercial and possibly administrative functions occurs, not as a result of their 'expulsion' from a conserved area, so much as a consequence of changing demands upon space which leave an abandoned or underused area, which becomes blighted and, apart from being scenically unattractive, may also house unwelcome activities such as prostitution (Ashworth *et al.*, 1988). The absence of pressures for redevelopment together with public concern to ameliorate the condition of such areas encourages the conservation of the remaining, largely relict, structures.

In either case the result is similar: a partial spatial separation of the CBD and the historic city. It is likely to be partial because the degree of compatibility of conservational policies and commercial exploitation varies between different sorts of functions. Some commercial activities can profit from the status, atmosphere and visitors in the historic city, despite the extra costs and inconveniences incurred, while others cannot, a theme pursued in Chapter 5.

The model hypothesises a fourth phase in which a partially relocated CBD overlaps with an historic city that occupies part of the area of the original city.

The moment such a developmental model is hypothesised, the possibility of variations from it become apparent. There are obviously many of these based upon the nature, distribution and valuation of the historic resources, on the one side, and the strength of pressures for redevelopment on the other. Many aspects of managing these relationships between the historic city and other urban functions will be considered later, and at this stage only a small number of major types of variation need be noted.

An obvious variable is city size. Small historic cities which have been preserved almost *in toto* can often accommodate their limited commercial functions without separating into 'old' and 'new' towns. In somewhat larger cases, such as Norwich, the original city may be extensive enough for selection within it to take place so that both conservation and redevelopment occur in different districts of it, with the various commercial activities being divided between these areas according to their locational preferences.

Equally, in very large cities, in place of a single contiguous historic city a number of spatially separate 'islands' may emerge and both the new commercial city and the historic city will then be polycentric.

More than any other North American metropolis, the expansion of Boston (Chapter 8) has absorbed many early colonial nuclei (such as Cambridge, Lexington and Salem) which now stand out as 'islands' of historic city in a suburban 'sea'. Boston also illustrates the results of the failure of the CBD to migrate over time. Unlike most North American cities, Boston's location on its congested peninsula has inhibited the hypothesised lateral shift in central area functions. Intense land-use competition over several generations of redevelopment *in situ* has resulted in no clear-cut zone of discard and the city's surviving 'colonial' structures are few and scattered. The original physical heritage of such a city is thus largely the street-plan itself, which has constrained the character of all subsequent redevelopment, and successive generations of distinguished architecture expressing a continuous tradition through many changes of style and scale from the eighteenth century to the present.

Conversely the complete separation of historic and modern city may result especially when there is a pronounced physical barrier, such as a preserved city wall, or the height distinction, common among Mediterranean towns, between an upper historic 'acropolis' and a lower modern town. Many such physically or culturally based variants have become even more apparent when tourism becomes a major function of the historic city, and they will be considered later.

A common situation, so widespread in its occurrence as to be difficult to dismiss as an aberration, occurs in waterfront locations, where the basic geometry of circular development assumed in the model is not present. One-sided urban expansion, and the consequent inland migration of the point of maximum accessibility, leads to the creation of a zone of discard in waterfront districts, a process encouraged by the relocation of waterfront activities for technical and commercial reasons. The result is the possible creation of a waterfront historic city in the discarded area, even where (as in Boston) the zone of discard is otherwise poorly developed. The peculiar opportunities and management problems resulting from this waterfront variant will be considered later.

3 The tourist city

Having considered at length the concept of the historic city and outlined its main spatial dimensions and functional relations, the following task is to do the same with the parallel concept of the tourist city. In the same way that tourism is only one of a number of activities that occur in historic cities, the historic heritage is only one tourism resource among many in the tourist city. Therefore it is necessary first to outline the urban dimension in tourism and then consider two distinctly different viewpoints, namely tourism as a function, welcome or not, of historic cities, and the historic city as a resource within the urban tourism industry. Both viewpoints can then be combined in the concept of the resort city, which can be modelled in much the same way as was the historic city in the previous chapter.

Tourism in cities

Most tourists originate from cities, and either seek out cities as holiday destinations in themselves or visit the attractions located in cities while holidaying elsewhere. It would be possible to elaborate and justify these assertions statistically in terms of the sheer volume of visitor-nights generated by individual cities, by the concentrations of tourism facilities in cities or by the contributions to national economies made by the urban tourism industry. However the importance of towns to tourism is so central that such elaboration would inevitably result in a book on tourism. This would be an unnecessary duplication of Pearce's (1987b) world review or Ashworth's (1989) survey of urban tourism, merely to arrive at the uncontested conclusion that tourism is important to cities and that cities are important to tourism.

More specifically relevant for our purposes is to stress three characteristics of tourism in cities that will underpin much of the later discussion. First, the tourism activities of cities exist within a wider regional and national tourism context, whether in terms of organisational structures, visitor place-images, spatial patterns of visitor behaviour, or distributions of tourism resources.

The urban central place occupies a pivotal position within the functional networks in the wider regional hinterland. Secondly, and to an extent contradictorily, cities exist within functional networks with each other regardless of, and separate from, their regional or national context. This is particularly marked in tourism where a mixture of inter-urban co-operation and competition can create various sorts of national and international tourism circuits. Finally, tourism in cities is dominated by variety, in two senses. The variety of facilities on offer to visitors, and thus the variety of types of holiday experience, is in itself one of the main attractions of cities. Equally these facilities are rarely produced for, or used exclusively by, tourists but are shared by many different types of user: in short, the multifunctional city serves the multimotivated user.

These specifically urban characteristics of tourism in cities form the context for the addition of heritage resources and heritage-motivated visitors. However they equally make it difficult to isolate either tourism resources, tourism facilities, or the tourist, from other resources, facilities or users within the city, or indeed the individual city in this respect from other cities or from its regional and national context. These intrinsic difficulties may help to explain the double neglect that has occurred in the study of urban tourism: those concerned with the phenomenon of tourism as such have generally failed to consider it within its urban context, preferring instead to pursue systematic studies of various aspects of tourism; while conversely those interested in urban studies have generally failed to give a systematic consideration, commensurate with its importance, to a tourism function that is frequently rendered all but invisible by its very ubiquity and integration in the urban scene.

Tourism in the historic city

It is clear from the account of the shaping and location of the historic city in the previous chapter that the relationship between the urban-conserved resources of the city on the one side and the tourist function on the other has been so close and long-standing, at least in Europe, that the difficulty has been to separate the two rather than find links between them. From the eighteenth-century Grand Tour to the modern marketing of cities as heritage centres, the historic city has been consciously used as a major tourist resource. Samuel Johnson's contemptuous view of the historic-city tourist, 'who enters a town at night, surveys it in the morning and then hastens away to another place' with only a 'confused remembrance of palaces and churches' (quoted in Hindley, 1983, p.11), has been echoed many times since. This role of historic artefacts as a saleable tourism product needs to be considered here alongside the reciprocal, but by no means identical, relationship, namely the role of tourism, as an activity and an industry, in the shaping and functioning of the historic city.

The importance of the concept of heritage as the link between the historic city and its users, in this case tourists, has already been raised, but there are a number of problems inherent in the application of the concept that should be introduced in general here and considered in more detailed examples of management later.

The most obvious and well publicised of these is the series of conflicts than may arise as a result of the simple spatial coexistence of tourism and historic monuments. There have been numerous well-reported cases of physical damage, whether intentional or not, resulting from large numbers of visitors enjoying their heritage. Stonehenge cannot withstand the feet of visitors nor the caves of Lascaux their breath. Just the physical presence of 'the golden horde' of tourists, to use Turner and Ash's (1976) rather threatening expression, can destroy the ambience that the monument was designed to convey. One-way pedestrian circulation systems controlled by traffic lights in a cathedral where it is claimed that the physical density of visitors reaches a figure of 1.5 m^2 of space per capita (Binney and Hanna, 1978) does not leave much medieval piety to be experienced. It is difficult to experience much aesthetic pleasure from an Athenian Acropolis around which visitors are 'crocodiled' in continuously moving unbroken columns along roped channels, shepherded by guards with whistles. These are perhaps extreme, but inevitable, occurrences when the European heritage is visited by those for whom it is conserved.

However strongly they may be attracted to the conserved relics of the past, tourists are themselves citizens of the present and as such require modern support facilities. The attractions may be medieval but few tourists are prepared to sleep, eat or travel in medieval conditions. The large, purpose-built and architecturally standardised hotel is frequently an intrusive element on the skyline of the historic city that its guests have come to enjoy. Of the numerous possible examples York's Viking Hotel and Bath's Beaumont stand out as particularly disturbing to the cityscape. City-periphery hotel locations avoid this intrusion but only at the cost of aggravating the problems arising from transporting visitors to and around the attractions. The amelioration of these sorts of conflicts is a management task considered later; the fundamental point being made here is that tourism, while providing a use and justification for parts of the historic city, simultaneously and inescapably makes other less welcome land-use demands.

A less visually obvious discrepancy between customer and product lies in their financial relationships, which complicate the superficially attractive idea that tourism can provide an economic justification and support for the historic city. The sights of the historic city are generally enjoyed free of charge, or if payment is sought it is often either voluntary or below cost. The visitor pays for the secondary support services provided by the commercial tourism industry, but not for the provision of the primary historic attractions that may be the motive for the visit. Various fiscal mechanisms may be devised to bridge this gap in the cycle of finance, but there remains a basic discrepancy in the distribution of costs and benefits resulting from the curious situation that the historic city as a heritage product can only be indirectly marketed to those for whom it is ostensibly created; or viewed from the tourism industry, that a major commercial activity is based upon a resource it has neither created nor usually manages. This paradox has many implications which will emerge later when the historic city is related to the tourist city.

The tourist is necessarily selective and the tourism industry will generally make intensive use of only a limited portion of the historic city. The implications in terms of land-use are obvious but made more serious by changes in the development of the conservation movement itself. As was noted earlier, later phases of urban conservation are marked by a proportionate increase in the attention paid to smaller domestic buildings rather than the larger more spectacular monuments. Yet it is primarily these larger monuments that will be of interest to visitors, leaving extensive parts of the growing historic city of interest mainly as a setting for the few major sights. This land-use selectivity is only the spatial dimension of the wider question of relevance: 'whose history, or whose heritage, is being presented?' As far as tourism is concerned the answer will always be 'the heritage made relevant to the visitor'.

The visitor is likely to have a more limited knowledge of the city than the resident, as well as different expectations. The result may be a 'bowdlerisation' of history or a significantly different valuation placed on historical artefacts in their interpretation. The first is the reduction of the complexity and richness of the urban heritage to a few simple recognisable and marketable characteristics – Nottingham becomes exclusively the city of Robin Hood and Heidelberg of the Student Prince. For the American, history becomes 'reduced to a sanitised, idealised past peopled with pilgrims and frontiersmen' (Ford, 1979, p.211). The second is subtler but equally important, namely that an orientation towards the requirements of visitors will emphasise those aspects of the local history that can be related to the experience of the visitor while underemphasising or ignoring those that cannot. The problem that consequently arises is not that these 'heritages', tailored to the characteristics of the market, offend abstract tenets of authenticity or comprehensiveness, for the historic city as argued earlier is necessarily a selection from the many possible urban 'pasts'; it is that the heritage of the tourist and that of the resident may be different enough to initiate conflicts about the purposes, and thus applications, of urban conservation. Neither group is of course homogeneous, but it is likely that the heritage the historic city chooses to present to itself will be different in emphasis, irrelevant to, or at worst conflicting with, that presented to visitors. This is especially likely to be the case where the cultural backgrounds of visitors and residents are widely different and where conservation is a decentralised local activity pursued for largely local aims. An extreme case raised by Zetter *et al.* (1982) is that of the remaining architectural relics of the West African slave trade. The conservation of these major historic features would be of potential interest to foreign tourists, but not necessarily welcome to residents.

Such differences are easy to identify in general on the international scale, where the differences between foreign visitors and local residents are greatest. A clear example from the many possible would be the interest of Western tourists in the, to them, relevant Graeco-Roman and early Christian heritage of the cities of Western Turkey and their lack of interest in Islamic Seljuk, Ottoman or more recent Kemalist heritage, although this is of critical significance for Turkish national and local identity. The problem for the Ministry of Culture and Tourism in setting priorities in the national conservation effort between the requirements of tourism and those of residents has posed very real dilemmas about what to conserve in cities such as Istanbul (Aysan, 1982).

More generally, the question 'whose heritage?' clouds the conservation and marketing of urban heritage in all formerly colonial societies seeking to exploit the tourism markets of their former masters: this has been noted by Tunbridge (1984) in relation to Harare (Salisbury), Zimbabwe, and by Western (1985) with respect to Tientsin, China. The depression in commodity prices in the 1980s encouraged many less developed countries to turn to the relics of their colonial past as an exploitable resource. Ivory Coast sought the help of UNESCO in 1988 in the restoration of the colonial parts of Grand Bassam and Grand Lahou. A long-standing example is the West Indies, which routinely markets what to many residents must be not only socially alien but distasteful reminders of slavery and colonial rivalry. An example of a city whose origin and success is rooted in colonialism is Singapore. But here the consequences of economic prosperity and overzealous redevelopment rather than any conscious rejection of the past have all but eradicated both the city's sense of place and any appeal to heritage tourism. In 1988 the problem of how to conserve Raffles Hotel, the central symbol of colonial Singapore, now marooned in a sea of modern development, was recognised as acute. Fortunately the polyglot nature of Singapore society has largely prevented the arousal of the social discord in such conservation common in many ex-colonies.

Ultimately this problem of marketing discordant heritage must also apply to South Africa, where urban conservation and tourism still heavily emphasise the heritage of the governing minority; classic illustrations are found in Pietermaritzburg (Tunbridge, 1984) and Cape Town (Western, 1985). Western believes that a former colonial society can only identify with and value the heritage of its erstwhile masters when it no longer represents a threat to national self-confidence – as with Roman remains in Britain or even British remains in the United States. If this is the case it is difficult to be optimistic about the future of white urban heritage in South Africa.

This problem is less extreme and less obvious when both tourist and resident share a similar national cultural heritage, but it can still be detected. In the city of Norwich for example, where the selection and management of the historic city is largely at the local level, the needs of tourism appears only in the fourth place in the stated aims of conservation policy (Berkers *et al.*, 1986), and thus at its simplest, 'the list of monuments of tourist interest may be quite different from those of archaeological interest' (Lawson and Baud-Bovy, 1977).

These sorts of arguments can be taken further by considering the implications of variations in the expectations of tourists. Cohen's (1979a) phenomenology of tourist experiences suggests at least two contrasting experiences relevant to the historic city. The first is the search for 'authenticity' in the past in compensation for the perceived shortcomings of the present. This is MacCannell's (1973) 'pilgrimage' in search of 'reality' which would clearly be frustrated by a too apparent 'staging' by the tourism industry. The second is the expectation of entertainment and distraction through an acknowledged 'pseudo-event' (Boorstin, 1963; 1964) and the acceptance therefore of an obviously contrived experience.

In summary, therefore, tourism is never likely to provide direct financial support, effective occupation of conserved buildings or a justification for the choice of more than a portion of the historic area in a limited number of historic cities. Its seasonality, selectivity, capriciousness in the face of fashion, as well as its systems of organisation and finance, will render it an incidental windfall gain rather than a central support in all but a handful of the most favoured cities. However, most other possible justifications for the creation and maintenance of the historic city from among urban functions suffer from similar weaknesses. The use of conserved buildings for housing is also selective both in terms of social groups that find the historic city an attractive residential environment and the sorts of structures that will find residential uses. Non-commercial cultural and social functions similarly make little or no financial contribution to the costs of the historic city, and many rehabilitation possibilities for retailing or office uses have similar environmentally intrusive consequences for traffic flows, ancillary services and the like.

This less complacent view is essentially European rather than North American. Although strictly speaking heritage is a relative rather than an absolute condition, North America is generally perceived as having a scarcity in comparison with Europe's surplus. Consequently there tends to be more commercial exploitation for tourism than the perceived historic resource might strictly justify, giving rise to an over-commercialisation problem rather than the reverse. It can also be argued that the problems of congestion are less likely to arise, except in those few cities where a particular restricted street-plan is an integral part of the historic resource.

However although the possession of less supply to satisfy much the same demand may lead to higher financial returns per monument, the difficulties of dependence upon a capricious and selective tourism market remain.

The historic city cannot be conceived or maintained on formal morphological criteria alone. In 'preserving purposefully' the purpose is intrinsic to the conservation and the historic city must therefore be considered also in functional terms. The intention here is not to deny this proposition, still less to denigrate the role of tourism in this respect. It is merely to assert that the symbiosis between the conserved city and the tourism industry is complex and not automatic. The recognition that the relationship is in many respects partial, frequently one-sided in its dependency, and occasionally the cause of conflict, provides a salutary introduction to the discussion of the historic city as a tourism resource.

The historic city as an urban tourism resource

A tourist resource, broadly defined, is any facility which is, or could be used by tourists but 'as tourists make use of a wide variety of facilities but an exclusive use of very few' (Ashworth, 1985) such a definition presents difficulties in the city where the range of possible tourism services is especially wide.

An early classification of recreation sites, by the influential Outdoor Recreation Resources Review Commission studies during the late 1950s and early 1960s in the United States, produced a well-known list of types of site resources of which the last was headed 'urban sites', as if the many different attractions and urban services offered to visitors could be bundled into a single catch-all category. A subsequent elaboration of this category was the division of sites into 'resource-orientated', i.e. those sites necessarily located on the immobile point of supply, and 'demand-orientated', i.e. sites created to satisfy a demand at or near its origin (Clawson and Knetch, 1966). There was a strong presumption that such a spectrum corresponded to a rural-urban distinction, with urban facilities being examples of demand-orientation.

Certainly many subsequent studies concentrated analysis upon those urban facilities exclusively or dominantly used in tourism or deliberately promoted to tourism markets. These were both easier to identify and clearly related to traceable patterns of demand. The resulting models of tourism accommodation (for example, Gutirrez, 1977; Ritter, 1985; de Groote, 1987; Pearce, 1987a), shopping (Werner, 1974; Dumas, 1982), cultural attractions (Wall and Sinnott, 1980; Moreschi, 1985) and many other urban services are necessarily partial and necessitate an artificial separation of the facility and its users from the context in which it is enjoyed. Such a restriction denies the very variety that is at the heart of the attraction of cities to tourists and which comprises the package of related experiences assembled by visitors to the city. It also inevitably neglects those many aspects of the city which are important to the tourism experience but for which consumption by tourists is only a small part of total demand. This central paradox, whereby tourism may be of only marginal significance to a facility, or to the city as a whole, while the same facility or city can be an important tourism resource, is especially relevant to heritage tourism.

Heritage tourism makes use of a particularly wide range of facilities, which themselves serve a wide variety of different types of users. Therefore the starting-point for this analysis must be the city as a whole rather than any fruitless attempt to isolate a specific set of exclusive tourism resources.

Primary and secondary attractions

A basic simplifying division of resources is the distinction between 'primary', i.e. resources which attract visitors and are the principal motive for the visit, and 'secondary', i.e. resources which support visitors during their stay. It can be objected, of course, that an individual may be motivated to visit a city by its so-called support services and during such a stay visit a museum, while another may do precisely the reverse. But despite the variety of possible motivations, which can be particularly eccentric in leisure-time activities, the generalisation can be made that a distinction exists between 'intentional' and 'incidental' use of facilities, and that the former can be regarded as primary and the latter, being dependent, as secondary. A more serious objection is that a classification based on motivation rather than on any intrinsic quality of the resource itself implies that different groups of visitors classify facilities in the same way. However, a foreign visitor in search of culture may regard a museum as a primary attraction, and motive for the visit to the city, while incidentally using restaurants and souvenir shops, while conversely a visitor on a gastronomic or shopping excursion may make an incidental use of a museum on a rainy afternoon.

The distinction between primary and secondary does not imply a quantitatively more intense use of the former. On the contrary, visitors may come to cities for their primary attractions but spend most of their time and money on secondary facilities (see Ashworth and de Haan, 1986), which are often more suited to repeated use. Nor does it imply that primary attractions were created for tourists while secondary facilities were not. The reverse is more likely to be the case. The Berlin Wall, Niagara Falls and Westminister Abbey are primary attractions which tourism did not create while the hotels, cafés and souvenir shops that have sprung up around them are clearly secondary.

Although cities may possess many sorts of primary tourist resources, whether casinos in Las Vegas, natural phenomena in Niagara or Marienbad, modern architecture in Brasilia or the fun parks of Disneyworld, it is historic resources, as defined in Chapter 2, that are the most numerous, widespread and important. The inherited built environment of historical architecture and urban morphology, associations with historical events and personalities and the accumulations of cultural artefacts and associations with artistic achievements and individuals are the raw materials from which the tourist-historic city is created. It is our contention that these historic resources are the single most important primary attraction for tourists and thus tourist-historic cities are the world's most important tourism resorts.

This contention is difficult to demonstrate statistically for the reasons already argued, but a number of national studies have indicated the primacy of heritage, however labelled, as a motive for foreign travel in Belgium (de Groote, 1987), France (Garay, 1980) and Britain (English Tourist Board, 1981). History, usually portrayed as 'tradition', is the dominant element in the national tourism marketing images of most European countries (Dilley, 1986) and present in most city marketing, at least in Western Europe (Ashworth and Voogd, 1986a). If domestic holidays and day excursions are considered, then historic attractions are ranked among the top three types of destination in most West European countries. The size of the market available for heritage in general is impossible to delineate accurately but is indicated by such randomly available statistics as for instance 60 per cent of the French population make at least one annual visit to an historic monument (Busson and Evrard, 1987) or British medieval cathedrals receive more than 30 million annual visits (Binney and Hanna, 1978). The annual sales of Michelin or Baedecker *Guides*, both dominantly heritage-orientated, or the subscriptions to museum or historic attractions annual passes (such as Britain's National Trust or the Netherlands 'Museum Passport') are enough to demonstrate that an active interest in visiting heritage sites is a mass recreational pursuit in the Western world.

At the scale of the individual city it is difficult to assess the importance of historic attractions compared to others. London's around 12 million foreign visitors are unlikely to spend all their time in museums but equally it will be the exceptional visitor that is totally unaware of the heritage on offer. League tables of visitor numbers to particular attractions in individual cities or countries have obvious difficulties of comprehensiveness, comparability and means of measurement. Many sites have an unregulated free entry, or are part of a freely accessible urban scene. Amsterdam, for example, cannot really be said to possess a single internationally renowned historic building yet it attracts millions of visitors to the ensemble of *grachten* and *herenhuizen*. The *English Heritage Monitor* annually lists the numbers of recorded visits to the major historical sites, buildings, gardens and museums in England and indicates the enormous attractive power of the best-known sites. Not all are in urban locations but there is not only a clear concentration in cities but also in a limited number of major tourist centres.

It is of course possible for historic resources to be used as secondary attractions by groups of visitors primarily motivated by other tourism or non-tourism attributes of the city. Business and conference visitors frequently make incidental use of historic and cultural facilities (Labasse, 1984; Law, 1988) and it is salutary to remember that the numerically most important group of visitors to most museums and historic monuments are local residents on repeat visits. Similarly, cities dependent upon quite different primary tourism resources can make use of historic resources as secondary attractions. To relate one typical example, the seaside resort of Great Yarmouth (UK) offers the traditional primary attractions of the seaside holiday based on beach and promenade entertainments. The need for diversions during the stay, and especially in wet weather, has prompted the exploitation of the historic resources of the town, especially those related to fishing and the sea. A number of museums have been opened; the conservation of the fabric of the town has received a new impetus. Few visitors are attracted to the resort by these resources but they contribute to the general atmosphere and specific excursion possibilities for those already attracted by the seaside resources. On a regional scale the same phenomenon can be observed in the use of historic cities as recreational centres in or near seaside resort developments. Examples can be seen in the use of Aigues Mortes, Agde or Arles on the Languedoc coast (Ashworth and de Haan, 1987), Cadiz or Cordoba for sections of the Spanish coast, or Ravenna for the North Adriatic beach resorts of Italy. The same juxtaposition of historic cities and beach resorts can be seen in St. Augustine (Florida), Beaufort (South Carolina) and through much of the Caribbean. In much of the less developed world the linking of historic cities to beach resorts is viewed as a means of increasing the importance of tourism to regional development, by extending the length of stay, moving 'up-market' to attract higher spending visitors, as well as spreading the impacts of tourism: a case in point is Cancun, Mexico, and the associated development of the Mayan and Spanish heritage in Yucatan, centred upon the historic city of Merida. Further examples are discussed in Chapter 7.

Therefore the historic city is not only a major tourism resource and part of a number of quite different packages serving various tourism and recreational markets; whether in a primary or secondary capacity, it also fulfils different roles within the city, the region and beyond.

The resort city

The idea of the resort combines the function of tourism with the particular spatial setting of a town, and is thus of special interest here. Admittedly, studies of resorts have been overwhelmingly concerned with one particular type of tourism activity, namely seaside holidays, with only a few examples of applications to other sorts of recreation such as winter sports, and to locations other than the sea coast. However, resort studies are important to the tourist-historic city as the only substantial body of work that approaches a particular form of tourism as an inextricable part of a particular type of town. There is thus the probability that the sets of models developed may, with modifications, prove applicable to the case of cities attracting visitors through their historic resources.

Most commentators have tended to regard tourist resorts as a special category of town, distinguishable by its recognisable dominant function, and therefore exceptional. This provides an excuse for their exclusion from most further consideration. The assumption underlying many textbooks on urban topics is that towns fall into two unequal categories: resorts, where the dominant economic function and resulting social or morphological structure derives from tourism, and non-resort, or 'normal', towns where the mainstream of urban models and techniques can be safely applied. Such an assumption has two unfortunate consequences. It explains the general failure to apply the advances in the understanding of urban processes in recent years to resorts. Even more seriously, it denies the presence of the resort function, to a greater or lesser extent, in all cities. Resorts are also towns, but all towns are to an extent resorts. Lawson and Baud-Bovy (1977), among a few others, recognised that being a resort was a relative rather than an absolute condition with their attempts to measure the importance of the resort function through various numerical indices of visitors or visitor facilities. None of these are of much practical use in ranking towns according to the importance of the tourism function, but they do underline the necessity to root an analysis of the tourist city in more general models of resort development and structure.

Such resort studies stem from two main lines of geographical thought. The first is that the concepts and techniques of urban classification can be extended to include specifically tourist towns. This led to a categorisation of resorts and resort regions by a mixture of functional and locational criteria, combining features of the physical environment with aspects of tourism demand. This approach, originating in Defert (1966) and developed by a school of mainly French geographers, including Miossec (1976), Clary (1977) and Lozato (1985), provides a means of defining the tourist city in general and the tourism heritage city in particular. Secondly, the explanatory models of the internal structure of cities, developed mainly in the United States, can be modified to include the tourism function. This results in intra-urban regionalisations which allow the tourist city to be included as one element in functional-morphological 'ecologies' of the city.

Such ideas were first applied to seaside resorts, one of the oldest and most easily recognisable resort forms, by Barrett (1958), Lavery (1971), de Haan and Ashworth (1985b) among others for British examples, and were rapidly diffused to other parts of the world, including France (Pearce, 1978) and Australia (Pigram, 1977). Although the seaside resort has received most attention there have been some applications of similar techniques to other types of tourism centre, especially to Alpine winter sports resorts and health spas (for example, de Haan, 1982). Perhaps the nearest such studies have approached the analysis of the large multifunctional city, as opposed to the deliberate selection of towns whose economies are as monofunctional as possible, is the delimitation of specialised commercial areas within cities. Regionalisation, based primarily upon rent surfaces in the United States, allowed the recognition of Recreational Business Districts, as extensions of existing Central Business Districts (CBD) (Stansfield and Rickert, 1970). This idea was exported to other countries (e.g. Taylor, 1975) and ultimately extended to other intra-urban regions based on specific groupings of leisure facilities, such as models of entertainment districts (Burtenshaw *et al.*, 1981; Ashworth *et al.*, 1988), restaurants (Bonnain-Moerdijk, 1975; Smith, 1983) and recreational shopping (Dumas, 1982; Jansen-Verbeke, 1990; Jansen, 1989).

The common features of these various attempts to model the functional structure of resorts are the method of treatment of tourism supply facilities, the nature of the resulting regionalisations and the acceptance of the existence of an inherent dynamic element. It is these three features, which are differently stressed and labelled by different authors, which allow these models to be particularly useful for our purposes. Comprehensive inventories of tourism facilities are unnecessary and are replaced by the search for indicative variables and their application in the creation of tourism regions. Sets of tourism facilities, whether in exclusive tourist use or not, are extracted from the total on the basis of the extent to which they can be used to indicate the spatial patterns of tourism in the city. The ensuing regionalisation results in the delimitation of such districts as 'sea-front entertainment', 'beach activities', 'tourist shopping corridor', 'entertainment district' and the like, which in turn are spatially and functionally related to similarly derived non-tourism functional regions familiar in urban geography. In fact, some of the most interesting aspects of such studies have been the demonstration of relationships between the specifically resort elements and the more ubiquitous urban characteristics. Finally, functional trends can be accommodated in such regionalisations and thus developmental sequences can be modelled.

The duality of the definition of the tourist city as both a designation of particular cities and of functional regions within all cities closely parallels that of the historic city made earlier. Such a definition, and consequent delimitation, is thus heavily dependent upon the extension of these resort concepts and techniques to cities in general.

Modelling the tourist city

The purpose of modelling the tourist city, in the sense described above, is to describe the present characteristic spatial patterning in relation to the urban structure as a whole, explaining the processes that have produced it so that trends can be recognised. The resulting tourist city, or cities, is thus not an exceptional kind of city nor even a homogeneous and exclusive monofunctional area within cities. It is a pattern of spatially clustered sets of functional associations that relates the activity of tourism to cities in general, allowing the tourist city to be compared to the historic city described in Chapter 2, and to a wide variety of other possible 'cities'.

For these purposes it is necessary to select sets of variables from among the many available that can be used as regional indicators of the spatial characteristics of the tourist city. Such indicators should be capable of recognition, collection, cartographic or statistical comparison and manipulation. From the large number and variety of facilities used by tourists a selection is generally made from within the three broad categories of accommodation, catering and attractions.

Elements in the tourist city

Commercial accommodation establishments have an obvious central importance to the package of tourism services consumed by visitors, being generally the largest item of expenditure, and also have the advantage to the researcher of being easily recognisable, and measurable in terms of capacity statistics, as well as producing distinctive spatial patterns of location. A major disadvantage is that registered commercial hotels supply only a part of total tourist overnight accommodation needs, with non-commercial or informal unregistered establishments being often of larger numerical importance in many cities. Equally, if not all tourists stay in hotels, not all hotel guests are tourists. The significance for the use of hotels as an indicator of the regionalisation of tourism is that the locational requirements of non-tourist visitors may be substantially different, and furthermore, with the rapid growth of the convention sector of the business market, which is dominantly urban hotel-based, it has become increasingly difficult to define which visitors are tourists.

Despite these difficulties, much of the urban modelling that does try to incorporate the tourism function mentioned earlier, such as that of Lundgren (1974) or Lozato (1985), is effectively using hotels as surrogates for tourism facilities as a whole. Among the most persistent attempts to describe and explain various categories of urban hotel locations are those for individual large European cities (e.g. Vetter, 1985; Gutirrez, 1977), medium-sized towns (Pearce, 1987a) and the comparative examples within a national (de Groote, 1987) or continental context (Burtenshaw *et al.*, 1981).

Such existing work is however only relevant for our purposes of regionalisation if hotel locations can be used as an indicator of the existence of distinctive tourism regions within the city. Figure 3.1 offers a comprehensive typology of urban hotel locations on the basis of experience

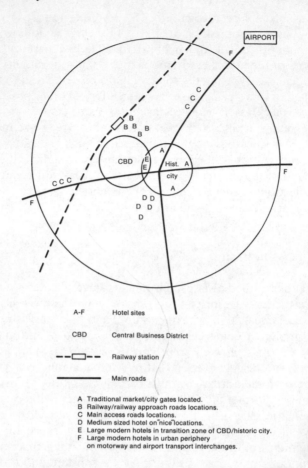

A-F   Hotel sites

CBD   Central Business District

-- --⬜-- --   Railway station

──────   Main roads

A Traditional market/city gates located.
B Railway/railway approach roads locations.
C Main access roads locations.
D Medium sized hotel on nice locations.
E Large modern hotels in transition zone of CBD/historic city.
F Large modern hotels in urban periphery
   on motorway and airport transport interchanges.

Figure 3.1   *Typology of urban hotel locations*

in medium-sized Western European provincial towns. Six types of locational cluster are hypothesised, each resulting from the responses of the hotel industry to such factors as accessibility, land values, environmental amenity, historic inertia and, more recently, land-use planning controls.

The most significant conclusion from such a typology is that recognisable concentrations of hotels can be identified, and these can be allocated to distinct categories. However these concentrations are themselves widely dispersed through the city in many types of central or peripheral location. A fundamental difficulty for our purposes is that the spatial and functional relationships between accommodation and other tourism supply elements is likely to be significantly different in each type of locational cluster. Locations in the historic core, for example, are likely to have strong functional associations with the attractions and facilities of the historic and central commercial city, in contrast to the urban-periphery hotel locations which are likely to be far more self-contained in the services they offer, less strongly associated with other tourism elements, and thus poor indicators of the tourist city.

Catering facilities form the second most frequently used set of tourism services but their use as indicative variables poses two particular problems. First, they are also widely patronised by residents, so that tourist demands are only of any proportional significance in relatively few establishments. Secondly, amongst the variety of different types of catering service there exist quite different patterns of distribution through the city and quite different spatial associations with other facilities, as Smith (1983) has demonstrated in detail for different types of prepared food outlets in a medium-sized Canadian city.

Thus such catering services as public houses, bars and taverns, cafés, fast-food outlets and take-aways have locational patterns that reflect the local distribution of residential or economically active populations in various parts of the city, rather than demonstrating the existence of concentrations of tourism activity as such. Thus, although many establishments in these categories play important roles in the tourism experience, generally in association with other tourism services, they rarely aid the definition and delimitation of areas of tourist activity. However restaurants and establishments combining food and drink with other entertainments, whether night-clubs, discos, casinos and the like, have two important locational characteristics that render them useful in this context: they have a distinct tendency to cluster together into particular streets or districts, what might be termed the 'latin-quarter effect', and they tend to be associated spatially with other tourism elements including hotels, which probably themselves offer public restaurant facilities.

The place of catering facilities within clusters of other entertainment and shopping functions raises issues which will be considered at length in the wider context of the users of the tourist-historic city, in Chapter 5.

The third category of tourism services, attractions, is the most hetero-geneous of the three but is taken to mean here the distribution of those urban facilities that themselves attract visitors rather than providing the support services mentioned above. Amongst the many possibilities, it is the historic attractions that are the most relevant in this context and in practice generally the most important. The distribution of tourist-historic attractions is not the same as that of the historic resources considered earlier. Tourists select from these resources a limited number, and restricted area, to be visited. Figure 3.2 shows the distribution of actual visits to historic attractions of a sample of visitors to Norwich (Ashworth and de Haan, 1986) and it is clear that not only are these a small fraction of the total available (cf. Figure 2.5) but that even within the small number visited there is an intense concentration upon a very few. This distinct and concentrated locational behaviour of tourists which stems from their constraints of time, money and knowledge, makes the use of this variable

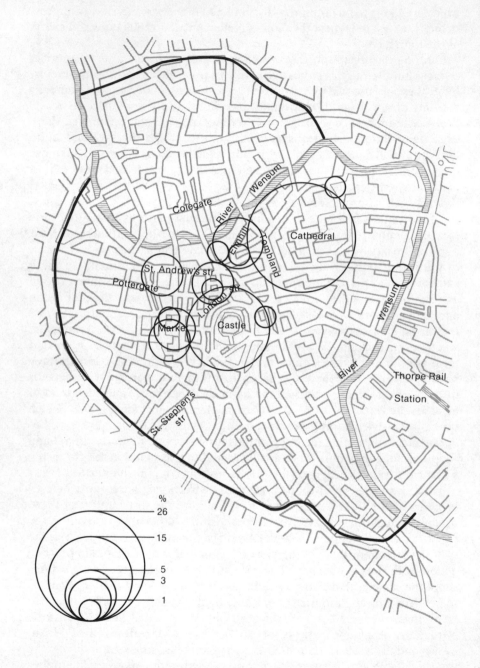

Figure 3.2   *Distribution of actual visits to historic attractions: Norwich*

for indicative purposes more effective. The only major problem is the variety of physical forms that can constitute an historic attraction.

MacCannell (1976) argues that the link between the physical site and the tourist is what he terms the 'marker', i.e. a designation that renders the former of significance to the latter. Thus an historical attraction may be such marked sites as a statue or monument, building, collection of movable artefacts, or groups of buildings and spaces that may encompass a whole district ('the old town'). It may even be a point indistinguishable in itself but associated with an event or personality. The cartographic difficulties of incorporating all such types of attraction into a spatial model are obvious.

Regional synthesis

The synthesising of these, and potentially other, tourism facilities into a regionalisation model has the obvious difficulties of comparing the significance of quite different types and sizes of establishments. Various weighting systems and methods of regionalisation can be used, but as the purpose is not to produce hard boundaries but to indicate areas of concentration, over-sophistication is unnecessary; and as with the delimitation of the historic city earlier, trend surfaces are useful measures of such spatial concentrations.

The results show that the city as used and recognised by tourists can be described as restricted in its selection of only a small portion of the total area; concentrated in its clustering; and contiguous in that the spatial concentrations are rarely widely separated from each other. The simple model has the tourist city overlapping both that part of the historic city selected for tourism functions, and part of the commercial city, where many of the related elements of tourist shopping, entertainment and catering can be found.

A number of modifications to such a simple model are possible. First, although some tourist accommodation is spatially associated with this central city region, a large proportion of the accommodation sector is often to be found outside it, as was discussed above, spatially and functionally isolated from other tourism services. Secondly, the model is based upon medium-sized towns in which tourism services and attractions will be concentrated into a single contiguous area which often measures no more than a few hundred metres. In Delft for example (VVV Delft, 1970), the action space of visitors was only some 200 metres from the central square. In much larger cities, however, a number of different spatially separate tourist cities can develop, sometimes separated by distances too large to be linked by walkable corridors. Conversely, in the small historic 'gem' cities the spatial distinction between historic, commercial and tourist cities cannot be so clearly distinguished, and in effect the town is small enough to be encompassed as a whole by a tourist's action radius of about 200 metres.

Thirdly, different groups of visitors may have significantly different zones of activity and thus in practice occupy different tourist cities. Although such an hypothesis is difficult to demonstrate clearly, there is some evidence that day, weekend and longer-term visitors (Ashworth and de Haan, 1986) and organised groups rather than individuals (Chaudefaud, 1981) may in practice patronise identifiably separate tourist cities, sometimes in different seasons.

The relationship between tourism facilities, tourist behaviour and tourism images is particularly important in delimiting such tourism regions in cities. Although there is an obvious triangular relationship between the location of tourism facilities, the spatial behaviour of the customers and the mental maps and preconceived expectations of the city that they hold, the direction in which this circular relationship operates is by no means clear. Each of these elements is not only influenced by the other two but also by exogenous factors. The location of tourism facilities is influenced by demands from other than tourists, and by factors relating to the structure and organisation of the industries of which they are a part, the economy of the city as a whole, especially the availability and costs of land and premises, as well as by locally implemented land-use planning policies. The spatial behaviour of tourists is controlled not only by their knowledge and experience of the city but also by the availability and accessibility of various modes of transport. Finally, the images and expectations of visitors can be influenced by deliberate promotional policies or the manipulation of information, as well as a wide range of opinion-forming sources well beyond the city.

The exact mechanisms through which all these variables, whether endogenous to tourism or not, operate to produce, reinforce or change the location of the tourist city are imperfectly understood. Consider, for example, one of many such circular processes that is especially relevant to historic-city tourism. An object, site, area or city is marked as of historic significance; tourists are drawn to it as a result of their changed image and new expectations; facilities to serve visitors are established. This very location of facilities is itself an attraction and the growing concentration of visitors confirms to each the importance of the tourism experience to be gained at the site, which in turn reinforces the marking in the information supplied to visitors. All three factors in this process seem to have an interest in increasing tourist numbers. Facilities are guaranteed a capacity market, tourists a valued experience and image promoters a clear method of selling visits to the city. If no countervailing centrifugal process exists, the logical end result is a concentration of all tourism in the city within a single area. Some portion of all three elements, however, have an interest in dispersion. The image promoters, especially if responsive to local authority goals, may adopt policies designed to encourage a spread of costs and benefits into the 'unknown city'; the innovatory minority of tourists gain satisfaction from pioneering and marking new areas; tourism facilities may be responsive to either official policies or commercial pressures to search out untapped

Figure 3.3 *The tourist city in Norwich*

markets in new locations. All these mutually reinforcing ways will lead to the expansion of the periphery of the tourist city.

These inherent trends towards concentration and dispersion lead to either an intensification of tourist activities or their expansion into new areas of the city. As tourism is rarely an exclusive occupier of urban space, these processes in turn affect other land-uses. The relationship of tourism to other uses of the same space may be one of functional association (i.e. the two uses are linked through either customer behaviour or various supply characteristics of the facility), functional competition, which can take many forms, or just spatial coexistence of two unrelated functions. Some of these possibilities will be considered in Chapter 5.

Figure 3.3 applies these various ideas to the single example of Norwich, a medium-sized multifunctional city with important historic resources which attract around a half million staying, and three million day, visitors annually. Despite modifications due to the peculiarities of the city's physical site and historical development, a clearly defined tourist city can be identified. Such a zone of tourist activity can itself be seen to be composed of a number of different combinations of land-uses. The tourist city is in part a selected area of the historic city, sharply concentrated between the cathedral and the castle; in part it merges with the eastern end of the commercial city, where the main shops and transport services of interest to tourists are located; and in part it occupies the overlap area between the historic and commercial cities, in this case focused on the market and surrounding streets. Although tourist accommodation is to be found in the last-named zone in particular (category 'E' sites according to the classification in Figure 3.1), much of the tourist accommodation is located outside the central area near to the railway station ('B' sites) and along the main access roads into the city ('C' sites).

Areas of association, competition and coexistence with other uses exist. These include the zone of overlap between historic, commercial and tourist cities, where controversy has been focused by a number of proposed developments (the Timberhill schemes) in which different combinations of shopping, office and hotel developments, involving various amounts of demolition, have been debated.

Expansion of the tourist city, an explicit policy of the city's tourism authorities (Berkers *et al.*, 1986), leads tourism into a relationship with the historic city in the south-east (King Street), north ('Norwich — over the Wensum'), and north-west (St. Benedict's). In most of these areas tourism is a welcome use of conserved buildings for which there is little alternative demand: but the council policy of encouraging the residential function in the central area, mostly in newly built infill developments, raises some problems of competition for land and of incompatibility between functions.

Such an analysis of change in the model of spatial structure, and the implications that can be derived from it, originated essentially from Western European experience. Although the tourist city, in various forms, can also be similarly modelled for the North American city, the processes through which it has been developed and the nature of the interaction and association between tourism and other functions may well be substantially different. For example, multifunctional conservation projects frequently include residential gentrification as an integral and supportive component of tourism developments. These and similar questions will be considered in the chapters on management and planning.

4 Modelling the tourist-historic city

The nature and use of a model

The attempts to conceptualise and regionalise the historic and tourist cities in the preceding chapters resulted in sets of intra-urban structure models that were necessarily based on an initial isolation of these functions from each other and from other functional areas of the city. Although the two concepts were distinct in their origins and development, it nevertheless became increasingly clear in the subsequent analysis that the historic city is at least in part being defined by tourist demand and that the tourist city is in part delimitable in terms of the location of historic attractions. Each was developed initially quite independently by different organisations for quite different motives, yet it was argued above that the historic city ultimately depends for its definition and justification upon users while similarly the artefacts of the past are marketable as tourism resources. Thus we arrive by the logic of evolution rather than the deliberate intent of policy-makers at the composite tourist-historic city. This concept has much in common with other attempts to delimit similar areas especially in relation to tourist and recreational uses of the city, such as the idea of the Recreational Business District (Stansfield and Rickert, 1970) or Central Tourist District (Burtenshaw *et al.*, 1981, p.172). Both of these however are narrower, being based upon recreational commercial services and tourism facilities respectively.

The tourist-historic city presents few new difficulties of conceptualisation or regionalisation, being merely the conjunction of the two previous models, so that overlap and interaction between the two constituent elements contribute towards a new synthesis. Thus the tourist-historic city can be conceived and modelled in the same way and with the same constraints as were earlier applied separately to the historic and tourist cities.

The bringing together of the two models into the composite tourist-historic city risks introducing a certain amount of circularity into the discussion as each part of the combined concept is, to an extent, dependent for its definition upon the other. The conjunction does not, however, necessarily imply an automatic compatibility and it is the interplay, whether co-operative or conflicting, between the two elements revealed by the synthesis that is in itself the justification for producing the composite model. The concept and model of the tourist-historic city both poses, and provides the framework for answers to, a number of important questions that are central to the management of such cities and form a leitmotiv in the subsequent chapters of this book.

From the viewpoint of the historic city two such questions are posed. Is tourism a realistic use of the conserved city? Realistic in this context might be assessed in terms of land or building occupancy, economic return or social and cultural benefits. Related to this is the question, does the implicit selectivity of tourism at best limit the usefulness of tourism and at worst distort the wider aims of urban conservation? In planning terms the question is frequently resolved into whether a single set of conserved resources can serve different groups of users equally effectively, or whether the commitment to tourism excludes, or restricts, opportunities for other users. 'The list of monuments of tourist interest may be quite different from the list of archaeological interest' (Lawson and Baud-Bovy, 1977). To this could be added many other such 'interests' and the broader implications of selling the city as different products to distinctly different consumer groups.

From the viewpoint of the tourist city there are similar intrinsic potential conflicts. First and fundamentally, many of these inevitably derive from the 'commodification' of the past, that is its treatment as a commercially exploitable product (see Ashworth and Voogd, 1989), in a volatile fashion-conscious and highly competitive market. Both conservation planning and heritage marketing are selective, but in each case the selection is based on different criteria and goals. Thus the delimitation and presentation of the urban past for tourism may lead to conflicts both within tourism, which is by no means a homogeneous market, and with other users of the historic city.

Secondly, the process of urban conservation, described above, was in practice largely a matter of the imposition of constraints upon the activities of land and building owners and users. The historic city was created by the imposition of controls on free markets in the community interest. The tourism industry requires many facilities which are usually provided by commercial firms in a competitive context. The question in simple terms is, to what extent is the successful use of the conserved city for this commercial activity dependent upon breaching the very protective regulations that created it?

Thirdly, there is a difference in the emphasis upon spatial scales that threatens the compatibility of the historic and tourist cities. The former is dominantly local in motivation and management, while the latter is inevitably related to demands from beyond the individual city. The tourist city is intrinsically part of a wider network of tourism places, whether these are defined in terms of visitor behaviour or facility supply, in a way that the historic city is not.

Three constraints, which also applied to the previous models, need reiteration. First, the composite tourist-historic city has two distinctly different meanings: it can be used as a description of a dominant set of functions, planning designations or the perceived character of the entire city, or as a description of that part of the city within which such characteristics are concentrated. The confusion arising from such a duality of meaning is unavoidable as both senses are freely used by customers, suppliers and urban managers. A city can simultaneously be regarded as tourist-historic, which has implications for the way it is perceived as a whole, and also include specified areas which are designated tourist-historic to distinguish them from others which are not. This seeming perversity is no different from the double meanings contained in many other functional designations such as 'industrial city', 'administrative city' or 'market town'. Secondly, the intra-urban functional models are based upon regionalisations of concentrations of particular uses and therefore lack sharp boundary demarcations. Thirdly, the recognition of such functional regions does not imply monopoly or even dominance: the uses and activities considered here can, and generally do, coexist in space with other related and non-related activities, the implications of which are discussed in Chapter 5.

Establishing the model

The tourist-historic city model, being derived from a conjunction of concepts, is necessarily constructed by superimposing the spatial patterns of the historic and tourist cities within the wider context of other urban functions. The resulting model is shown in Figure 4.1 in which phase III represents the fully developed ideal situation where the historic city, the tourist city and the central commercial district all partially overlap. This pattern is a result of the shift of some central area commercial functions out of the conserved original city and the spread of the tourist city over both a selected part of the historic city and a portion of the modern commercial area. Both of these processes were discussed earlier. Logically the tourist-historic city can be defined as the area of overlap between the historic and tourist cities, this being the part of the city where historical artefacts and associations are being actively used for tourism, whether as primary attractions, secondary supporting services or merely as a background environment for the enjoyment of visitors engaged in non-historic activities.

Although such an area of overlap represents the currently exploited tourist-historic city, the entire area of both the historic and tourist cities could be included, both because an appreciation of the overlap depends upon a prior understanding of the independent development of the two constituent parts, and also because the excluded parts of the historic and tourist cities contain the latent resources for the potential expansion of the tourist-historic city. The planning and management of the tourist-historic

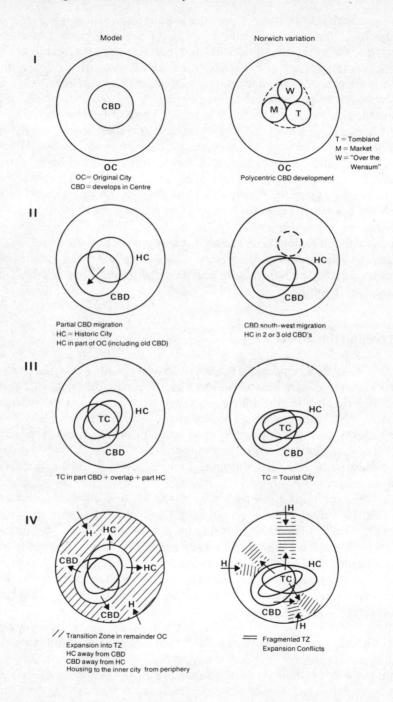

Figure 4.1 *An evolutionary model of the tourist-historic city*

areas must consider the wider entities from which they are derived: policies for tourism need to recognise that historic attractions are only one part of the package of facilities assembled from within and outside the historic city for tourist use, while conversely policies for conservation are concerned with more than just the historic highlights which have been, or could be, selected for visitor consumption.

It is clear that the tourist-historic city is not a separate functional zone in quite the same sense as a shopping district or office quarter, nor can it be delimited in purely morphological terms corresponding to the buildings and spaces of the conserved city. It is an integral part of the formal and functional complex that comprises the central area. It should be seen as an extra dimension of that complex rather than a specific function to be accommodated alongside existing central area functions, or a spatially separate demarcated district alongside other functional zones.

The empirical basis for the model derives from the regionalisation of the concentrations of historic and tourist facilities described earlier. One aspect of this complex relationship is spatial congruence between the various elements in the tourist-historic city and other urban features. Figure 4.2 shows an example of some of these sorts of spatial relationships in a medium-sized tourist-historic city as described through trend surfaces, which display significant concentrations rather than abrupt boundaries. 'Central area shopping functions' is used as an indicative variable of the central commercial area and includes an extensive part of the inner city within which protected (i.e. 'listed') buildings, as an indicator of the historic city, occupy only the northern part. The tourist city is indicated by two different variables, catering facilities and tourist attractions. The latter includes and thus tends to correspond to the distribution of historic resources, while the former also extends into the modern commercial area outside the historic city.

The spatial coincidences upon which the model is based can also be inferred statistically. For example Table 4.1 shows a set of results which, while not unexpected, do suggest some of the spatial relationships that underpin the model and need further investigation later. There is for example a positive relationship between the distribution of catering and tourist attractions but not between tourist accommodation and other tourist facilities. Similarly the central commercial area, indicated by the presence of higher-order shopping, office and banking functions, the absence of housing at ground-floor level and high rateable values (i.e. taxation assessments), correlates closely with the distribution of tourist catering facilities but not with tourist accommodation. Listed historic buildings correlate strongly with the interrelated complex of central commercial functions and especially with shops and offices.

In terms of change over time, the preceding evolutionary phases of the model are clearly those of its two constituent elements as discussed earlier. Expansion of the tourist-historic city however raises some new

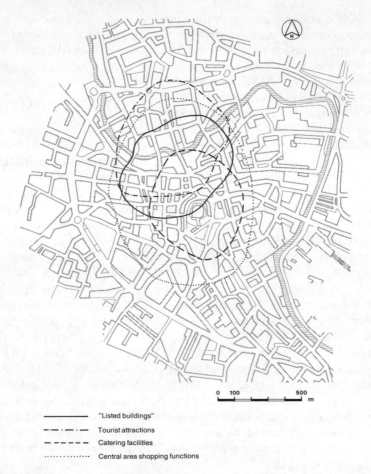

————————	"Listed buildings"
—·— ·— ·—	Tourist attractions
— — — — —	Catering facilities
··············	Central area shopping functions

Figure 4.2   *Trend surfaces for some functions in central Norwich*

issues. It is assumed that the historic city reacts to possible pressures for
expansion by extending protective cover outwards from the core of the
original city, which also generally implies an extension forward in time
into more recently built areas. Such expansion is also more likely to occur
in a direction opposite to that of the expanding commercial area within
which redevelopment rather than conservation is likely to have occurred,
thus into zones of discard where the pressures from other land-uses are
less and new functions may be sought for existing premises. The tourist
city has limited possibilities and incentives for physical expansion within
the central area. Increases in tourism demand are more likely to lead
to an intensification of tourism uses within the existing tourist city, as
a result of increased competition between tourism facilities and other
users. Some expansion of that part of the historic city used by tourism is
possible as tourists widen their selection of historic attractions, a process

Table 4.1 Matrix of Pearson correlation coefficients of the distribution of selected characteristics of the central area of Norwich

	RV	Cat.	T.At.	H(gf)	Acc.	C.S.	OBPB.	LB.
Rateable values	–	+0.19*	–	−0.27	–	+0.24*	+0.26*	+0.19*
Catering facilities		–	+0.16*	–	–	+0.74*	+0.46*	+0.41*
Tourist attractions			–	–	–	–	–	+0.31*
Housing (ground floor)				–	–	–	–	–
Tourist accommodation					–	+0.18*	–	–
Central shopping						–	+0.34*	+0.50*
Offices/Banks public buildings							–	+0.45*
Listed buildings								–

* significant at 99.9%

Source: Ashworth and de Haan, 1986, p.91

often encouraged by the dispersal policies of local tourism management agencies. Similarly expansion of this part of the tourist city may follow in the wake of expansion of the historic city as suggested above, while equally possible is expansion, especially of catering and entertainment facilities, in the opposite direction following the shift in location of the commercial city. The tourism facility most likely to expand as a result of increases in demand is purpose-built tourism accommodation, but much of this expansion is likely to be peripheral to the central area, although again intensification is as usual a reaction as physical expansion, with the zone of triple overlap between tourist, historic and central commercial cities being under particular pressure to include new tourism accommodation in redevelopment projects. Examples of the results of these processes in particular cities are illustrated later.

Variations from the model

The model described above is clearly derived from the experience of the medium-sized Western European multifunctional city. This is explicable by the early pre-eminence of this area in both urban conservation and tourism, as well as its continuing importance in these respects. However two questions must be posed, namely, would distinctly different sorts of city result in fundamentally different spatial structures, and is such a model robust enough to admit variants in response to particular physical and functional characteristics and different cultural contexts?

In searching for variants two contradictory processes can be observed, namely individualisation and standardisation. In the sense that the history of any place is a unique experience resulting in a unique historic city, and the tourist is travelling in pursuit of variety, then it might be expected that there would be substantial, widespread and deliberately cultivated deviation from any model that attempts to generalise the tourist-historic city. But against this tendency towards distinctiveness must be set one towards standardisation which is equally intrinsic to both tourism, in its search for an instantly recognisable product, and conservation planning, as a result of the internationalisation of tastes and techniques discussed earlier. In part this individual/standard paradox is explicable by the scale of the examination; none the less particular sets of variations from the model can be identified.

Variations in the site

Waterfront A fundamental set of variations can be expected when the classical assumption of a circular city, equally accessible in all directions, is relaxed. The most widespread occurrence is cities located on water frontages, whether seacoast, lakeside or riverside. This implies more than that only a portion of the circle is available for the evolution of the functional regions hypothesised, for the waterfront is more than a negative boundary. The partial separation of central commercial functions from the evolving historic city described earlier receives a new and special impetus. The waterfronts and surrounding area were often the fundamental reason for the initial establishment of the settlement and important nodes of early commercial activity. Two factors in particular are likely to encourage the discard of the waterfront area by many commercial functions. These are changes in the requirements of transport technology, and the inevitable inland migration of the geometrical centre of an expanding semicircular urban area, and thus also of city-serving commercial activities which relocate at the point of maximum accessibility. Such a loss of functions, together with the area's previous historical importance, may result in the survival, on or near the waterfront, of an architectural heritage and historic associations usable in the creation of an historic city, with the added advantage to tourism of the attraction of waterfront views and linear promenades. The exploitation of such possibilities will form an important theme in later chapters: the point here is that these physical site conditions tend to accentuate and qualify this phase of the model rather than form a radical departure from it.

Acropolis Another site attribute that is equally fundamental and widespread is that of differences in physical relief. Where these are minor they can be regarded as local detail, but there is one case in which the variations are neither minor nor exceptional: this can be termed the 'acropolis city'. It is not confined to Mediterranean countries but is so widespread in them as to be more usually the norm than the exception. Such towns originally developed on defensible higher ground in regions of chronic insecurity, expanding in more peaceful interludes beyond, and necessarily below, the original city. The functional shift of modern central commercial activities out of the historic city is thus reinforced and made physically more obvious by the distinction between the upper and lower towns. The former preserves its architectural heritage as a result of its abandonment rather than redevelopment, creating the possibility of the separate spatial development of the tourist-historic city and the modern commercial city. The results of this can be seen most clearly in a number of the medium and smaller towns of Italy, Spain, Turkey and Greece which combine both an important architectural heritage and sufficient modern development to motivate expansion beyond, and below, the original city. In extreme examples, such as Corinth, the modern city has developed some distance away from the ancient settlement; but in cities such as Bergamo, Urbino, Carcassonne or Gerona there is more continuity in both time and space, leading to the evolution of two contiguous 'cities', with tourist-historic attractions and most tourist accommodation and commercial services occupying the clearly defined upper town, and most modern commercial activities concentrating in the physically separate lower town.

Even in far larger cities, where the scale of modern development dwarfs any earlier urban development, acropolis sites may form islands of historic architectural survival and thus actual or potential tourist attraction and commercial clusters. The Turkish cities of Ankara and Izmir, for example, have small but distinctive partially walled 'upper towns' where historic functions dominate, although surrounded by modern urban developments.

While the acropolis city is particularly characteristic of the Mediterranean, similar cases occur in other regions, notably the 'burg' phenomenon (variously 'burcht', 'berg', 'borgo', 'borg' 'burgh' or 'bourg'), which was defensible high ground, whether natural or contrived, on which military and governmental functions were located. Although in most Western European towns such developments were generally gradually absorbed into the expanding settlement, they have survived in some towns to act as a focus for a wider tourist-historic city, as in Salzburg or Edinburgh.

Thus again the site variations tend to underline and reinforce the hypothesised model rather than contradict it.

Variations in size

The origin of the model in the experience of the medium-sized city implies a number of assumptions that will not necessarily apply in either the small town or the large city.

The model assumes a town large enough to possess sufficient historic, tourist and other central commercial functions to allow each of these types of facilities to cluster in recognisable regions. In other words, the sort of functional segregation envisaged in the model is dependent upon attaining a size threshold sufficient to allow spatial segregation to occur. The small historic town, which is conserved more or less *in toto*, is frequently too small to allow a spatial distinction between the conserved city and the location of tourism facilities, and also between the concentration of tourist-historic and other central commercial functions. The small conserved town, however attractive to tourists, will rarely detain them for more than a short stop, and its limited tourism facilities will rarely form a recognisable, spatially distinct, urban region. There is, however, an additional difficulty with such towns in that their charm is derived from the absence of the evolutionary pressures for change, and consequent abrupt fossilisation of their development. The interactive processes assumed by the model have just not occurred. Such towns are thus not really variants of the model so much as not relevant to it, being in their entirety a tourist-historic facility rather than tourist-historic cities: they are more open-air museums than urban places in a full sense. Examples, such as Willemstad, Bourtange, Ribe or in North America, Williamsburg or Saint Andrews will be discussed in Chapter 7.

Conversely, cities large enough to develop more than a single major concentration of a particular set of facilities can produce multiple nuclei variants of the model. Both the tourist and the historic cities will tend to develop around a number of distinct nodes, in the former case possibly linked by corridors of tourist movement between them. In the major metropolitan cities such a fragmentation of the tourist-historic attractions, based around groups of major monuments, museums or neighbourhoods with historic associations, is clearly identifiable, and best developed in the cities that combine a long history of importance, a substantial visitor inflow and a large resident population. The planning and management of a number of examples of these cities is discussed in Chapter 8.

There appears to be a critical mass of historic attractions, tourist visits and consequent development of secondary tourism services that must be reached for the successful development of such a polycentric model, which confines its occurrence to the major cities. In any case, only the major cities are likely to have absorbed enough spatially distinct historic nodes during their development to provide the resource base for such polycentricity.

Many smaller cities have seen advantages in the deliberate stimulation of the development of secondary or additional tourist-historic districts in order to encourage the spreading of the impacts of visitors, whether positive or negative, by utilising underexploited historic resources. The methods and problems of such management strategies will be considered later, but it can be noted here that the strong tendencies towards concentration found in both the tourist and historic cities, as assumed by the model, are generally only countered by genuine multiple nuclei development in the largest cities.

Cities which are both large and contain tourist-historic functions important on a national or international scale will not only tend to develop multiple nuclei but also intensify these functions within the existing areas, allowing on occasion a near monopolistic pattern of uses to occur. It is in the cities with a national show-case function, such as the larger Western European capitals, and those with a major international tourism reputation based on their historic attractions, such as Venice or Salzburg, that extensive contiguous areas of the inner city can be devoted almost exclusively to these functions, at least during specific times of the year. The complex relationships with other central area urban functions described below become, in these cases, of minor importance, at least within the districts concerned.

Cultural and historical variations

As every city is a product of a particular historical experience and reflects a particular culture, the set of tourist-historic resources will, at least in detail, be unique. Variations from any generalising model will be inevitable on these grounds alone and any attempt to describe each such variant in detail would ultimately become a Michelin *Guide* to the historic cities of the world. However this, or similar structural models, can be applied to a number of broad cultural regions other than North-western Europe, from where it was derived. The extent to which other cultural and historical experiences result in significantly different spatial generalisations, produced by different processes, will determine the universal applicability of the main suppositions of the model.

The Spanish variant An important assumption of the model is the partial functional separation of the original city, now conserved as historic, on the one hand, and the modern commercial city on the other, with the overlap between the two playing an important role in the tourist city. These aspects of the tourist-historic city have received particular attention in the work of

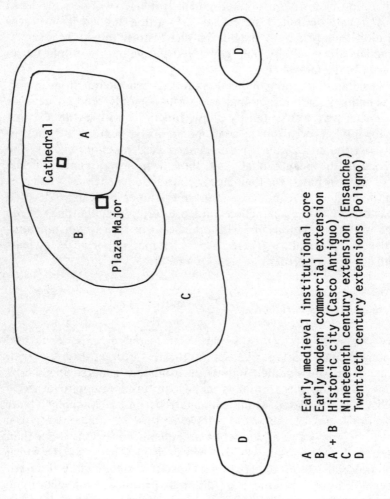

A   Early medieval institutional core
B   Early modern commercial extension
A + B   Historic city (Casco Antiguo)
C   Nineteenth century extension (Ensanche)
D   Twentieth century extensions (Poligno)

Figure 4.3   *A morphological model of the Spanish city*

Ford (1985) on the Spanish city. This study is one of the few to consider the development of urban morphology in relation to the conservation and tourism functions in a sample of medium-sized non-metropolitan provincial capitals in a single country. Thus general conclusions can be drawn about what amounts to a national model of the tourist-historic city. This national variant, although derived from the particular history and institutional structures of Spanish urbanisation, and not consciously related to experience elsewhere, nevertheless has features in common with other parts of the Western Mediterranean, and provides an elaboration of some of the aspects of the more general model.

The early medieval core of the Spanish city (see Figure 4.3) was typically walled, compact and dominated by ecclesiastical land-users. The growth of commercial activity and individual prosperity after the 'reconquest', and subsequent colonial expansion, led to an extension outside the walls in the late medieval and early modern periods. These two 'cities', taken together, form the *casco antiguo*, corresponding to the 'original city', and generally coinciding with the subsequently preserved *conjunto historico*, the historic city. Beyond this is the nineteenth-century expansion of the *ensanche*, often 'Haussmannised', as in Barcelona, which developed to accommodate both the rural immigrants and the suburbanising inhabitants of the old city. The twentieth century provided further planned and unplanned peripheral extensions.

In terms of tourist-historic functions, the medieval core was spared severe pressures for redevelopment by its early extension, which reinforced a spatial distinction between institutional and commercial land-uses. The physical and functional link between core and extension was typically provided by the *plaza mayor*, located outside the gates of the walled town. This important morphological feature is composed of a substantial open space used for trading and civic displays together with a development around it of commercial premises. The *plaza mayor* is thus often both an historic attraction in itself (as in Cordoba's *Plaza de Corredera*, for example) and the focus for tourist-oriented commercial activity. It thus performs a bridging function between the dominantly ecclesiastical monuments of the core and the commercial city. Thus that part of the medieval core nearest to the *plaza mayor* forms part of the overlap between historic and tourist zones. Conversely on the opposite side of the core it is usually possible to identify a frequently extensive discarded area of the medieval city which is peripheral to both the protected historic city and the areas of the old city penetrated by tourism. Beyond the medieval core and its early extension, the later expansions of the Spanish city have generally little of interest to offer the heritage-motivated visitor, apart from accommodation.

The Spanish variant, therefore, despite its special cultural features and particular chronology of urban development, reiterates the importance of a number of features of the general model such as the partial separation of the conserved monumental city from the tourist commercial city, the significance of the zone of overlap, aptly portrayed by the *plaza mayor*, and the spatial selectivity of tourism within the historic city and of the preserved historic city within the medieval core.

The Morocco variant If cities outside Europe were placed along a spectrum that ranged from those of purely indigenous origin and development to those whose creation and shaping owed much to Western influences, then cities such as Cuzco, Chiang-Mai, Mandalay or Zanzibar (McQuillan and Laurier, 1984) would cluster near the former end while Santo Domingo, Singapore (Turnbull, 1977), Hong Kong or Nairobi would be closer to the latter. There would however also be an identifiable middle group of cities where pre-existing, invariably pre-industrial, urban forms have been squarely confronted by Western economic and social processes which have resulted in a more clearly dualistic colonial/indigenous urban structure. Although many such examples can be found, such as Delhi and Chinese treaty ports like Tientsin (Western, 1985), this situation has been particularly well documented in a number of Moroccan cities, especially Rabat (Abu-Lughod, 1980) and Fez (Segers, 1989), which can represent many similar cases throughout the post-colonial world.

Rabat's old city, like others in Morocco, was explicitly avoided by French urban development at the turn of the century, ostensibly to preserve it from the pressures of modern urbanism, but equally to accommodate a social apartheid which effectively excluded its inhabitants from political and economic power. On the withdrawal of the colonial administration the new city was occupied by the new indigenous social and political élite, whose abandonment of the old city thereupon threatened its conservation, along with concurrent urbanisation pressures. In Fez, there are three morphologically distinct cities: the 'original' medina of the eighth century, the 'palace city' constructed in the thirteenth century as a government centre and the 'new town' dating from around 1910, which was constructed to house French residents and administrators. The first two have received various amounts of architectural protection since 1923 and together form a relatively compact historic city. The third, as in Rabat, now accommodates an indigenous élite and modern commercial and administrative functions.

At the present time the tourist-historic importance of this variant is relatively muted. It is, however, steadily growing as a result of both increasing demands of Western tourism and the expanding horizons of tourists, and of economic pressures in such countries to capitalise upon this. Where such 'schizophrenic' cities exist, the tourist-historic city will naturally be identified primarily with the indigenous component, and this will be politically most desirable in light of the 'whose heritage?' problem addressed earlier; but Western interest in the colonial heritage of the new city is also to be expected.

The Jerusalem variant Jerusalem is a special case of such dualistic cities but represents not so much a national or Middle Eastern cultural variant as a city of such remarkable longevity and particular international historic significance as to warrant separate mention.

The historic, political-symbolic and religious importance of the resource, together with the resulting long-standing reception of visitors, must be considered within the context of two distinctive characteristics of the city. These are, first, the very rapid population growth over the last century, and concomitant growth in the city's importance as a modern commercial and administrative centre, and, secondly, the omnipresent, and frequently violently expressed, political conflict within which the city has occupied a critical role. Although in this case the long and varied historical fortunes of Jerusalem render the term particularly inexact, the 'original city' is a clearly defined physical entity, referred to by both contemporary planners and citizens as the 'old city' (see Figure 4.4, phase 1). This 'old city' was largely contained within its sixteenth-century walls throughout the Ottoman period, but was subject to two sets of pressures for change after the First World War (Cohen, 1977). The first of these was the extension of preservational legislation by the British Mandate authorities over many of the historic buildings and sites, and the adoption of an urban planning philosophy within which conservation was given a high priority. Secondly, the city's population and commercial importance grew rapidly. These circumstances led to a clearly defined spatial separation of functions in phase 2 of the model, with the development of new commercial focuses outside the walls, especially in the direction of the coastal towns, such as along the Jaffa road (Turner, 1988). Intercommunal violence in the inter-war and immediate post-war period, and the armed conflict over the city itself in 1947–8, resulted in a social and political division into an Arab old city within Jordan and a Jewish West Jerusalem within Israel. This reinforced and made visible the functional separation of the historic and modern cities, leading in phase 3 to the strengthening of the modern commercial and residential functions in both West Jerusalem and north of the old city in Jordan. The *de facto* removal of the political boundary in 1967, and further rapid population growth, has led to a tendency towards the consolidation of the modern commercial city in West Jerusalem and the increasing dedication of the old city in the current urban plans to tourist-historic uses. This process was made easier by the departure from the old city of not only many of the remaining non-tourist commercial functions but also part of its Arab population.

A Japanese variant An opportunity to examine the development of tourist-historic cities in a non-Western culture is provided by the work of Satoh

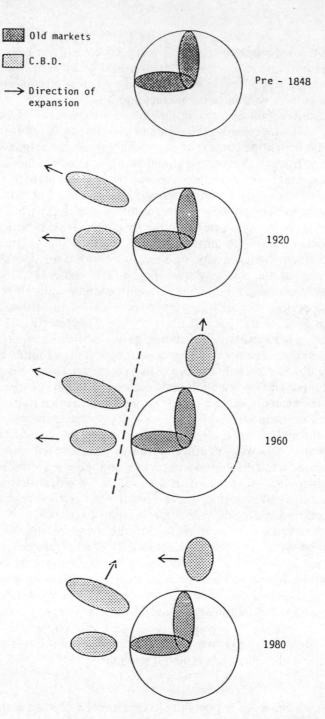

Figure 4.4   *Evolution of historic and modern commercial area in Jerusalem*

(1986) on the origin, subsequent evolution and planning problems of Japanese castle towns. Although the historical experience, building techniques and materials and methods of administration are quite different from those of Europe, it is notable that a series of generalisations have been drawn, which result in a clear spatial and functional distinction between a conserved historic city and a modern commercial city, relevant to the approximately 100 generally small or medium-sized castle towns in Japan. The processes through which this pattern emerges are, however, significantly different from those of North-Western Europe.

For much of the period before the seventeenth century the Japanese feudal system of administration and economic order led to the familiar 'acropolis' pattern of hill-top castle and administrative buildings, located for a mixture of defensive and symbolic reasons, together with the more or less spontaneous evolution of a lower commercial town. Such a pattern of settlement was widely superseded from the early seventeenth century, the beginning of the Edo period. The 'new' settlements were deliberately conceived as having two main components, namely a castle district that functioned as the seat of local administration and, separated from it by extensive defence works, a commercial and residential town. Rapid urbanisation from the end of the nineteenth century, the Meiji period, occurred mostly in the commercial town, leading to its expansion usually in a particular favoured direction, with the castle district generally acquiring mostly new administrative functions as a centralised national government replaced the local feudal structures.

The development of town planning, beginning with legislation in 1919, but becoming a major preoccupation in the period of post-1945 reconstruction, allowed a restructuring of these towns and especially the introduction of some conservational measures. A combination of earthquakes, highly combustible building materials and aerial bombardment has determined that it is the street patterns and the major landscaping features that are the main preservable attributes rather than the buildings as such. The principal axioms of this planning are the maintenance of the pre-Meiji morphological patterns in the castle districts and their use as parks, museums and other leisure-based activities, while new transport, commercial and residential developments are deflected into peripheral districts.

Satoh (1986) has described a large number of variations in the pace, timing and magnitude of development in various physical settings but the basic pattern of a clear tourist-historic district and separate, one or more, commercial districts remains. The similarity with the Western European model is obvious, despite the differences in what constitutes the historic city and the processes through which it has been created, especially the original in-built functional segregation and the absence of an extensive zone of overlap between the two.

North American variants No urban model can aspire to universality until its relevance to the North American city, and to the New World city more generally, has been established. In essence the concepts discussed above are as applicable in the New World as in Europe, given the similarity and interactivity of their market economies, conservation philosophies and tourism industries; hence the frequent reference to North American examples.

In some important respects, however, it is suggested that a difference of degree exists, which will be manifested in many of the cases discussed later. An obvious difference is in the quantity and antiquity of urban historic resources in a, by definition, more recent and less culturally varied urban system. This in turn has led not only to a higher valuation being placed on what remains but a difference in methods of exploitation and presentation, in particular a larger proportion of contrived attractions (discussed in Chapter 7). In addition, the locations of many tourism facilities tend to be more widely distributed than in Western Europe, as a consequence of the early development of private transport. It is thus more difficult to define the tourist city in narrowly inner-city terms and the concept of a regional tourist city assumes a greater prominence.

In the final analysis, in North America as elsewhere, the delimitation of the tourist-historic city, and its two components, is dependent on the functional interrelationships of its elements and how it is perceived and used by the consumer. These matters will be addressed in the following chapter.

Limitations of the model

The intra-urban structure model presented, developed and exemplified in various forms here is essentially a description of resource and facility locations, a regionalisation of these spatial concentrations in relation to other functional distributions and an account of some simple but fundamental evolutionary developments. Such modelling, like all such approaches in urban analysis, is not in itself a complete explanation of the regionalisation of tourist-historic facilities but is rather a necessary basis for further analysis. It is a series of more or less inductively derived spatial hypotheses that require investigation if the operational dynamics of the model are to be understood.

In particular there are two such lines of further development which are suggested but not pursued by the model, and need further investigation. First, although either a spatial coincidence or a spatial aversion between the locations of different sorts of urban activities has been delimited, the actual functional relationships that cause such behaviour have not been investigated and cannot be left as self-evident.

Secondly, the approach so far has been almost exclusively pursued from the supply side; from the facilities provided for, or used by, tourists and the morphological features of the conserved city. The questions about who actually uses the facilities of the tourist-historic city, in what way and for what purposes, have yet to be answered. The model constructed from uses needs peopling with users.

These two tasks will be the subject of the following chapter.

5 Uses and users of the tourist-historic city

Cohabitation and coincidence

The preceding accounts of the origins of the historic and tourist cities culminated in their integration into the intra-urban regionalisations of the tourist-historic city models. This necessarily involved a systematic abstraction, and isolation from their wider urban context, of each set of processes which had led to the historic and tourist cities respectively. Their complexity was reduced to a set of manageable and largely intrinsic criteria. It was equally evident in the above chapters however that such isolation results in a serious divorce from reality. Such an approach, which abstracts a single or small related group of functions for study, although common in the investigation of many aspects of the city, fails to appreciate that the city is more than a coincidentally existing cluster of different functions cohabiting within a morphological structure.

This failure is particularly serious in this case because few cities, or parts of cities, are exclusively tourist-historic in their functions; the behaviour of few users of such urban spaces is explicable exclusively by tourist-historic motivations; and the urban planning and management so critical in shaping such areas is usually a compromise resulting from attempts to accommodate many other interests and pressures. In short, the tourist-historic city normally has been brought into being and continues to exist as an integral part of the multifunctional city and caters for a wide variety of consumers with an equally wide variety of motives. Such multifunctionality is more than just the coincidence in space of quite different land-uses; it is a central condition for the creation, character and development of the tourist-historic city itself. Thus a study of the tourist-historic city without an understanding of its place in the wider urban synthesis is not only incomplete, it is incomprehensible.

The purpose of this chapter is to go beyond a recognition of the existence of such a context of the tourist-historic city in the service of the multimotivated user of multifunctional urban space. Logically it is the totality of the urban environment that comprises such a context and thus it is the whole interrelated complex of urban functions, and the demands made upon them, that must be explained in order to place the tourist-historic city in its proper perspective. This is of course neither possible nor necessary, and, as with the study of any other aspect of the city, a selection of the potentially most important relationships with coexisting land-uses has to be made.

In particular there are a number of recognisable functions and activities which are commonly found in the tourist-historic areas of the city other than those intrinsic to either heritage tourism or the conserved historic city. Such functions may be positively attracted by the tourist-historic character of the area, or equally but more indirectly, be attracted to the area by its other characteristics, by the presence of other activities themselves attracted by the tourist-historic possibilities, or be merely inertial survivals of a previous locational pattern. Examples of each of these explanations may be found within the same tourist-historic area. It is these other urban activities, existing for whatever reason in close proximity to the direct tourist-historic functions, and forming their immediate operational context, that must be considered here.

Such an integrated context can be approached from three directions, themselves interrelated, namely from the side of supply, i.e. from the facility or function; demand, i.e. the attitudes and behaviour of the consumer; and intervention, i.e. the marketing, management and planning for public or private goals.

Clusters and associations

The concepts of facility clustering and association, originally devised to explain spatial patterns of retailing, have been developed as a means of describing more general urban functions by Ashworth and Jansen-Verbeke (1989). Here it is assumed that the spatial pattern of facility locations for each function can be described in terms of the degree and type of clustering and also by the associations that can be traced with quite different facility distributions. Such facility associations can themselves vary in intensity and type, most simply with different sorts of uses being attractive, repellent or indifferent to each other. Equally such associations between functions can be mutually experienced or, as is relatively common in the tourist-historic city, asymmetrical in their operation. Finally, locational patterns may be associated with each other through the characteristics of the location itself, the requirements of the product or the spatial behaviour of the consumer. Although the distributions resulting from these three forms of association may be very similar, the processes through which they have emerged, and which maintain the present patterns in being, are quite different and therefore amenable to quite different policy interventions for the management of the tourist-historic city.

The complementary concept on the demand side to that of 'uses' on the supply side is that of 'user'. Various references have been made in the analysis so far to tourists, visitors, customers and other categorisations of users of facilities within the tourist-historic city. The question must now be raised, 'who are these people?' and 'how do they interact with the formal and functional characteristics of the tourist-historic city already described?'. It is clear from the variety of terms already used that the existing classification systems are likely to prove inadequate for our purposes. The myriad of different people who live, work, recreate, or seek goods and services in the tourist-historic city again logically determines that from the user viewpoint there is not one objective city but an individual tourist-historic city unique to each user experience and purpose. The practical impossibility of describing and generalising from such a quantity of individual cities determines that the answers to the above questions must be sought through taxonomies of users; but these taxonomies must be derived from the use of the tourist-historic city itself and not based initially on other social, economic or demographic dimensions.

The third approach, through management, is necessarily integrative and fundamental to the second part of the book. It will be considered in detail then, but it should be borne in mind that such holistic management is itself dependent upon an understanding of the supply and demand sides discussed here.

The tourist-historic city as a location for urban functions

The tourist-historic city has a number of distinctive characteristics that can make it attractive or repellent as a location for particular functions. These general characteristics can be summarised as relating either to the area as a whole or to the individual historic buildings within it. The distinction, although artificial, can be important to a number of activities which are attracted for various reasons to historic areas but not necessarily to historic buildings. The reverse situation is much less usual.

Area variables

The most obvious area characteristic is that it has become endowed with an atmosphere of historicity as a result of the preservation of its fabric, attention to features of public urban design that accentuate a chosen atmosphere and the 'marking' of its historical associations in the ways already described. This may be regarded as advantageous in conferring an

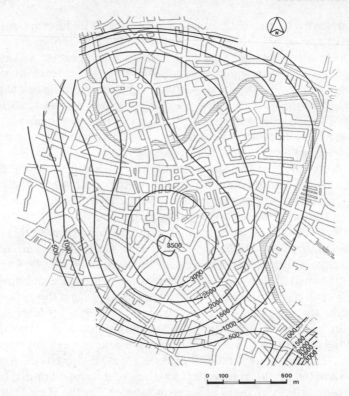

Figure 5.1 *Land values in the central city: Norwich*

element of status on activities located within it. The historical continuity of the area's morphology allows the address itself to convey an association of long-standing credibility and probity. Such address associations will be a valued asset of those activities dependent upon conveying such attributes to potential clients and customers. Conversely this very transference of an atmosphere of tradition and continuity will be unattractive to activities that wish to associate themselves and their services with novelty, modernity and progress. In some instances an inference of adaptive change is deliberately sought so that the unfamiliarity of the new is tempered by the familiarity of the past. Equally there will be a substantial category of functions that are largely indifferent to historic address associations, if only because they predate the creation of the tourist-historic city.

The role of centrality and accessibility is less easy to summarise. The tourist-historic areas of the city are likely to be centrally located in relation to the city-region and thus theoretically accessible to the rest of the city. The conservation of the historic morphology however will probably have preserved a street pattern and imposed constraints on vehicle circulation, loading and parking, and thus reduced accessibility within it. This poses a clear dilemma for many activities that are dependent upon a high density of casual pedestrian consumers drawn to the area by its historic atmosphere and yet conveyed to it by modern transport media.

The most attractive feature of these areas to many commercial enterprises is the presence of people and of other activities. The former are potential customers, the latter may be customers, suppliers or mutually dependent partners in the production of a package of goods and services for joint consumption. The extent to which this presence is valued is probably the single most important locational characteristic for enterprises in the tourist-historic city.

Conversely the cost of historic atmosphere, centrality and the presence of people and other activities will be reflected in land values and thus rent levels. Figure 5.1 shows an example of such levels based upon rateable values (i.e. local property tax assessments). It is noticeable that although land values are high in the well-established historic areas of this city as a result of competition for sites within it, yet the land values peak, not in the historic city, but in the neighbouring modern commercial city. In part this can be explained as an anomaly resulting from the presence among the users of the historic city of a number of occupiers exempt from this tax but it also reflects the lower density of plot occupancy. Floor-area rents are as high in the historic as the modern city but fewer usable floors per plot result in a lower total rent per plot. Yet it is dangerous to generalise in this way, as land values in the less well-established historic areas may in fact be low by the standards of the central area, reflecting a lack of developed tourist functions and of competition by users other than housing. In the New World case, the tendency for the historic city to be located in the long-standing zone of discard means that while its land values mostly now reflect the Norwich case, in the poorer 'blue-collar' cities they may well be quite low.

Building variables

Similarly, the intrinsic characteristics of the conserved buildings themselves will be valued differently by different types of user. The historicity of the restored structure itself conveys an atmosphere of historic continuity and, by implication, reliability, integrity and probity which is transferred by inference to the occupier however recent that occupation. In addition, there is an implication of the status of artistic patronage implicit in such occupation. The extent to which such a status and such transferred qualities are valued as assets, treated with indifference or even regarded as liabilities, depends upon the nature of the activity conducted in the building.

The occupation of historic buildings incurs extra direct costs of maintenance which are likely to be both higher than in new premises, as a result of the age of the building itself, the higher than average standards expected and the use of relatively rare and thus expensive materials and techniques. A varying portion of this cost in different countries can of course be offset against subsidies and tax concessions, but a negative balance usually remains.

The indirect costs are less easy to assess but probably more important. The most obvious of these are the costs of inflexibility imposed by the constraints upon alterations to the building. The severity of such constraints varies with the particular legal, but also social, pressures in the area involved but can amount to major restrictions on the freedom of occupiers which in turn is a major financial imposition. External structural changes and even external façade decor are normally strictly controlled, which has implications for external design, recognition logos and advertising displays important for many shops and direct customer services.

Internal space divisions are generally less strongly protected legally but nevertheless expensive to alter and in any event must conform to the existing fenestration. Similarly, modern services needed to conform with contemporary standards of lighting, heating, plumbing, in accordance with legally enforceable, or socially acceptable, codes of working and living conditions, including health and safety standards, will be expensive to insert into an existing building. In addition to these basic conditions, there is a whole range of modern communication technologies and office management practices which may prove expensive, or all but impossible, to incorporate into the existing internal space divisions of older buildings not originally designed for them. The difficulties of installing modern equipment in old buildings has received some attention in relation to computerisation but the equally difficult but less obvious problems of accommodating particular business management practices (such as, for example, the fashionable *burolandschaft*, open-plan) has received less attention.

The extent to which these restrictions on external alterations, and the organisation of internal spaces, are regarded as a cost depends once again upon the nature of the activity conducted on these premises.

Coexisting functions of the tourist-historic city

The reactions of different sorts of activities to the area and building-related variables summarised above can be considered for different groups of functions. There are many omissions in these 'marketing synergies' (Snedcof, 1985) which are not intended to be an inventory but only the most commonly encountered coexisting uses. These can be brought together into four groups:

1. services provided directly to individual customers, usually in person, which includes within it such clusters of related activities as leisure shopping, arts/crafts/antiques, catering and both private and public personal services;

2. services provided indirectly, and normally impersonally, to customers;
3. services offering culture, the arts or entertainment, whether 'live' or not, to 'live' audiences;
4. housing.

Direct customer services

The historic atmosphere, together with access to a high density of potential customers themselves attracted by that historicity, are attractive to establishments in the private or public sectors offering goods or services directly to clients on a face-to-face basis. It is difficult to separate the three related elements of the trilogy, customer density, historic location and clusters of associated service facilities, let alone trace the cause and effect relations between them. These elements can, however, be examined in more detail.

As far as any individual service is concerned, access to potential customers in this situation depends upon the existence of a large, probably pedestrianised, market which has been drawn to the area by its historicity and by the cluster of services as a whole rather than by any particular establishment. It is therefore a market characterised by impulsive purchase from any particular establishment, by decisions made on the basis of short-term and spatially restricted comparison, and by a combination of purchases of widely different goods and services. Such a description fits the urban tourist, especially those engaged in heritage sightseeing, but is by no means exclusive to this group of users of the tourist-historic city, as will be discussed later. A result of this definition of market access is a detailed micro-scale locational relationship between such services and specific areas of the tourist-historic city. This, however, is not the only important definition of access relevant to these services. Sites within the tourist-historic city are likely to be physically central to the city region as a whole as well as being well known and promoted; thus locations in Quincy Market, Boston, Covent Garden, London or Stroget, Copenhagen, benefit from centrality and clarity in the mental maps of customers. Physical access between such areas and the rest of the city-region by private transport, however, may be restricted as a result of conservational measures which affect not only car-borne customers but also delivery of materials.

The second element, the historic nature of the area, has three main influences upon coexisting direct customer facilities. The most important is the indirect effect through the attraction of people to the area who then form the market for such services. Secondly, these facilities can themselves be directly linked to the historicity. This may be because the goods or services on offer contain elements that can be related to history in some way; or because an historic atmosphere endows the location with qualities such as tradition, longevity and aesthetic taste, which are transferred from the historic area or building to the occupier, who becomes associated with feelings or stability, reliability and continuity. The third and more prosaic influence is on the size and nature of the individual premises. In so far as these are part of the historic city and subject to individual monument or conservation area designations, many of these will be small, difficult to enlarge, inflexible in their internal space divisions, unsuited to many modern fittings and utilities and subject to constraints on external alterations and display. The chief partial exceptions are often warehouse or factory premises, which accordingly may be at a premium for adaptive reuse by space-consuming functions such as restaurants.

The locational requirements of few activities correspond precisely to the criteria outlined above but it is possible to identify sets of direct customer facilities for which the advantages of location in the tourist-historic city outweigh the disadvantages. Some commonly encountered examples can be grouped under the following headings.

Leisure shopping This is a broader category than directly tourist-related shopping although it may include the sale of souvenirs, and is not the same as the 'recreational business district' (Stansfield and Rickert, 1970), which includes catering but is much narrower in its definition of both the customer and the facility.

The concept of 'leisure shopping' can be investigated from the side of either supply or demand. Although such a category of shopping clearly exists as an important activity of favoured areas in the tourist-historic city, it is difficult to identify in terms of the nature of the shops themselves which may be offering for sale a wide variety of products, whose only common characteristics may be that they are inessential, lend themselves to comparison and thus to a large element of display and impulse purchase, and are small relative to their value, thus generating a high turnover per square metre in the relatively small premises. (See Kuhn's, 1979, description of the leisure component in shopping streets in West German cities.)

However, by definition such leisure-shopping complexes can really only be identified through the characteristics of the demand for them. This demand depends upon the purpose and state of mind of the customer as much as on the assortment of goods on offer, as the objective of the trip is not so much the purchase of specific goods as the enjoyment of the observation, comparison and, possibly but not necessarily, the largely unplanned purchase of goods. Such leisure shopping is a well-known major activity of tourists but is also an activity of other groups including residents, who usually form the majority of such customers. The motives and behaviour of these sorts of shoppers have been studied by Jansen-Verbeke (1986; 1988) in a sample of ten small and medium-sized Dutch towns. She identifies 'recreational shopping' as an activity defined by the customers' immediate intent rather than the principal overall purpose of the trip, thus residents engaged in 'normal' shopping trips, central-area workers, and a wide range of recreational or business visitors can become 'recreational shoppers' for short periods. The definition is to be found in the enjoyment of a recreational experience as investigated in Jansen's (1989) study of the psychological reactions of shoppers to particular streets in Amsterdam, and its reflection in behaviour, in particular the high inspection/purchase ratio typical of 'window-shopping'.

Such leisure shopping is not uniquely associated with historic environments, and almost all shopping can possess an important recreational element, whether pursued in modern out-of-town shopping malls (Jansen-Verbeke, 1990) or historic 'themed' settings, such as London Court, Perth, Australia. But some characteristics of historic areas, especially small premises with direct access to high pedestrian flows, render them especially suitable, particularly if combined with other attractions. The individual establishment is dependent upon the existence of a cluster of numerous enough facilities to offer the consumer the necessary comparative experience within the very short distance that the pedestrian is prepared to cover. Such facilities are associated with each other through the possibilities of comparison of the products on offer rather than through their physical similarities.

Arts/crafts/antiques This set of activities is really only an aspect of the above leisure shopping with which it can imperceptibly merge but is especially related to the historic atmosphere and even to its broader associations with culture so as to include modern arts and handicrafts. Indeed the practice of the latter can serve as a form of entertainment and attraction to a passing trade to whom the resulting artefacts can then be retailed. Antiques and bric-a-brac are clearly particularly suited to locations in the tourist-historic city, being both appropriate land-uses for historic premises and attracted by the presence of potential customers who have a predisposition to favour historic objects. In fact from the customer's viewpoint it is only the existence of price tags that distinguishes a visit to a museum from that to a retail display of antiques: visitors to antique shops have a notoriously low propensity to purchase.

In addition these sorts of facilities have a particularly strong association with each other that derives in part from the comparative behaviour of customers but also from the strong purchasing links that exist between such establishments. Antique shops in particular are their own best customers. The result is a tendency not only to cluster but to monopolise so that whole streets can become dominated by this activity. A complicating factor however is that both the trade in antiques and arts and crafts can vary enormously in quality. This ranges from the high-priced luxury end of the market which associates with leisure shopping and historic and

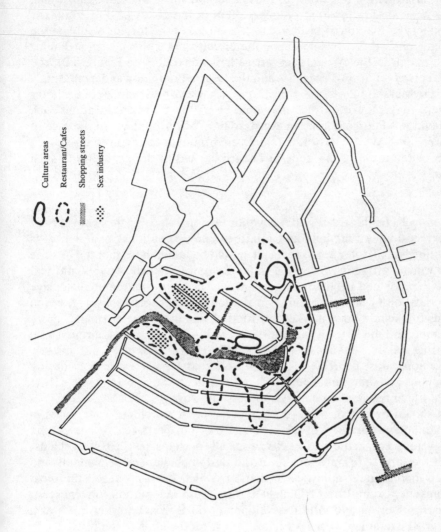

Culture areas
Restaurant/Cafes
Shopping streets
Sex industry

Figure 5.2 *Some functional districts in central Amsterdam*

cultural attraction locations, to the 'junk' and small workshop end which is associated with low-rent premises often in the zones of discard on the periphery of the tourist-historic city. Examples of the former would be the antique and art districts adjoining major cultural facilities, such as Paulus Potterstraat in the Amsterdam 'art galleries district' (see Figure 5.2), the area between Forum-Les Halles and the Centre Pompidou and increasingly into the Marais in Paris, and King Street, Charleston. Examples of the latter type acting as tourist attractions would be the 'flea market' locations such as London's Petticoat Lane or Amsterdam's Waterlooplein. In the case of Lower Town West, Ottawa, the 'junk' environment has evolved up-market and revitalisation of this zone of discard has led to the expulsion of such uses.

Catering Refreshment services have an obvious place in these clusters of direct customer functions and reinforce the recreational experience as described in Chapter 3. However, it should be added here that the historic city will be attractive to only a limited variety of such services and will tend to repel 'bad-neighbour entertainment' or those that require extensive modification of historic premises or blatant, inappropriate display, which tends to exclude mass market fast-food chains in favour of smaller more discreet and historically appropriate establishments. In addition those catering establishments associated with leisure shopping and historic attractions must contend with a clientele that largely exists only during shopping and museum hours rather than necessarily being part of the night-life entertainment complex discussed below.

It should be noted, however, that some fast-food chains have shown a remarkable propensity for adaptive reuse of old premises, or compatible redevelopment, in the historic city; ironically perhaps it is the largest chains, with the largest resources to meet the design challenges of planners and of an increasingly sophisticated market, which have produced the most impressive examples. McDonald's warehouse adaptation on Museum Wharf in Boston and infill redevelopment on Byward Market in Ottawa are good examples. Social attitudes to fast-food chains in the historic city may, however, lag behind their adaptive capacity, perhaps through reaction against the clientele they tend to attract; thus a second fast-food proposal for the Byward Market has met with stiff resistance.

Private personal services Establishments offering services directly to clients on a face-to-face basis may benefit from the same density of a passing, pedestrianised potential market as those offering goods for sale. Such 'counter-services' as travel agents, estate agents and some personal financial services may thus be dependent on, as well as contributing to, the leisure shopping described above. Locations on the major routes within the tourist-historic city are advantageous, maximising the opportunities for comparative 'window-shopping' and impulse buying, while the constraints on size of premises or display are not serious disadvantages.

There are other direct services, frequently found in the historic city, that are not part of the leisure-shopping and entertainment complex. Personal medical, dental, legal, financial and similar 'professional' 'counter', or more accurately, 'consulting room' services, may benefit only indirectly from the site advantages within the historic city. These are not so much the potential direct impulse sales from a passing market but the advantages of location within a recognised area. This address status recognition may stem from association of the particular establishment with the area as historic, or as a well-known location for similar services. The 'Harley Street' phenomenon can be found in most cities for various professions. This sort of popular functional labelling of streets and districts has an intrinsic inertia, with such street images being slow to develop and to dispel: thus many such professional service districts, in European cities particularly, are in fact continuing a functional specialisation that predates the conservation of the historic city rather than being a new function attracted to it. Castles, cathedrals and major civic buildings attracted a penumbra of clerks and lawyers through their original administrative functions rather than their later conserved form.

Once conserved, the potential disadvantages of historic premises in terms of constraints on unit size, external display and the inflexibility of internal space partitioning may be disregarded by what are normally small firms with few large specialised equipment demands. Indeed it is precisely these sorts of services that may value the intangible feelings of confidence that the occupation of conserved and restored historic premises may convey to clients. Vries-Reilingh (1968) traced a strong connection between the 'free professions', especially lawyers, and formerly residential properties of the eighteenth and early nineteenth centuries in Amsterdam, a relationship confirmed much later in the quite different city of Glasgow by Sim (1982). Rosenberg (1984) described the existence of a certain tension in physicians' choices of location in Toronto between prestige sites, which included conserved neighbourhoods, and sites accessible to hospitals and other medical services.

A variety of private direct customer services can thus be expected in association with the historic city, taking advantage of its centrality, its attraction to other uses and the inherent historic qualities of the area and its buildings. Those more dependent upon casual customer access will compete for sites, and coexist, with retailing, entertainment and catering functions: those not so dependent, and uses tending towards monofunctional professional clusters, will be especially attracted to locations on the periphery of the main tourist-historic areas, or in the less accessible upper floors of the shopping districts.

Public personal services Many of the services described above could as well be offered by public as private institutions: the same locational considerations would apply, for example, to tourist information services operated by public authorities. Similarly there are a range of social, educational and financial services offered by government agencies dealing directly with the public that can derive the same benefits from locations in the tourist-historic city, and in historic premises, as private services. The main distinction is that such public services may be prevented from occupying such locations, however beneficial to their efficiency, because they do not produce a direct financial return and thus cannot compete with private services able to pay free-market rents. Paradoxically, public agencies may be compelled to occupy premises in the historic city which have failed to attract commercial financially viable functions, as a 'last-resort use' of otherwise vacant premises. Public services are thus being used for wider town planning objectives regardless of the optimum locational or building requirements of the service itself.

Examples in the first category are necessarily hypothetical, but there is no reason to suppose that a wide range of social consultative services would not benefit from the same aspects of customer behaviour as many of the private services discussed if they had the financial resources to compete for such locations. Examples in the last-resort category are widely found in public administrative, educational and social agencies, usually operated by local governments, occupying historic premises, though less commonly in North America where such premises have a relative scarcity value.

Case studies of direct customer services

The isolated description of particular types of direct customer services, in terms of their locational relationships with the tourist-historic city, needs to be reintegrated into a multifunctional micro-regional setting. Two pairs of contrasting examples can illustrate something of the variety of such settings.

Two pedestrian streets in the centre of Norwich, Elm Hill and London Street (see Figure 3.2), illustrate two distinctly different types of these functional clusters within an important tourist-historic city.

Elm Hill, saved from demolition by a single vote in the local council, became the cherished show-piece of conservation planning in the 1960s, and the third most visited tourist attraction in the city (Berkers *et al.*, 1986). Its renovated, and in some cases reconstructed, façades, newly cobbled street surface and appropriate street furniture, created a seventeenth-century stage set. The pre-conservation residential and commercial land-uses had effectively disappeared by 1960, leaving a functional vacuum, which has been filled on the ground-floor level by a mixture of leisure-shopping functions, including craft shops and a stamp and coin collector's shop (a variation on the antique theme), and a number of tea and coffee establishments, most closed outside shopping hours. The upper storeys have few financially viable functions and are used principally for storage: the lack of direct accessibility to the ground level excludes both leisure-shopping functions and residential uses.

There had long been pedestrian areas, squares, alleys and walkways in many cities, especially in older districts where many of the streets were just physically impenetrable to motor traffic. But the rebuilding of many of Europe's bomb-damaged cities after 1945 included deliberately planned pedestrian streets (as Kuhn, 1979, has exhaustively catalogued in West German cities). Rotterdam's Lijnbaan was the archetype for many such general comparative shopping streets, while some developed specifically as centres for art and fashion, such as Bremen's Bottscherstrasse.

The distinctive features of the London Street scheme, completed as early as 1962, however, was that changes in the existing traffic circulation pattern were not planned in isolation from conservation policy and adjoining land-uses. London Street was a major location for shopping and commercial services whose pedestrianisation was intended to provide a walkway between the two most important monument and tourist clusters in the city, and thus inevitably alter the nature of the commercial functions along it. The more or less simultaneous development of a new central area retailing concentration in the St. Andrew's Street area to the south-west of the market encouraged the division of commercial functions between the two areas; the one increasingly specialising in the leisure-shopping activities described earlier and direct counter services, together with a growing number of catering establishments, especially occupying upper floors; the other housing the department stores and multiples and non-counter office functions. The distinction is by no means complete but it is apparant.

Two New World examples, namely Ottawa's Byward Market and the Historic Properties development in Halifax, have some important differences. The first evolved organically, although with an important element of government planning, while the second was an integrated revitalisation scheme largely by private initiatives for largely commercial objectives (see Chapter 9).

Lower Town West in the Canadian capital, Ottawa, was the 'original city', being the early nineteenth-century nucleus, the lumber town of Bytown, around which the chosen capital developed. It was however effectively bypassed by the planned developments which shifted the focus of administrative and commercial activity distinctly westwards and until the early 1970s was a largely working-class residential area surrounding a local provision market, Byward Market. Government intervention in the 1960s initiated a general rehabilitation of the area which included a series of functional changes. Thus the creation of an historic district encouraged changes in land-use, which in turn made the area attractive to tourists by providing secondary tourist resources for visitors drawn to the 'capital' attractions nearby, as well as to the newly nurtured historicity of Lower Town itself.

The detailed process of change has been documented by Tunbridge (1986a; 1987a). Since the late 1960s a wave of new commercial activities has diffused eastwards from Sussex Drive (see Figure 9.6), the focus of initial government intervention, and has transformed customer services to the extent that by the late 1980s they were almost entirely of the types described in this chapter. This process involved both a replacement of the preceding lower-grade functions, and also a substantial increase in the total number of businesses as a result of infill redevelopment which augmented the rehabilitation of older premises. Retail and service categories such as boutiques, restaurants, pubs and related leisure services have grown disproportionately. There are considerable definition problems in detail between traditional and contemporary businesses, but in all categories there are clearly identifiable growth and decline components; in retailing, for example, second-hand stores have given way to antique-related establishments, kitchen boutiques etc. The link between this commercial growth and both historicity and tourism is clear and will be considered in more detail in Chapter 9. However this growth has occurred at the expense of other land-uses, both directly, and indirectly through the voracious demand for car parking space; the residential function has retreated in the face of this double onslaught during the last twenty years, an illustration of the relationship between commercial and residential uses discussed later in this chapter. Beyond the zone of immediate land-use competition, Lower Town remains a residential area; and, predictably, it has experienced progressive gentrification during the 1980s as the neighbouring amenity increased. This has not only displaced working-class residents but has also put pressure on particular types of customer service geared to the poor: charitable institutions, including the Salvation Army, have been forced to form alliances with other social agencies in order to remain in the area. On the periphery of the expanding commercial area, and in its upper storeys, a variety of indirect customer functions, which are considered later, have also joined the growing competition for space. Overall, ironically, this competition has frequently resulted in damage to the heritage resource which initiated it.

Historic Properties in Halifax (Nova Scotia) is a private commercial revitalisation with local authority support, which has acquired and renovated a series of waterfront buildings dating from 1813 to 1870. The area, once the centre of Nova Scotian privateers, was left vacant by the migration of port facilities, nearly redeveloped, but through the persistence of a few conservationists designated a National Historic site in 1963. Although it is adjacent to a number of ship and land-based museum attractions (see Figure 5.3) and to a newly built 360-room Sheraton Hotel (for which it was the primary locational motive),

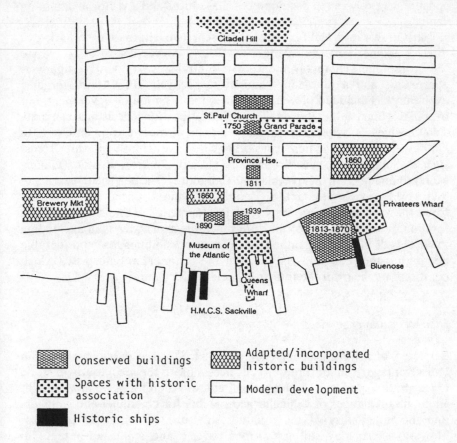

Figure 5.3 *Historic land-uses in central Halifax (Nova Scotia)*

the renovated warehouses are principally leased to revenue-earning commercial establishments. These have been turned effectively into enclosed malls with shops on the ground floor and small offices above. The shops are an archetypal mixture of the leisure-shopping functions described earlier, including crafts (Inuit and Nova Scotian sculptures and paintings, traditional confectionery manufacture), art and antiques and quality woollens, china and jewellery (especially objects imported from the British Isles, thus stressing the historic ethnic links of the region) and refreshment establishments. The ensemble provides a principally recreational experience both for tourists attracted to the waterfront by the historic sites and accommodation and for shoppers and business visitors to the main modern commercial district, directly adjacent inland. The upper-floor offices lack direct access to the pedestrian flow and are mainly occupied by small financial, legal and consultancy companies. In addition, Parks Canada, the national parks authority, which played a major collaborative role in the development, has offices and a visitor information centre.

The Ottawa and Halifax cases represent two alternative scenarios of direct customer services in the New World tourist-historic city, where the entrepreneurial involvement of a central development company is a recessive and a dominant element respectively. In Ottawa, organic evolution has included piecemeal contributions by major developers, but overall it is the result of the amalgam of many locational decisions by mainly small businesses, which is also characteristic of most European cases. In Halifax, however, as in numerous other cases, particularly on waterfronts, such as Saint John, New Brunswick (Market Square), Boston (Quincy Market/Faneuil Hall Marketplace), Baltimore (Harborplace) or, in an 'old world' city, Southampton (Canute's Pavilion), corporate enterprise forms the leading edge in commercial development and thus the nature and location of services is constrained in much the same way as in a shopping mall. This dichotomy, or rather spectrum of possibilities, has considerable bearing on the scale and character of the commercial enterprises which constitute the heart of the tourist-historic city's customer services.

Indirect customer services

Services which have less need for direct face-to-face public contact gain less advantage from locations directly accessible to the main tourist-historic concentrations of facilities and people, and will therefore give more weight to the disadvantages of vehicular accessibility for personnel and suppliers and the inflexibility of the building structure of conserved premises. However there may still be various psychic and status advantages to be gained by an address in an historic neighbourhood and a location in a restored historic building. Although there has been little research on these locational considerations, the nature of the enterprise may be critical in determining the valuation placed on these factors. A study of the requirements of large multinational companies seeking locations for branch offices (Dunning and Norman, 1987) revealed that 'local image', i.e. the ascribed status of the site and area, scored more highly than the availability of local subsidies, labour, transport or amenities. However Sim's study of the relationship between building life cycles and functional change among small local offices in Glasgow (1982), suggested that the important variable in the case of the large number of converted Georgian properties was rent levels rather than conserved status.

In Ottawa's Lower Town West various familiar indirect services such as consultants and architects have located for reasons including proximity to profession-specific amenities, the relative availability of parking and the low rent levels relative to the CBD. Motives also often include historicity-related factors, such as psychic satisfaction in the character of the area or building, a perceived professional appropriateness of a restored older building and an appreciation of the value of the area's amenities to employees. There also frequently remains an element of personal idiosyncrasy, whose importance must never be overlooked in the locational decision of many of these small enterprises (Tunbridge, 1987a).

The obvious method of gaining the benefits without incurring the costs is, whenever feasible, to divide office functions: a relatively small headquarters 'front office' in the historic city reaps the benefits to public relations and the association of the firm's name with the historic area or building; and a main set of offices, handling the more space-consuming indirect contacts, information processing and storage functions is located elsewhere in purpose-built premises with better vehicular access. The extra costs of spatial disintegration of the office functions are compensated for by the appropriateness of each location to the particular functions of the site.

Figure 5.4 shows the distribution of some commercial offices in Amsterdam. Banking and insurance frequently have a number of the above characteristics. They are clearly concentrated in part in the prestigeous seventeenth and eighteenth-century restored buildings lining the Amsterdam *grachten*, especially the *Heren* and *Prinsengrachten* which are generally both too large and too expensive for private housing, and are thus largely occupied by the front offices of commercial firms and government agencies.

Such a reaction can equally occur in the public sector. In fact a common situation is the occupation of large, key historic buildings in the heart of the historic city by government offices because town, provincial and state capital buildings are themselves important historic buildings, on which have been lavished many centuries of artistic effort because of their symbolic importance. The function is at least as old as the building and predates its conservation. Public agencies will benefit from the status associated with such symbolically important buildings. Indeed the general public is likely to associate the public service very directly with the building itself, even more so than with private firms, so that city government becomes 'City Hall' which citizens have little difficulty in identifying. The problem, as with private offices, is that for many office functions such premises are at best unnecessary and at worst inefficient. The solution with the rapid expansion of government services in the post-war years was often the same as in the private sector, namely the division of functions between those requiring a central prestigous location (for example public information services, local legislatures and political decision-making chambers) and those quantitatively much more important departments engaged in indirect communications and general administration. The former remain on the traditional site, the latter are rehoused in purpose-built accommodation elsewhere. This situation also occurs in North America, such as Charleston; but the process has occasionally been taken further with City Hall being

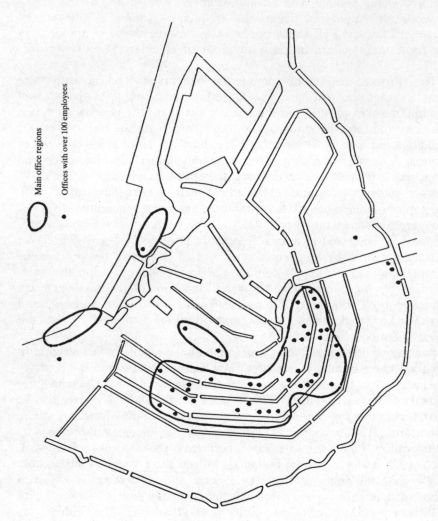

Main office regions

Offices with over 100 employees

Figure 5.4 *Office districts in Amsterdam*

lured away from its historic downtown building entirely, and relocated to new functional and motor accessible premises, sometimes in association with a shopping mall development. This may create problems of reuse of the original building, as in Saint John, New Brunswick.

It is noteworthy here that office functions that do not require direct access to the general public may often be a realistic use of underutilised upper storeys in areas where the ground floors may be in use for direct customer services and residential uses are inappropriate.

The culture/entertainment complex

There are a number of difficulties in identifying a distinctive complex of coexisting interrelated activities that can be labelled culture/entertainment. The thread linking together such diverse facilities as opera houses, theatres, cinemas, night-clubs and concert halls is less easily understood than that connecting the functions considered above. With culture/entertainment the customer is rarely assembling a packet of different facilities, such as a ballet, a play and a few films, for consumption within the same entertainment experience, thereby encouraging a spatial clustering of locations for comparative purposes. A single pre-booked, or at least predetermined, performance is more likely. Nor is it usual for most of the varied facilities included here to be serving the same customers; on the contrary, this market is noted for a severe segmentation into habitual users and non-users of particular services. This segmentation creates the additional difficulty that the specialised market for any one of these activities is necessarily a small proportion of the total population, thus enormous threshold populations are needed to sustain them. They tend therefore to be 'higher-order' activities found only in small numbers with most towns having only a few examples of some facilities and only the largest cities, which operate within a world market, having a collection that can be regarded as complete or large enough to form a distinctive spatial cluster.

Therefore an explanation is needed of why a tendency to cluster does exist among such facilities and, central to our argument here, why such facilities have a strong locational affinity to the tourist-historic city and why, despite existing in very small numbers and serving small markets, they have an important influence upon that city.

The most significant common feature of these otherwise diverse activities is that they occur dominantly in the evening. They therefore bring customers into the central area of the city outside the opening hours of most of the commercial and historic activities already described. This 'animation' function is often regarded as so important to the maintenance of a populated evening streetscape as to be deliberately encouraged as an essential support of the tourism industry, the hotel and catering sector and even the security services. Cultural facilities which are themselves not economically viable are nevertheless included in mixed-use downtown office and shopping developments and even free street entertainments and 'happenings' (as in the public spaces around London's Covent Garden or Paris' Centre Pompidou for instance) may be encouraged for this purpose (Snedcof, 1985). A second, and related, common feature is that the nocturnal nature of these activities determines that planners will attempt to concentrate them away from housing by dedicating a portion of the central city to culture/entertainment, as is illustrated by Boston's Theatre District, which occupies a prominent position adjacent to the historic Common (see Figure 8.3). Thirdly, some of these activities are related through customer behaviour, although rarely during the same trip, so that a cinema or theatre district is habitually visited. Finally, on the production side there are management economies to be gained by clustering a variety of buildings of different size and purpose in close proximity, or even on the same site, hence the 'Arts Complex' (such as London's Barbican, or South Bank or Paris' Les Halles-Beaubourg).

When considering the relationship between these activities and the tourist-historic city, the idea of a culture/entertainment complex composed of all facilities offering performing entertainments before an audience divides into its two main components. The urban locational patterns of what on the one side can be termed 'high' culture (defined as including those activities labelled the 'performing' or sometimes the 'podium' arts) and, on the other, 'popular' culture (such as cinemas, night-clubs, cabarets) are significantly different and thus have a distinctly different relationship to the tourist-historic city.

'High' culture shares in, and contributes to, the historical and aesthetic atmosphere of the historic city, partly because it is patronised by the same social groups whose values and enthusiasms shaped the climate of opinion that allowed that city to be created. Thus, for example, the conserved central area of Norwich accommodates the Theatre Royal and the Maddermarket Theatre, as well as a number of cultural functions in conserved churches, all serving a market which is dominantly local but includes tourists.

There are other less fundamental connections, some of which are consequences of this set of joint values. In terms of civic consciousness and pride, and the personification of this through the creation and projection of place images, 'culture' (meaning 'high' culture) is strongly linked with the buildings and associations of the historic city. Tourist-historic cities are promoted as 'art cities' (the Flemish *Kunststeden* for example) and cultural performances and achievements loom large in the publicity material used to market such cities, even to those who rarely attend such performances. Whitt (1987) has argued strongly that the performing arts are a 'centrepiece for urban growth strategies' (p.16) and 'not merely symbolic but material shapers of cities'. However it remains their symbolic values which account for the government-business-arts coalition that is motivated by the assertion that commercial firms, especially those already described as attracted to the historic city, will not wish to locate in a 'cultural desert'.

Finally, there is a link between conserved buildings themselves and cultural activities. Although the contemporary technical demands of many performing arts determines that their use of conserved buildings is frequently inappropriate, it is nevertheless widespread. In part this is because the buildings themselves are considered worth preserving (for example many urban Victorian theatres, such as the Theatre Royal, Portsmouth (Windle, 1981)), or because the building possesses an association with past performances that are themselves an historical legacy. The building and the artistic company jointly contribute to the character of the monument. Thus famous opera houses (such as the Vienna Staatsoper, La Scala, Milan, London's Covent Garden or the New York 'Met'), concert halls (the most notable being the Amsterdam orchestra that is actually known by the name of the building it plays in, *Concertgebouw*) and theatres are tourist-historic attractions as a result of both the building and its association with artistic performance. Indeed the cultural association, which is itself in part historic, relating to past performances elsewhere, can be so strong as to be transferred to new and modern premises, so that Sydney Opera House or London's Festival Hall can become part of the tourist-historic city.

This relationship between the use of conserved buildings and cultural performances can be however somewhat one-sided. Culture frequently provides a use for large conserved buildings, especially churches, that is so widespread as to deserve special mention. Religious buildings provide a peculiar and burdensome paradox within the tourist-historic city. The fervour of past piety has resulted in the single most architecturally important and tourist-attractive category in the historic building stock, while the loss of that piety has removed the only reliably significant use for such buildings. Therefore church buildings, which were after all designed with both 'audience' and 'stage' facilities, have eagerly sought culture as an appropriate use. In the Netherlands for example, the large, mostly seventeenth-century, city-centre churches (such as The Hague's *Jacobskerk*, Arnhem's *Nieuwkerk* or Groningen's *Martininkerk*), fortunately in this respect designed for the Calvinist 'performance' of preaching, find uses as concert and congress halls as well as exhibition spaces. However appropriate such uses may be for the buildings, they are often less than ideal for the users who would frequently prefer to be housed in modern purpose-built structures but are financially constrained and dependent upon support from public bodies. In a sense these are therefore involuntary users who rarely provide an economic return for the building concerned and are only a preferred alternative to a functional vacuum.

Popular entertainment can be related on the one side to the catering functions of the tourist city, forming a part of the Recreational Business District whose locational characteristics have already been described in

Chapter 3. Equally, however, elements such as bars, night-clubs, reviews, 'adult' cinemas and video establishments relate to downtown 'red-light' districts, which usually have a different spatial and functional relationship with the tourist-historic city. A classification of night-life entertainment districts in the European city through its functional relationships (Ashworth *et al.*, 1988) drew a distinction between the respectable complexes of clubs, cinemas and associated catering establishments (such as London's Leicester Square, Amsterdam's Rembrandtsplein, Paris' Place Pigalle, West Berlin's Kurfurstendam) and the less respectable, more explicity commercial sex-orientated complexes of bars, strip clubs, massage parlours and prostitution (such as de Wallen, Amsterdam, St. Pauli, Hamburg, Rue St. Denis, Paris). The former category is strongly related to the tourist city as part of the package of tourist activities and attractions but is rarely found in the historic city, being typically a 'West End' rather than an 'historic core' function. The latter however is frequently a zone of discard use being attracted to low rent neighbourhoods. Ground-floor prostitution is a commonly found function of old, possibly preserved but not yet rehabilitated, districts within the historic city, for example Barcelona's Barrio Gotico adjoining the 'respectable' entertainment and tourism of the Ramblas. Such 'red-light' districts provide a link between the historic city and an underworld of commercial sex, drugs, crime and marginalised social groups, which is in sharp contrast to the relations the 'respectable' entertainment districts have with tourism, and 'high culture'. However, these two types of area may exist close to each other, in part for logical marketing reasons, such as London's Leicester Square/Piccadilly and Soho; and in smaller cities, such as Ottawa, the clear-cut spatial distinction between them may become blurred. It may also be in a state of flux as the forces of revitalisation seek to replace the red-light uses with more appropriate alternatives; this is well illustrated by the gradual displacement of Boston's notorious 'Combat Zone' from its location close to the Theatre District mentioned earlier.

Thus the culture/entertainment sets of coexistent uses of the tourist-historic city have many characteristics in common but normally result in two distinct functional regions. These perform a number of bridge functions between tourism and the wider service functions of the city, as well as between the buildings of the historic city and a range of distinctive social groups and socially marginal activities.

Housing

The residential function is undoubtedly the most important user of space in the tourist-historic city, occupying around three-quarters of all protected buildings in most European cities (Ashworth, 1984b) and a comparable proportion elsewhere. The success of the conservation movement, described earlier, led to an increase in the proportion of domestic buildings within the protected stock. This is partly because such buildings predominate in the areas subject to the 'second wave' of conservation after the major and usually non-domestic buildings have been protected, and partly because the extension of conservation from individual buildings to ensembles inevitably conferred a protected status upon myriads of smaller, usually domestic, properties which formed the spatial setting for the major monuments, whether or not they were intrinsically valuable. The historic city, therefore, is likely to possess a copious supply of such buildings. In the typical European case of the Netherlands, 30,000 of the 43,000 national listed monuments are in use as housing, predominantly by owner-occupiers (National Commissie Monumentenzorg, 1989).

Similarly on the demand side, almost all the coexisting functions considered so far in this chapter are highly selective in their occupation of premises, favouring either the most prestigious properties, or the most commercially advantageous locations. The storeys above street level and the less accessible sites in the interior of the building blocks will be unattractive to direct customer services (see Slater and Shaw's, 1988, discussion of this problem in Exeter). Thus although tourism and other service activities appear to dominate historic-city land-use, this is generally an illusion encouraged by their conspicuous occupation of the most visible sites: in terms of the contribution to land occupancy, as opposed to economic impacts, housing is in practice the only possible use of large areas within the historic city.

Residential use is further encouraged in many cities by housing policies, which for various political and social reasons aim to strengthen the central area residential function. These public policies, especially noticeable in Western Europe (see Burtenshaw *et al.*, 1981), are of two main types. First they may be defensive in attempting to conserve the existing residential communities as well as the buildings they occupy. The extension of the historic city in the second wave is likely to have included not only premises originally intended for housing but also those currently in residential use. The maintenance of not only a residential use but the same residential use, after renovation, can be attempted through a range of rent subsidies and controls and by rigorous controls on land-use change (see Nelissen, 1975, and Cervellati and Scannarini, 1973, for examples of such policies in Dutch and Italian cities respectively). Similar controls are commonly attempted in non-European cities, albeit, as in Ottawa, with limited success. Secondly, more active policies may be pursued to insert new housing into the central area which almost inevitably implies also into the historic city. Such 'back to the city' policies do not necessarily imply the occupation of the existing conserved building stock but can equally involve new development on existing infill sites. The extent to which this process has occurred in even a particularly renowned historic city can be appreciated in Figure 5.5, which shows the extensive areas in central Norwich which were designated for new residential developments (Berkers *et al.*, 1986). Nor is it likely that such policies literally return back to the central city those groups which left it, or were displaced by conservation. They are more frequently part of a wider 'gentrification' process described by many observers of the North American and West European city (Ley, 1988).

There is a copious literature on the relations between renovation and residential change in general (e.g. Burtenshaw *et al.*, 1981). The link between housing demand and conserved property in particular has been questioned by Ashworth and Sijtsma (1987). The superficially harmonious symbiosis between the apparent over-supply of conserved domestic buildings, especially in Western Europe, and the demand for inner-city housing contains some fundamental dilemmas.

First, the dependence is not mutual. The historic city needs the residential function as the only practical alternative to widespread vacancy. Also,

0   100   500
                            m

Public sector

Private sector

Housing associations   Source: Boukema et al, 1985.

Figure 5.5 *Residential development in the inner city: Norwich (Boukema et al., 1985)*

although the economic returns from housing are lower than those from most commercial uses, private housing provides the most effective means of obtaining private investment for the rehabilitation and maintenance of many smaller historic buildings. Local authority building and area designations, together with the private investment that results from the effects of these on the housing market, is a form of public-private 'partnership' upon which conservation planning has been long dependent. However this dependence is asymmetrical. The housing function makes a major contribution to the historic city but the historic city makes only a minor contribution to the city-wide housing function. Only a minority, and in most Western cities a small minority, of the urban population live in the central area and 'back to the city' movements are unlikely to have more than a marginal and socially selective effect upon this. In any event, much of this housing, although in the historic city, will be in new developments. Less than 1 per cent of the annual housing demand is met by renovated historic buildings in the Netherlands (Schelleris, 1978).

The second dilemma stems from the heterogeneity of residential demand. The important relevant distinction is between those who live in historic premises or areas because of historicity, and those who, although resident in the same properties or areas, have a different set of motives and priorities. The first group values the historic city as such, has generally chosen to inhabit it because of this historicity and makes a useful financial partner, through its investment in the properties, and a political ally, through its support of amenity societies, in its conservation. The second group places a higher priority upon the centrality, accessibility, tenure flexibility or low rent levels of the central area and is indifferent to its historicity as such. The significance of this distinction is that the second group will be displaced by the first in the classic 'conservation = deportation' confrontation (as described by Castells, 1978) between historic-city gentrifiers and low-income inner-city residents, or will choose to occupy where possible new housing development within the historic city. An example of the first process (see Table 5.1) is found in three architecturally and historically similar neighbourhoods within the central area of Colmar (France), where the stage of conservation can be compared with the composition of the social structure of residents. The second process which can involve both high and low-income groups is evident in the Norwich example (see Figure 5.5) where since 1970 around one-half of the new residential developments inserted into the central area have been subsidised housing largely for lower incomes. It is worth noting that in the more vibrant 'white-collar' cities in North America the possibility of the low-income group being rehoused in the historic city is constantly diminishing, having reached a crisis situation in Canadian cities such as Toronto and Ottawa (Ley, 1986; 1988).

The relationship between the inner-city residential function and the tourist city can be summarised in a series of assertions which, although forming the basis of public policies in many cities (see Berkers *et al.*,

Table 5.1   Renovation and social change in some districts of Colmar (France)

	Quartier Vauban	Place de la Cathédrale	Quartier des Tanneurs
Physical Condition:			
Renovation	Barely begun	In progress	Complete
Housing in poor/ moderate condition %	77	60	0
Length of residence:			
< 5 years %	37	20	64
>10 years %	29	30	0
Occupations of residents:			
Manual workers	51	56	2
Crafts/trades	13	22	12
Service workers	8	15	21
Free professions	4	11	49

Source: Adapted from Ashworth and de Vries, 1984

1986), are extremely difficult to test empirically. On the positive side the contribution that housing makes to the occupation and upkeep of the fabric of the historic city necessarily maintains the fundamental tourist resource. Mathieson and Wall (1982) had no doubt that tourism development 'can aid in the rehabilitation of historic areas and rejuvenate decaying parts of the city'. Indirectly the existence of a substantial inner-city resident population provides a pool of customers for entertainment, cultural and catering facilities which could not be sustained by the demands of tourists alone. In more general terms residents help maintain a 'living heart', especially outside shop and office hours, which is valued by tourism.

Against these positive features should be weighed the costs of neighbourhood rehabilitation to the historic tourist resource which include the demolition of buildings for modern infill housing and the creation of modern standards of access and services needed by contemporary life-styles. Secondly, the demands of residents and those of tourists are not always compatible and land-use competition can occur. Infill locations suitable for new housing may be equally suitable for new hotel development, and increases in tourist accommodation demand are likely to give rise to a 'creeping conversion' (as was noted in London in the 1970s (Greater London Council, 1978)) of suitable larger residential buildings to hotel use. Pressures on visitor accommodation in the middle 1970s in Britain, and most noticeably, but by no means exclusively, in London, led to widespread and politically expressed anxieties that in a 'homes against hotels' competition the former were economically weaker and would be expelled from parts of the central area.

Although there is some evidence, again drawn from the major cities, that the private low-rent housing sector in particular has been displaced in some areas by tourism accommodation in periods of strong tourism demand (see Young, 1973, for an account of this in London), the overall relationship between housing and tourism accommodation demands is more complex. Most of the housing stock is protected from such encroachment by its small building size, relatively inaccessible locations within the tourist city or social tenure type. Even with the remaining vulnerable categories the relationship can be supportive rather than threatening. Work on the economics of the guest house industry in British seaside resorts (Stallibrass, 1980) has shown how supplementary income from tourism may support the housing function. This use of tourism accommodation demands is not confined to resorts but is a widespread phenomenon in the central areas of many cities. It allows the existing housing stock, and otherwise underutilised household labour, to be used, often on a casual or seasonal basis, by tourism to support the central area residential function.

In North American cities the 'bed and breakfast' phenomenon grew prolifically during the 1980s: it began as an answer to the problems of affordability of hotel accommodation, especially in the larger cities, but was rapidly co-opted by the tourist-historic 'heritage' economy. It has become a means to market explicitly the heritage attributes of historic homes to tourists, thus emphasising both the building itself and traditional standards of service (Brown, 1986). The 'historic inn' tradition, long established in New England, has found many imitators in other areas. It is no coincidence that the entertainment of visitors is a plausible way to meet the likely high costs of maintaining such a scarce resource as a North American historic home. In certain historic 'gem' cities, such as Charleston (see Chapter 9), the housing-tourism link is further enhanced by 'homes and gardens' tours. This phenomenon is transitional to rural 'stately homes' tourism in both Europe and North America, and in the urban context is most feasible where a social structure like that of the *ante-bellum* South allowed the development of urban mansions.

Finally, there is the problem that although tourists may welcome a populated historic city, this population may not equally welcome the presence of large numbers of visitors. Stress may result, which although vaguely felt is nevertheless often strongly articulated in local political arenas. Some tourism facilities, especially those operating at night or generating traffic and parking problems, are 'bad neighbours'. Such stress however is not only specific to particular tourism activities but also to particular residential groups (see Ashworth and de Haan, 1985), and is usually susceptible to sensitive local planning and management measures.

The relationship therefore between the tourist-historic city and the coexisting housing function is important, intimate and necessarily complex. This is most clearly demonstrated in the expansion of the tourist-historic city, as described in Chapter 4, into the zone of transition on the periphery of the central area. The residential function in one form or another is likely to play a spearhead role in the rehabilitation of such areas, and their incorporation into the tourist-historic resource. Finally it should be remembered that in most Western cities the structure of responsible local government is such that the economic weakness of the residential function, relative to tourism, is counterbalanced by its local political strength. 'The management of the cities is run on behalf of the residents by elected city councils or their equivalents. They undoubtedly equate the needs of the city with the needs of the city's residents and would suffer electoral embarrassment were they to do otherwise' (Young, 1973).

The users of the tourist-historic city

One of the strongest conclusions to emerge from both the description of tourism in Chapter 3 and the above account of coexisting functions is that the tourist-historic city is used by many different sorts of users. As it is in the nature of cities to be multifunctional, this is in itself not unique to these sorts of cities and areas. A consequence however is that a more detailed analysis of this intrinsic variety is hindered by the absence of a relevant classification system of such users. Most existing taxonomies divide users into a series of simple categories based usually upon a single motive. There are thus 'tourists', 'shoppers', 'workers' or 'residents', each of which must be identified in isolation from the rest and then further subdivided according to a wide range of demographic, social or behavioural characteristics.

Tourism studies in particular have concentrated upon defining 'the tourist', and subsequently labelling subcategories by length of stay ('day trippers', 'holiday excursionists', 'period visitors'), motives for travel (business, conference, pleasure), or by set of primary attractions ('heritage tourists' as opposed to 'shopping', 'gambling', 'gastronomic', 'acquaintance visiting' or countless others). Clearly there are ultimately as many possible subdivisions of such classifications as there are tourists themselves.

However necessary such an approach may be for the initial systematic study of a particular set of activities, it is clear from the above discussion about the functions of the tourist-historic city that it is ultimately inappropriate here. Neither 'the tourist' nor 'the tourism industry' exist as exclusively delimitable individuals or facilities. Both are really only definable in terms of the individual intent of the user at the moment of use. An historic monument is a tourist resource in so far as it entertains visitors, although it may also service residents. Equally a renovated historic street at any one time may be fulfilling many functions, including tourism and transport, to a range of users. Similarly from the viewpoint of the user, an individual may successively work, shop and recreate in the same area of the tourist-historic city, moving rapidly and largely unconsciously between categories. This phenomenon of the multimotivated user in the multifunctional city is not unique to tourism nor to the tourist-historic city as such, but the varied nature of coexisting uses of such cities and areas renders it particularly relevant in them.

If disintegrated studies of behaviour are inappropriate then different taxonomies relating users to uses must be found. Market segmentation approaches may appear superficially similar in their division of actual or latent users into categories but these are based upon the actual nature of the use itself rather than any general characteristics of groups of users (see Ashworth and Voogd, 1988). The following therefore is not only a search for clarity in taxonomy but also a ground-plan of such a segmentation approach for the multifunctional tourist-historic city.

Among the primary divisions of the consumer market based upon the nature of the use itself commonly employed in such analysis are customer motives in terms of 'buyer-benefit' (i.e. ultimate purchasing intent), AIO (ie. attitudes, interests, opinions) analysis of the product, or frequency of use. The most fundamental is the use/non-use dichotomy. There are two main types of relationship of groups of users of the tourist-historic attributes of the multifunctional tourist-historic city, namely the 'intentional' users i.e. those whose use is to a greater or lesser degree motivated or enhanced by the tourist-historic character of the city, and the 'incidental' users i.e. those for whom the historic character is a chance irrelevance. The first group are 'recreationists', at least at the moment of use, regardless of other activities or motives that may be combined in the particular trip: the second are 'non-recreationists' in a similar sense.

A slightly more complex fourfold classification of user attitudes and participation is suggested in Table 5.2. Onto the simple incidental/intentional distinction can be superimposed the spatial dimension of those from inside the city and its region ('residents') and those from beyond the city's daily urban system ('visitors'). The relationships between these two dimensions produce four possible combinations (see Figure 5.6), namely:

1. Intentional users from outside the city region, who may be holiday-makers staying in the city or outside it using the city for excursions—

Table 5.2 A classification of users of the city

Participation	Attitude	
	Favourable	Unfavourable
High	Enjoyers	Users
Low	Sympathisers	Abstainers

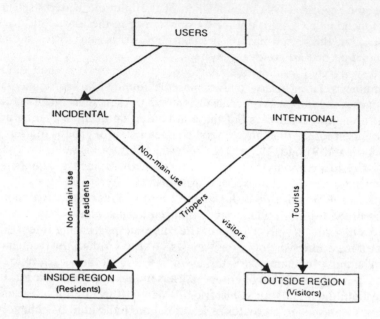

Figure 5.6 *A typology of users of the tourist-historic city*

    Tourists and in the case of these resources quite specifically *Heritage tourists*.

2. Intentional users from inside the city-region, making use of the city's recreational and entertainment facilities or merely enjoying its historic character while engaging in other activities—*Recreating residents*.

3. Incidental users from outside the city-region, which would include most business and congress visitors and those on family visits—*Non-recreating visitors*.

4. Incidental users from inside the city-region, the most numerous group, being ordinary residents about their ordinary affairs—*Non-recreating residents*.

    These four combinations can be recombined in various ways according to the aspect of the use of the historic city being considered. For many individual facilities, whether multi-storey car parks or cafés, all four are important and distinction between them is unnecessary. For much of the tourist industry, such as the accommodation sector for example, users fall into categories one and three, being *Visitors* regardless of the relevance or otherwise of the historic attributes in the motive for the visit. Equally, for many recreational and cultural facilities, and for those planning and managing them, the attitude rather than the place of origin is the determining factor, and users fall into categories one and two.

Thus the categorisation of users is dependent upon the aspect of use being considered. The user as employment generator, as export income earner, as cause of congestion or damage, as competitor for space, or as political constituent, is definable in terms of a particular combination of these basic dimensions.

A difficulty in obtaining information within such a framework of analysis is that users tend to classify themselves according to a general role they have assumed for the visit as a whole rather than their specific purpose in using a particular facility. Thus regardless of the actual facilities being used within the tourist-historic city, users may label themselves as tourists, shoppers, business visitors, etc. The mix of users at any given facility is thus likely to include all of such categories.

Among the few studies of actual use, a study in the central area of the tourist-historic city of Norwich compared these general labels with the motives and actual uses of people in the area (Ashworth and de Haan, 1986). Users' self-allocated categories (such as holiday-maker, long-weekender, day tripper, business visitor, or shopper) were compared with other variables, such as the stated most important reason, or reasons, for being in the area. Something of the expected multimotivation begins to be apparent in Table 5.3. Holiday-makers, understandably, have a wide variety of main reasons, with only around a half being 'intentional' users of the historic city as such. The other groups are similarly mixed; only around half of those classifying themselves as shoppers or business visitors are also claiming these activities as their main reasons for the trip. A more subtle picture is revealed by the degree of importance attached to various attributes of the tourist-historic city (see Table 5.4), attached to particular activities (see Table 5.5), or facilities actually used (see Table 5.6).

A recent study of the visitor behaviour in museums in Nijmegen, Netherlands (Tuynte and Dietvorst, 1988), specifically investigated the

Table 5.3 Main reasons for visiting Norwich (percentage)

	Holiday-makers	Day visitors	Business visitors	Shoppers	Total
Castle/cathedral	18.9	19.5	2.2	0.0	15.6
Other historic site	2.5	9.5	11.1	9.1	6.3
General sightseeing	26.9	23.3	4.4	18.2	23.3
Shopping	2.5	10.0	4.4	54.5	7.5
Family/friends	22.3	10.0	2.2	4.5	18.1
Sport	0.8	1.7	0.0	0.0	1.9
Business/congress	0.4	1.4	55.6	0.0	3.9
Other	25.6	24.6	20.0	13.6	22.4

n = 907

Table 5.4   Aspects of the city regarded as important by visitors to Norwich (percentage)

	Holiday-makers	Day visitors	Business visitors	Shoppers
Museums	70.2	51.3	50.0	63.6
Shops	52.9	47.9	50.0	77.3
Historic attr.	85.2	79.0	54.3	68.2
Culture	55.1	49.0	39.1	59.1
Restaurants	41.1	41.7	54.4	59.1
Sport	9.9	9.3	23.9	13.6
Night-life	12.4	10.1	26.0	22.7

n = 907

Table 5.5 Most important activities of visitors to Norwich (percentage)

	Holiday-makers	Day visitors	Business visitors	Shoppers
Visit castle/cathedral	16.5	24.3	2.2	14.3
Visit other historic site	3.0	10.4	6.5	14.3
Sightseeing	51.7	26.5	10.9	9.5
Shopping	4.2	15.4	4.3	47.6
Visit family/friends	7.6	3.9	2.2	0.0
Sport	0.4	1.0	0.0	4.8
Business	0.0	0.7	56.5	0.0
Other	16.5	17.8	17.4	9.5

n = 907

extent to which such visitors also made use of other facilities (see Table 5.7), whether commercial (cafés, shops etc.), non-commercial (parks and other free-entry facilities), or 'historic' (other museums). A number of different sorts of user associations emerge: as well as visitors combining a number of historical attractions, there are also a 'museum + general sightseeing' activity cluster (22 per cent of the sample), a 'museum + shops' cluster (26 per cent), and a 'museum + shops + café' cluster (7 per cent).

Jensen-Verbeke's various studies of the patterns of use of the central areas of ten medium and small Dutch market towns (1986; 1988) again conclude that classifications such as 'tourist', 'recreationist' or 'shopper' rarely coincide with clear-cut patterns of use of particular facilities, such

Table 5.6 Use made of urban facilities by visitors to Norwich (percentage)

	Holiday-makers	Day visitors	Business visitors	Shoppers
Restaurants	35.1	21.0	32.6	42.8
Cafés	39.4	25.4	47.8	33.3
Pubs	30.7	16.6	37.0	9.5
Antique shops	19.8	12.4	20.0	14.3
Department stores	35.0	26.5	32.6	61.9
Theatres	6.5	4.0	6.5	4.8
Cinemas	5.2	3.8	13.1	14.3
Night-clubs	4.7	3.4	15.2	9.5
Window-shopping	53.2	39.4	52.3	81.0
Car parks	21.4	15.8	28.3	40.0
Buses	10.5	7.6	8.9	23.8
Taxis	7.9	1.5	15.5	0.0

n = 907

Table 5.7 Use of other facilities by visitors to Nijmegen museums (percentage)

All visitors to museums	100
	/ \
Used other facilities	Yes No
	55 45
	/ \
Commercial facilities	Yes No
	28 24
	/ \
Other 'historic' facilities	Yes No
	6 22

Source: After Tuynte and Dietvorst, 1988

as catering establishments or periodic markets. In terms of the relationship of users to facilities, she suggests the division of the supply side into three categories of urban facility, namely primary, i.e. facilities that form the main motive for the visit, secondary, i.e. supporting catering or shopping facilities, and conditional, such as transport accessibility, parking, or information. But again the problem is that different users, or the same user at different stages in the trip, will allocate the same facility to different categories.

The general pattern revealed by all of these comparisons reinforces the argument that multifunctionality of the tourist-historic city depends not only upon offering a range of different facilities to separate groups of consumers, but stems also from the multimotivation and multi-use of the consumers themselves. So-called 'business visitors' make extensive use of catering and shopping facilities and value the presence of museums and historic attractions. Similarly 'shoppers' not only make use of catering facilities but may also include visiting museums, historic and cultural attractions as motives for the visit, thus re-emphasising 'leisure shopping'. It is therefore clear that uses and users are not independent variables but are so closely related as to be only definable in relation to each other. A final point to underline the complexity of the relationship is that many of the users of the tourist-historic city derive from the existing uses, and their employees. A significant component, for example, of business in Ottawa's tourist-historic Lower Town West is dependent upon the demands of the area's existing commercial community, to the extent that a locally intense use-user subculture develops.

6 The planning, management and marketing of the tourist-historic city

The previous five chapters have been essentially conceptual and descriptive, endeavouring to isolate and define the various elements that compose the tourist-historic city, trace their origins and describe their relationship with the form and functioning of the city as a whole. In so far as these processes can be broadly labelled 'theory', then the remaining chapters can be grouped under the general heading of 'practice'. An almost inevitable consequence of such a shift in emphasis is a parallel shift in the balance between the systematic description of processes and their exemplification in particular cities. When the focus of attention is upon application rather than analysis of the tourist-historic elements, then the studies of individual cities become the central structuring elements rather than illustrative case studies in a more general argument.

However, before such cases are examined in detail, there is a need for a brief restatement of the justification for conscious management, a review of the main types of such management practised and an explanation of the method of classification of the urban cases used below.

The inevitability of management

It is clear from the accounts related above of the origins and development of the tourist-historic city as a formal-functional entity in the city that it is a phenomenon that has been created and shaped by a series of intervention decisions, whether made consciously with this end in mind or not. It has in no sense emerged through time as the end result of a series of abstract random and uncontrollable processes, rather its existence is the clear result of planning and its maintenance depends upon management, whether such intervention occurs from the public or private sectors and whether in pursuit of collective or individual goals.

Secondly, there are many instances in the above account of the nature and development of the tourist-historic city where conflict, if not inevitable, is at least predictable. Most obviously there are potential conflicts between the wide range of motivations that have led to the creation of the historic city. In most cases the 'what is heritage?' and 'whose heritage?' questions receive multiple answers. Equally clear are the large number of implicit tensions, described earlier, that are encompassed by the conjunction of the two elements in the tourist-historic city especially as the costs and benefits are asymmetrically allocated. More broadly, the potential for conflict between the large number of possible coexisting functions, each with its distinctive demands upon, and expectations of, the area and its historic attributes, as described above, is again intrinsic to the application of the concept. A paradoxical conclusion that can be drawn from the account of such coexisting functions is that the tourist-historic city in practice invariably coexists within a number of possible functional mixes, as part of a particular residential, commercial or cultural complex. This in turn is generally a condition of fundamentally unstable equilibrium, as the development of individual functions threatens the harmony of the mix as a whole. It creates therefore at least the desirability of sensitive management, if the appropriate balances between functions are to be maintained, and frequently the necessity to prevent or remedy resulting possible conflict.

Thirdly, this very variety of goals and objectives, and this diversity of functions, introduces a multiplicity of organisations with an interest in, and responsibility for, the operation of the tourist-historic city. The case studies already described, and those that will be discussed in more detail below, have introduced the important roles played by a large number of governmental, pseudo-governmental, commercial and non-commercial private associations and groups as well as concerned individuals in such operations. The balance of responsibility between them varies enormously in different national systems, but the very plurality of such groups, and the fragmentation of effective controls between them, together with the concomitant variety of objectives, underlines the necessity for some co-ordinating intervention. Such a central role has been assumed, in the varied cities already discussed, by national or local government agencies, by philanthropic and charitable bodies, by associations of commercial businesses, by profit-seeking financial or property investment organisations, or by particular combinations of all of these, depending upon local circumstance. The simple point is that in almost all the cases investigated it was possible to identify a critical intervention which exercised a catalytic and co-ordinating function without which the tourist-historic city would not have come into being or could not have been maintained.

Once the necessity for such intervention is recognised, through either the co-ordination or conflict resolution arguments, then it can be seen to possess two main dimensions. There is first the need to synthesise between the functions and objectives of various organisations and secondly to co-ordinate between different levels in the hierarchy of spatial scales. The interaction, whether contradictory or complementary, of local, regional, national and international elements and interests is again evident as a central theme in the application in particular cities described in the following chapters.

Types of planning and management

An equally wide variety of planning and management philosophies, organisations and techniques are available for the performance of such tasks. It is not possible to describe in detail the particular individual legal and administrative structure that forms the context for each of the cities mentioned below. The following list of the most commonly encountered is not a comprehensive inventory but only a salutary reminder that the tourist-historic city is in practice managed in a variety of quite different ways, even within the same national or urban situation, and that no single administrative or executive model for its creation can be deduced from the applications in particular cities examined below.

These 'philosophies' of public-sector urban intervention provide an introductory framework for the detailed cases of management discussed below, even when they are implicitly practised as professional norms rather than explicitly stated. The essential differences in objectives, instruments and values of these approaches, as relevant to the planning and management of the tourist-historic city, can be briefly restated. It must be stressed at the outset, however, that although the ordering of the approaches reflects a certain chronology in their adoption as working methods, at least in the countries of North-western Europe,

Table 6.1   Some public-sector planning approaches to the tourist-historic city

Philosophy	Focused on	Instruments	Selection criteria	Determined by
Preservation	Buildings	Protective designation	Intrinsic qualities	Taste leaders
Conservation	Areas	Area designation	Professional norms and practice	Professional planners/ politicians
Land-use regulation	Conflict resolution	Local plans		
Market planning	'The urban product'	Marketing promotion	Market	Users

there is no implied progression in the sense of either logical inevitability or desirability, and most of the case studies considered later will contain recognisable elements drawn from more than one approach.

The development of 'preservational' and 'conservational' approaches to the built environment, with their focus upon the intrinsic qualities of buildings and areas, has already been examined in Chapter 2 as part of the evolution of public attitudes towards the protection of the built environment. Both depend heavily upon legislative designations conferred upon buildings or areas which provide a critical legal framework, constraining development to a greater or lesser degree.

The distinction between conservation planning and the much broader local land-use planning is one of both goals and methods. Conservation planning contains within itself a clear statement of its broad objective, whatever element of the townscape is to be so conserved and however complex the wider functional context in which it is set. Local land-use planning contains no such explicit objective. It aims at regulation and control of the various demands for space made upon the city in the 'public interest', whether this is interpreted as the neutral refereeing of conflict or redressing of perceived discrepancies. The essential point is that such 'regulatory' planning has as its objective a series of compromises about the role of the tourist-historic elements in the city, the nature of which are not predetermined. The main instrument for this type of intervention is the plan, whether this is a detailed cartographic statement of a desirable and attainable future pattern of forms and functions or a series of policy objectives to be approached through continuous monitoring and control.

Market planning as discussed here relates specifically to the application of terminology, techniques and philosophies drawn from marketing science to public-sector, non-profit, organisations with collective goals. The development of concepts and procedures necessary for this translation has been undertaken in general terms in the work of Kotler (1972, 1987) and many others. It is notable here that marketing approaches within public-sector urban planning have been found particularly appropriate to the management of the tourist-historic city which,. at least in the Western European context, has often formed the leading sector within public agencies for the experimentation with such approaches (see for example the market planning procedures for local authorities outlined in theory and practice in Ashworth and Voogd, 1986b; 1988). The essential relevant differences between this approach and that of regulatory land-use planning is the focus upon the city as 'product' and its various users as 'consumers'. The tourist-historic product, however it is constructed (see Ashworth, 1990b), is 'sold' to targeted consumers by means of a range of marketing techniques according to particular selected marketing strategies. Each of these elements in the marketing process could be discussed at length but most significant here are the obvious differences in management instruments and institutional organisation. In terms of objectives, there

Table 6.2 Types of marketing strategy for tourist-historic cities

Character of demand	Marketing strategy	Example
Full demand	Maintenance marketing	Colmar/Quebec/ York
Latent demand	Developmental marketing	Antalya/ Lincoln
Negative demand	Conversional marketing	Lille/Wigan/ Belfast/Pittsburgh
No demand	Stimulational marketing	Rotterdam/ Genoa
Faltering demand	Remarketing	Amsterdam/ Scarborough
Over-full demand	Selective de-marketing	Bath/Florence/ Ribe

Source: Loosely after Kotler, 1975

need in practice be much less pronounced differences with conventional regulatory land-use planning, as the aims of market planning are by no means self-evident, and need not necessarily be measured in terms of maximising 'sales' or 'profits' however these are measured in the public sector. Table 6.2, for example, outlines some possible marketing strategies relevant to the tourist-historic city which result from differences in the nature of the demand, reactions to that demand and thus differences in the possible objectives of such intervention through market planning.

The above discussion of approaches to planning and management of the tourist-historic city is clearly incomplete, being confined to public-sector philosophies, whereas in every case considered below the shaping and operation of the tourist-historic city in practice results from a combination of public and private-sector intervention. Although the terminology of public-private partnership is generally related specifically to marketing approaches, in fact all the above planning philosophies discussed imply some degree of such a 'partnership'.

Even with preservational or conservational planning approaches, where the objectives are determined by public authorities, and the instruments are statutory designations that restrict the operation of private rights over property, there is still a dependence, to a greater or lesser degree, upon the same free market that is being constrained. The search for economically viable occupiers of such premises within mixed economies has already been discussed. With regulatory planning designed to manage functional change to achieve desirable collective goals, the partnership is between an active initiating private sector and a public sector reacting where necessary to resolve conflict, support or restrain particular functions and encourage the attainment of particular functional mixes. A contrast is frequently drawn between what could be termed North-west European social democratic planning practice with its dependence upon statutory instruments, and a North American model where local planning intervention is more likely to manipulate the market to produce acceptable compromises; although in practice considerable variation exists between particular jurisdictions on both continents. In the following chapters such a comparison between approaches is exemplified by the Dutch and Canadian cases respectively. However, despite the differences in choice of instruments of planning, the approaches have in practice frequently much the same basic goals of intervention.

Market planning approaches, however, are an intrinsically different form of public-private partnership. The distinction is not so much in the nature of the organisations that engage in the process as their methods. The philosophy, procedures and terminology of market planning have been translated from private-sector experience but are largely operated by public-sector organisations with collective goals. The management of the tourist-historic city through market planning is more than just a terminological substitution of 'product' for 'facility' or 'customer' for 'user'; it implies a way of viewing the 'historic product' and the 'tourist customer', as well as the assumption of their conjunction within a market. Viewed in that way, the previously important distinctions between public and private-sector organisations and methods no longer apply and a quite different form of partnership emerges. The elements that contribute to the urban product for example may be publicly owned museums or privately owned theme parks, which may be marketed through public promotional agencies or private advertising services, but both are 'sold' on the same market. The distinction in form of ownership has less importance than the nature of the objectives.

Classifying tourist-historic cities

The multitude of tourist-historic cities around the world can be grouped in almost as many different ways as there are examples. Each case is necessarily the product of a unique set of resources, resulting from a particular historic experience, and presented as a distinctive product on a targeted tourism market. The purpose of attempting to impose a system of classification rather than just proceed with a descriptive glossary of unsorted unique examples is that sets of identifiable common characteristics may result from similarly comparable histories of development and subsequently in comparable problems and management policies. This statement of purpose immediately exposes the three principal bases upon which classification could be attempted, namely through the nature of the historic resources, the way in which those resources have been exploited, or the planning and management approaches that are exercised upon the city. A classification system based on each of these has its attractions, not least because a typology based upon any one element in such a triangle would allow the variations in the other two elements to be isolated and examined.

However the central contention of this book is that tourist-historic cities remain cities and a classification must therefore be based upon the characteristics of urban places rather than upon aspects of the tourist-historic function as an isolated element. The classification that has been used is therefore not based on the characteristics of the historic resource itself (the 'Georgian historic city' as opposed to the 'Victorian'); nor its continental or culture region location (the 'West European' or 'Latin American' city); nor its stage of development ('the latent' or 'fully exploited' tourist-historic city) or method of exploitation ('the centrally planned' or 'free-market' city); but upon the more general urban characteristics of the cities themselves.

From among the many such possible characteristics, three alone have been chosen as the main structuring dimensions for the classification, with a further two elements playing a subsidary role. Each of these three characteristics is a continuous spectrum raising the problem of separation into discrete categories. The only practical solution to this is necessarily somewhat arbitrary and depends in the final instance upon the self-definition of the cities themselves. But in terms of planning reactions this can be justified. If Amsterdam with 700,000 inhabitants considers itself to be a major metropolis, while Birmingham although twice as large does not, then their respective management of tourist-historic elements will reflect these beliefs. Similarly a tourist resort is ultimately a town that considers itself to be such and acts accordingly.

These three characteristics are:

1. Population size. The assertion that large cities are more than scaled up versions of smaller ones is especially noticeable in this context; they are significantly different in a number of ways relevant to the tourist-historic dimension. The essential paradox is that the larger the city, the more important is the tourist-historic function in absolute terms. The dominance of one or a very few large cities in both national tourism industries and national historic and cultural resources have both already been demonstrated, as have some of the effects of size upon the tourist-historic regionalisation models. Equally, however, the larger the city, the wider the diversity of other functions and the less important proportionately is the tourist-historic element and the greater its proportional susceptibility to attrition by forces promoting redevelopment for other ends. Both these situations have implications for planning and management.
2. The extent of the diversity of the functional mix. Population size relates to, but does not necessarily determine the diversity of the

urban functional mix and in particular the dominance of tourist-historic functions within this. The contrasting labels of 'monofunctional' and 'multifunctional' city can be used, not as absolute conditions, because obviously no city can exist with only a single function and remain by definition an urban place, but as a spectrum with two main identifiable sets of clusters along it. Two sorts of monofunctionality, which may be related, are relevant here, namely those towns whose historic legacy is so dominant, and so significant on a national or international scale, as to render this function central to all subsequent urban management—these could be termed the 'historic gems'—and secondly, those towns where the tourism function has such a relative importance that they can be labelled 'resorts'.

3. The position on a resource-demand spectrum. Clawson and Knetch (1966) introduced the distinction between 'resource-orientated' and 'demand-orientated' recreation locations as opposite ends of a continuous spectrum. Transferring this idea to tourist-historic cities produces a distinction between those places where the existence of a fortuitous legacy of non-mobile historic buildings and associations has brought into being a resource-based city regardless of the existence or location of demands for it, compared with the reverse situation, where demand for the historic city, whether motivated by tourism or not, has led to the creation of dominantly demand-based historic cities, whose location therefore is determined principally by the spatial patterns of that demand. At its extreme, the distinction is between Stonehenge and Disneyland, but almost all of the cases discussed below occupy intermediate positions, albeit with a recognisable tendency towards one or other end.

		Size		
		Small	Medium	Large
Monofunctional	Demand-based	Legoland Disneyworld U.Canada Village	unlikely	unlikely
	Resource-based	Ribe Williamsburg Heidelburg Lowell	unlikely	unlikely
Multifunctional	Demand-based	unlikely	Ottawa Groningen	London Paris Amsterdam
	Resource-based	unlikely	Pietermaritzburg Norwich Quebec Savannah Charleston	Brussels Sydney Boston

Figure 6.1 *A classification of tourist-historic cities*

The distinction between urban examples drawn from more and less economically developed countries frequently overlaps this resource/demand spectrum, in so far as tourism demand at least is generated principally in the richer countries, for which the resources of the poorer countries compete as destinations. The overlap is of course incomplete, with resource-based historic cities being found also in richer countries and demand-based ones being developed within poorer countries, but the general tendency remains.

As well as these three primary dimensions, there are two others which will reappear where appropriate as structuring elements for the case studies. These are:

1. The nature of the policy objectives of urban management, in particular the distinction between defensive or protective policies that are reactive to external pressures on the one side, and more active, stimulational policies on the other.
2. The physical characteristics of the urban site, when these are dominant features. The most obvious are waterfront sites which have common developmental characteristics, but there are others such as island or 'acropolis' sites which provide sufficient common factors to require comparison on the basis of this element alone.

The three dimensional classification results in the matrix in Figure 6.1, not all the cells of which are either interesting or occupied.

The case studies presented for comparison in the following three chapters will therefore be grouped in the first instance into those that are dominantly monofunctional, as defined above, and those which are clearly multifunctional. The first category (Chapter 7) includes both resource-based 'historic-gem' cities and the more demand-orientated tourist cities: despite their obvious differences the common characteristic in both is that the tourist-historic elements are a major preoccupation of management, whether the goals are dominantly conservational as in the first case, or economic developmental, as a tourist resource, in the second.

The history of development, the resulting characteristics of urban form and function, and thus the objectives of planning intervention, are quite different in the second category, that of multifunctional cities (Chapters 8 and 9). Here the management of tourist-historic elements must take account of a much wider set of management objectives, within which it will often form only a minor consideration. Despite this relegation to a more or less subsidiary role, it must be remembered that the multifunctional cities are in absolute, if not relative, terms the most important repositories of the historic heritage and the most important attractors of tourists; some in fact contain historic 'gems' embedded within their core areas. This importance however is matched by the two obvious intrinsic difficulties of analysis caused by their very multifunctionality and the diversity of what amounts to a 'rest' category. Attention will therefore be focused upon two groups of cities, classified according to size and development strategy, namely the major world cities (Chapter 8) and the medium-sized multifunctional cities (Chapter 9).

7 The management of monofunctional tourist-historic cities

The context

Our exemplification of planning and management begins with those cases where either the historic or the tourist elements are so relatively prominent as to be categorised as either 'monofunctional' historic 'gems' or tourist resorts. We consider a diverse group of resource-based historic gems which range from international to regional in their significance, and from organically evolved to highly orchestrated in their development. Similarly, a wide-ranging exemplification of demand-based tourist cities and related phenomena is considered, in order to demonstrate the diversity inherent in this dimension. Our attempt to provide a global perspective begins, as in the following chapters, with examples of the European cases in which we consider the genesis of the tourist-historic city to lie; both parallels and subtle distinctions will frequently be apparent between European and broadly 'New World' cases, but perhaps most important is the mutual influence which the rapid contemporary global diffusion of information permits. We make use of the spectrum, suggested by Clawson and Knetch (1966) for recreation sites, that allows cities to be ranged from resource-based to demand-based extremes.

Resource-based historic gems

We describe as historic 'gems' those usually small communities in which the historic resource dominates their morphology and identity, as internationally or at least regionally perceived. In Europe they are typically medieval/renaissance survivals, whereas in the 'New World' they may appear in various guises associated with pioneer settlement, and in the less developed world they are inevitably diverse. They normally share the characteristic that they are relics bypassed by economic progress until the twentieth century has, more or less, redefined their economic resource in terms of their history.

Western Europe

Ribe (Denmark) Ribe is in a number of ways archetypal of the small conserved historic gems in Western Europe, especially in those countries with a long tradition of regulatory land-use planning. It possesses the three critical elements generally associated with the survival of such towns, namely:

1. It has enjoyed a period of spectacular commercial prosperity, especially during the sixteenth and seventeenth centuries, that resulted

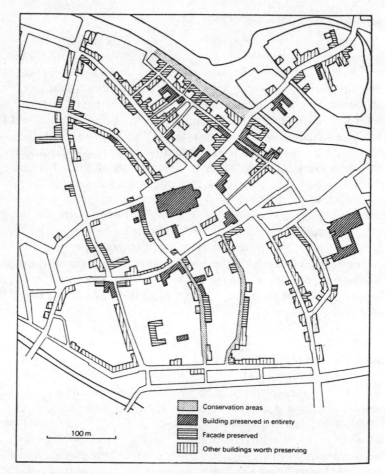

Figure 7.1   *Ribe: preserved buildings and conservation areas*

in a large quantity of building. (It contains 103 nationally listed buildings from this period (see Figure 7.1), the largest concentration of listed buildings outside Copenhagen.);
2. It then suffered, fairly abruptly, a period of commercial stagnation for a mixture of economic and political reasons that discouraged growth and removed much of the pressure for redevelopment;
3. Finally, it has had the good fortune to be located in a country in which the awareness of the value of architectural preservation, and subsequent implementation through appropriate protective legislation, largely predated the encounter with the modern pressures for re-development.

Although it is Denmark's oldest city, incorporated around AD 700, the street layout is essentially from the fifteenth century and much of the building from the following two centuries. The shifting of the Baltic-North Sea trade routes away from the base of the Jutland peninsula undermined the town's entrepôt function, and the loss of Schleswig-Holstein in 1864 placed Ribe on the international frontier, further restricting its local hinterland. The result is a compact town closely surrounded by open meadows with only around 8,000 inhabitants, a quarter of whom live in the historic core.

Some notable buildings were demolished in the course of the nineteenth century but an antiquarian society was formed in 1855, and the Protection of Historic Buildings Act offered national protection from 1918. It was however largely local initiatives, symbolised by the founding of a local Tourism Association as early as 1899, that led to a recognition of the need for systematic conservation and the development of a suitable town plan. In 1963 general controls on change were imposed on an area of the old town, including no fewer than 550 buildings. This was followed in 1969 by a comprehensive building-by-building survey and the adoption of a conservation plan (Bevaringsplan Ribe), which thus predates the national enabling legislation of the 1977 Municipal Planning Act for the designation of conservation areas. The small, compact extent of the town, together with the completeness of its architectural ensemble and its visibility as a result of its setting in open country, raised a number of special problems and justified quite rigorous detailed measures. For example, not only are roof-lines carefully controlled but so also are the types and colours of tiling used on them. Again the small size of the town has made it relatively easy to consign non-conforming uses, such as large-scale modern retailing and car parking, especially for the million annual visitors, to the periphery (Court, 1987).

Rothenburg (Bavaria) Rothenburg ob der Tauber repeats the critical elements of gem survival, with variations. It was founded as a castle

Figure 7.2   *Rothenburg ob der Tauber. Tourist map (courtesy Fremdenverkehr-samt, Rothenburg)*

town in the early Middle Ages, in common with many other German towns, and in the thirteenth century it achieved the status of a Free City of the Holy Roman Empire; its economic and political importance were sufficient for the Imperial Diet to convene in Rothenburg in 1377, and it played a significant role in the Thirty Years War (1618–48). Its free status was lost with incorporation into Bavaria in the early nineteenth century, since when it has been functionally marginalised relative to the major cities in the strategic Rhine and Main corridors.

Rothenburg's site and morphology provide a further constraint upon its contemporary functional possibilities but also a highly distinctive scenic and historic tourist resource; it shares with Ribe (and most European gems) a high visibility but in a quite different physical context. It is a completely walled town on an escarpment overlooking the Tauber valley, the contours of which are precisely reflected in the alignment of the walls. Modern functions are necessarily concentrated in the limited suburban development

Plate 7.1a Rothenburg: town wall with tourist-leisure reuse of moat (JET 1976)

beyond the walls; the historic town is highly constricted in its ability to handle vehicles, or activities other than some of those geared to serving the tourist trade. This has been generated by its fame as an exceptionally complete medieval/renaissance gem, both in its internal streetscapes and in its aggregate townscape as seen from its fortifications and from across the Tauber valley (see Figure 7.2, Plate 7.1a).

The survival of Rothenburg's historic resource was dependent upon its economic and political eclipse before the industrial period. Its discovery by nineteenth-century Romantics as a symbol of a vanishing Germany led to early heritage awareness, the founding of the *Verein Alt Rothenburg* (a conservation society) in the 1890s and the enactment of civic controls in 1900 which, as in Ribe, largely forestalled insensitive redevelopment. Rothenburg's eclipse is particularly critical in the context of recent German history. It was, none the less, substantially damaged in 1945 and its emergence from this national trauma is credited to the forbearance of an American general who halted his attack when he saw the town's quality, and who is duly remembered as a vital figure in the town's history. This survival through a single military decision to respect historicity is not unique, other famous examples being Savannah (Chapter 9) and, in the present context, Heidelberg (see Plate 7.1b). There is a likely factor in the tourist-historic survival of Rothenburg that could be·labelled the 'Student Prince' phenomenon, although it is Heidelberg that can actually claim Romberg's operetta. The life or death issue in these two German cases is

Plate 7.1b Heidelberg: town gate and castle from across Neckar River (JET 1976)

that artistic fiction shapes expectations which a city may fortuitously fulfil, or a role model for the city to emulate. Cause and effect, reality and myth are impossible, and for our purposes unnecessary, to disentangle. What is important is the popularity of the Andersen images in Ribe or the Brothers Grimm in Rothenburg, however subconsciously, among potential users of the historic resource.

The tourist-historic city has been the principal preoccupation of Rothenburg's recent planning and management. The municipal controls ensured that post-1945 reconstruction adhered to the historical character; as in Ribe they predated higher authority but were reinforced at the *Land* level by the Bavarian *Denkmalschutzgesetz* in 1973 and by tri-level cost-sharing provisions, including the federal government, for related urban management. The entrenched preservation of historic Rothenburg has provided a fertile centre-piece for highly sophisticated tourist marketing, which includes conference facilities and an annual calendar of events making good use of a store of legend, and has given rise to over sixty hotels and as many restaurants in a town of 12,000 people. Tourist success has a predictable price, however: there is a concern to balance tourism with suburban industrial development without visual intrusion, and to spread tourists more evenly through the historic city. As in Ribe, major parking facilities are provided in relatively unobtrusive locations outside the walls and moat, where tourist information is available; in this way tour buses, which cause particular environmental stress, are deflected from the narrow gates and streets. Note that Rothenburg is marketed in a wider regional framework, which we will show to be common elsewhere; here there is a particularly linear dimension since it is a prime attraction on the Bavarian *Romantische Strasse*.

Western Europe: overview Ribe and Rothenburg are typical of many such West European historic gems in the series of chance occurrences that have contributed to their survival and enhancement, and in the sort of detailed, regulatory planning made possible, and publicly acceptable, by their undisputed historical value. What is equally clear however is that such cities are rare, and that this very rarity confers a substantial consensus about the objectives of their planning. The planning problems tend to be technical and architectural rather than political or economic. Functions other than those directly related to the historic city, even those concerned with tourism, will only be tolerated so long as they conform with, and offer no threat to, the preserved historic fabric. The town's economic viability, retailing structure and the social and demographic balance of its residential population have all in effect been sacrificed to the single goal of preservation. Most European countries consider themselves fortunate in possessing a few such gems, but would not be prepared to pay the price, in terms of urban fossilisation, of too many.

Although there are many categories of such cities, two are especially prevalent. Fortress towns are often built in one historical period to meet a particular military threat; reassessment of defence needs and abandonment of the military function may then result in stagnation and ultimately preservation. Many of Europe's most renowned gems fall into this category, including Willemstad and Bourtange (Netherlands), Palma Nova (Italy) and Neuf-Brisach (France), and even the New World contains a few, such as Louisbourg (below).

Secondly, a recurrent geographical environment in which historic gems tend to be found is the obsolete port location; Rye in Sussex, England, Aigues Mortes in the south of France and to a degree Dubrovnik in Yugoslavia illustrate this type. Reference to this classic gem location expands our discussion, however, for again it occurs also in the New World (Portobelo, Panama; Nantucket, Massachusetts) and in colonial gateways to the less developed 'old world' (Malacca, Malaysia; Goa, India) and furthermore it touches upon the tourist-demand base represented by the proximate coastal amenity, considered later in this chapter.

The New World

The concept of an historic gem in the continents of post-Columbian European settlement might seem, to European minds, a contradiction in terms. Aside from any urban heritage of indigenous peoples, however, the first settler towns are now essentially five hundred years old; Santo Domingo (Dominican Republic), the oldest, is a direct extension from the European medieval heritage, as its extensive 1970s restoration testifies. The older Iberian (Latin America), Dutch (South Africa), French and British settler cities include a number of gems which bear comparison with European renaissance contemporaries. The historic gem in the New World also appears in forms which have received relatively scant consideration in Western Europe. There is a wealth of nineteenth-century urban heritage which generates tourist interest because it is the beginning of settlement, and lately there has been an awakening of industrial heritage tourism parallel to Western Europe (Weiler, 1984). One very recurrent type of historic gem which provides a common thread throughout the New World is the pioneer mining town, which dates chiefly from the gold rushes of the nineteenth century; many classically possess the critical elements in the survival of historic gems, having passed from boom to bust to tourist-oriented revitalisation in a century or less, the brevity of their history being more than compensated by its romance. Examples include Ouro Preto (Brazil, seventeenth century), Hill End (New South Wales), Pilgrims Rest (Transvaal), Georgetown (Colorado) and Dawson City (Yukon), the latter two now experiencing heavy tourist pressure. Dawson exemplifies the truly resource-based nature of these mining gems in that demand must overcome difficulty of both access and environment, this including permafrost in Dawson's case, a direct impediment to conservation and a financial drain for Parks Canada, which owns various buildings as part of Klondike National Historic Sites. In contrast, some small market towns with uneventful histories are now finding an identity as historic gems of regional significance.

Whatever the provenance of the New World historic gem, it has usually organically evolved like its European counterpart. A sufficient number have experienced some corporate enterprise in their revitalisation, however, that a spectrum could possibly be identified between organic and corporate extremes. Among the latter are interesting cases such as Pilgrims Rest and Matjesfontein (South Africa), both of which have been restored as hotel complexes by a single enterprise. The most famous corporately restored gem, however, is Williamsburg.

Williamsburg (Virginia) Williamsburg is an outstanding, if unusual, example of the tourist-historic city and its marketing in North America. It clearly illustrates the continuum that exists between the New World corporate-enterprise historic gem and the historic theme park (discussed below), since it could be regarded as a hybrid between a Disneyland environment, in which popular entertainment is paramount, and a town seeking to portray the idea of historic authenticity. As the eighteenth-century colonial capital of Virginia, it is unquestionably an historic city,

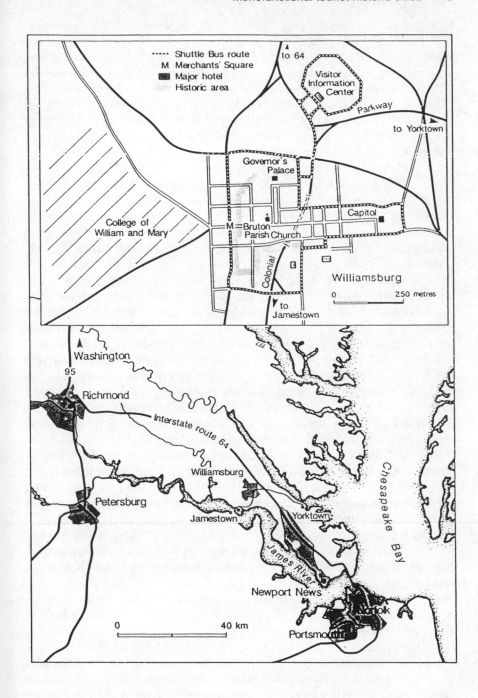

Figure 7.3   *Williamsburg and region*

having rich associations with contemporary statesmen and over 80 pre-1776 buildings remaining. Their survival was aided by the transfer of the seat of government to Richmond in 1780 (see Figure 7.3), which removed Williamsburg's main *raison d'être* and also spared it the destruction and the prejudice to which Richmond (as capital of the Confederacy) was subjected during and after the Civil War. Thus Williamsburg is a classic historic gem in that past economic failure permitted contemporary success by sheltering the physical fabric from economic and political hazards until its value as an historic resource was recognised.

Local promoters of the historic resource prompted John D. Rockefeller, Jr., to fund the restoration of colonial Williamsburg, from 1926 through the 1930s (Hosmer, 1981). The restored area comprises 173 acres, the essence of the colonial city; a further 3,000 acres were acquired as a 'cordon sanitaire', including Carter's Grove Plantation, an outlying attraction. It was among the first notable examples of urban historic preservation in the USA, and in consequence it was undertaken with what is now regarded as an artificial 'pickling' philosophy, in which it has been restored to a sanitised interpretation (with little reference to slavery) of what it was like in the eighteenth century, without respect for intervening evolution (Coopersmith, 1976). This entailed the clearance or moving of nearly 600 later buildings, the restoration of 88 colonial buildings, and the reconstruction on original foundations of over 400 which had disappeared since the eighteenth century; it has thus become an open-air museum, based upon detailed research, and has largely ceased to be a normal evolving community (Plate 7.2). To compound this, it has acquired a *secondary* heritage identity as a period piece in the evolution of conservation philosophy, and as a home of the Rockefellers. Since it is operated and marketed as a commercial enterprise by the Colonial Williamsburg Foundation, with Visitor Center, shuttle buses, interpretive programmes and staff in period costume, and since there are admission charges (with theme park package options) to most buildings, it has become scarcely distinguishable from a theme park in which the heritage is entirely artificial, reconstructed or relocated. The fact that it is a pedestrian precinct reinforces this image; so does the emphasis upon theme retailing of period crafts, food and activities, and the provision of official hotels and recreational amenities.

The tourist city of Williamsburg also includes a variety of outlying parasitic attractions (where space allows), and the fast-food facilities of the small central business district, a prime function of which is the servicing of the seventeenth-century College of William and Mary. The College is both an activity compatible with the historic city and an autonomous part of it; it predates the town and participates actively in tourist-historic cultural events such as lectures and concerts. Bruton Parish Church (1715) is a further autonomous historic component which also contributes to Williamsburg's active arts/culture profile (cf. Chapter 5).

Plate 7.2 Williamsburg: tourist activity on main street (Duke of Gloucester) (JET 1977)

The marketing of Williamsburg, and its largely theme park quality, is greatly enhanced by its proximity to Jamestown, the first permanent English settlement in North America, and Yorktown, the site of the strategic American victory in the War of Independence. The three locations are linked by the landscaped speed-controlled Colonial Parkway and are co-marketed ('Virginia's Historic Triangle'), even though different controlling authorities are involved; they can be considered a *dispersed tourist-historic city.* The controlling authorities are principally the National Parks Service (the Colonial National Historical Park includes parts of Jamestown and Yorktown, and the Parkway); the Commonwealth (State) of Virginia (a historic theme park at Jamestown and museum at Yorktown); the Association for the Preservation of Virginia Antiquities (Jamestown collaboration); the Colonial Williamsburg Foundation; and the Williamsburg Area Convention and Visitors Bureau (a division of the Chamber of Commerce concerned with area event promotion, hotel bookings, etc.). Overall, tourist marketing is highly sophisticated, employing co-ordinated literature, advertisement and a toll-free telephone system. However it is neither exclusively urban nor exclusively historic in its focus; regional attractions are marketed together, and in this case the dispersed tourist-historic city is co-marketed with the James River plantations, which fit the historic theme, and other nearby historic towns and waterfront attractions. This regionalisation of the resource and its marketing corresponds to a similar regional patterning of visitor behaviour. The long-standing dominance of the automobile in the North American situation has encouraged the development of regional visitor circuits, with the key attractions forming nodes ideally linked by recreational parkways that are themselves part of the excursion experience. Such regionalisation is increasingly encountered elsewhere in the world (cf. Chapter 4).

St. Andrews (New Brunswick) While other New World historic gems have experienced degrees of corporate tourist-historic enhancement (such as St. Augustine, Florida), some have evolved organically. An example is St. Andrews, New Brunswick, which has effected a natural transition from a small seaside resort to a contemporary tourist-historic city. St. Andrews has a history of great national significance to Canadians: its foundation in the 1780s was a monument to the determination of Empire Loyalists to escape the new United States at all costs, for it was a second relocation from Castine, in Maine, when the Passamaquoddy rather than the Penobscot River was finally agreed upon as the international boundary in 1783. Many of its houses date from the period of first settlement, and a few have added interest to the national ideology in that they were dismantled from Castine (where their former locations are still marked) and rafted round the treacherous rocky coast to their final safe haven. As the first secure landfall, St. Andrews is in general very poorly located within both New Brunswick and Canada as a whole, and accordingly it failed to grow and thereby to suffer erosion of its heritage; in the nineteenth century it found a limited economic base as a small, select seaside resort, a function which (with the addition of retirement in recent decades) has proved highly compatible with slow growth and with conservation. In the late 1970s, the Heritage Canada Foundation attempted to establish a heritage conservation area in St. Andrews; this was subsequently voted down by the local electorate on the grounds of unwarranted interference with private property rights, but there is an influential local civic trust, and in practice the community contains neither the development potential nor the motivation to disturb what is, in effect, a virtually total conservation area. The revitalisation of its main street has, in any case, enhanced both its historic image and its capacity to service its moderate (seasonal) tourist trade, for which the Loyalist heritage is exploited to retail British goods.

The small town as regional historic gem The New World historic gem may also be a small central place of regional rather than national significance. The small town plays such a central role in the romantic vision of the recent North American past (in Canada portrayed in the books of Montgomery, cf. Squire, 1988) that it can be an ideal candidate for conversion to an historic gem in which architectural, historical and literary associations can be combined. The typical decline of such towns, as a result chiefly of changes in agriculture and in the scale of industrial production, both conserves the historic resource and provides the need for an alternative economic activity. A multifunctional, if local, economic base may be converted into a near monofunctional historic gem of at least regional tourist interest, where both resource and market are favourable.

The decline of these towns has been complicated, since the 1970s, by the invasion of enclosed shopping malls, undermining the remaining vitality of their 'Main Street'. Growing concern over the economic and often physical threat to this, the focus of the town's heritage and identity, has caused both the US National Trust for Historic Preservation and the Heritage Canada Foundation to give priority to a 'Main Street' conservation programme, frequently taking advantage of a variety of parallel state and provincial assistance schemes. This has enabled many small communities with sufficient enterprise to tap these sources and turn blighted structures into their central tourist-historic resource; where the main street abuts a waterfront, typical in formerly pioneer communities, there may be a regionally impressive heritage of early commercial and industrial buildings, of which the widely encountered mills offer a variety of tourist-oriented adaptive reuse potential. However, the successful realisation of tourist-historic cities from these regional gems depends upon additional geographical attributes favouring tourism: accessibility both to other recreational resources and to a potential market.

The relevance of these points may extend to communities of populations of 50,000 or more and may include those with varying degrees of national significance, such as St. Andrews, and Kingston (Ontario), a thriving lakeshore tourist-historic city.

The Ontario small town: Perth and St. Jacobs The historic gem potential of New World small towns is well exemplified in Ontario, particularly since here the waterfront makes a practically ubiquitous contribution to both the heritage and the wider recreational resource. Perth is an early nineteenth-century town particularly noted for its Georgian limestone architecture, 100 km west of Ottawa, to which it is connected by the Rideau Canal system, historically fundamental to both communities (and to Kingston) since its construction in the 1820s. Perth's quality caused it to be selected by Heritage Canada as a national 'Main Street' pilot project for co-operative revitalisation by the Foundation, the municipality and local business. Its subsequently successful economic and physical revitalisation in the 1980s has rested upon the expansion of its tourist appeal, now largely based upon heritage and related commerce (Plate 7.3). In Perth's case, the wider resource and market factors are highly positive: the canal terminus, adjacent to the main street, is owned and landscaped by Parks Canada (like all 'heritage canals') and is the site of a proposed retail-leisure facility; the town is a service centre for the nearby Rideau Lakes resort area; and it is one hour's drive from a major metropolis with the advantages this implies for residential potential as well as for a nearby day-excursion market. However, a controversy between the municipality and an external developer over a potentially damaging suburban shopping mall, before provincial arbitration in 1989, indicates the vulnerability of these regional gems in the North American context; given that the geographical advantages otherwise enjoyed by Perth are seldom as strong elsewhere, a point little acknowledged by Heritage Canada, the tourist-historic success of such regional gems is rarely guaranteed. Nevertheless the subsequent national 'Main Street' programme, and Heritage Canada's many other urban involvements, are important testimony to the positive tourist-historic influence of the voluntary conservation sector.

In Ontario, similar processes can be detected in Prescott, Brockville (both Heritage Canada-sponsored) and Port Hope along the St. Lawrence, and Elvira, Fergus and St. Jacobs in Western Ontario. In the last two, the tourist promotion of cultural and ethnic minorities is combined with the conservation of the built environment. Fergus, the site of the 'Highland Games', markets its Scottish origins, while the attraction of St. Jacobs is its Mennonite community. Such towns are gems of social as well as architectural history.

Plate 7.3 Perth: Georgian-Victorian main street ambience (Gore Street) (JET 1982)

St. Jacobs provides an interesting example of both the preservation and marketing of a living community, as well as the deliberate adoption of a tourist-historic strategy as a defensive measure. The old-fashioned clothing, transport and farming methods of the Christian fundamentalist Mennonite denomination is a marketable curiosity that 'peoples' the conserved landscape. The realisation by the Mennonite community itself that such curiosity is inevitable led to the deliberate development of St. Jacobs as an attraction with a free museum and interpretation centre, so that visitors will be concentrated in one manageable place and not intrude further into the life of the inhabitants. The managed, concentrated historic attraction is further anchored, in particular, by a craft-oriented shopping complex in an adaptively reused mill and grain silo. There is a paradox for social groups whose desire for isolation, for religious or political reasons, has led to their preservation, but whose very isolation from the social mainstream renders their way of life a visitor attraction and thus invites intrusion. The St. Jacobs solution is relevant to many similar communities world-wide, such as Calvinists at Staphorst (Netherlands), monks on Mt. Athos (Greece) or 'Dancing Dervishes' at Konya (Turkey).

Armidale (New South Wales) Armidale, an Australian example of the regional historic gem, provides an interesting counterpoint to the Canadian context discussed above. It is not a national gem in the care of national parks authorities or national or local trusts, such as Hill End, Berrima (NSW), Richmond (Tasmania) or Childers (Queensland). Armidale is, rather, a regional capital of the New England tableland district and is an archetypal manifestation of the rural central place. The heritage by-product of its central place status is the possession of two distinguished cathedrals, several museums and art galleries, and a small main street with numerous public and commercial buildings of historic interest in its vicinity. Its centrality also generates a tourist market for the historic city, tourists being drawn both by the scenic and historic interest of New England, which contains important national parks, and by Armidale's location near the Newell Highway between Melbourne/Sydney and the Queensland coast, which is another route receiving linear tourism promotion. The rationale for its development as a tourist-historic city is enhanced by the presence of the University of New England and a major college; this raises its visitor profile, creates a substantial white-collar community favouring conservation, and generates a student work-force.

The main street revitalisation problem of small North American communities has a comparative relevance here. However, Armidale has been able to organise retail expansion so as to be supportive rather than destructive of the existing main street; new shopping centre developments built behind the main street feed into it by way of covered arcades, and the traditional retail frontage (which was converted into a pedestrian mall in the 1970s) remains the central economic and morphological focus of the town. Such a solution is found elsewhere in Australia and indicates that the heritage quality of small New World central places does not have to be subverted by alien commercial megastructures. Since the threat of such subversion continues to hang over even successfully revitalised towns such as Perth, the comparison has pertinent lessons for the continuity of regional historic gems in North America, making due allowance for Australia's climatic advantage.

Although Armidale does not require the intervention of the voluntary conservation sector in defence of its main street, the National Trust owns an historic homestead on the edge of the city and classifies over thirty other buildings as historically significant. This is both a measure of the city's significant historicity and a further indication of the widespread significance of the conservation movement in promoting this in historic gems and more generally.

Demand-based tourist cities

Creation of historicity

The growth of tourism and its increasing orientation to 'heritage' has generated market demand to enhance or contrive an historic resource. The logical progression from preservation to creation was described in Chapter 2 and the relationship between historical authenticity and the tourism experience was raised in Chapter 3. Historic creation will now be examined in particular situations.

Pressure to expand heritage resources is most understandable in those societies which perceive themselves as having the least historic heritage, or as having squandered it most recklessly before the market perceived heritage as a resource. We may look to the capitalist societies of the New World, particularly North America, for the origins of this; but the concepts developed have subsequently spilled over into other parts of the world, including back into Europe. While the creation of historicity is largely associated with monofunctional centres, hence its inclusion in this chapter, many creations exist in or near large cities, most particularly those New World cities which have placed a premium on growth at the expense of conservation.

It is difficult to separate the creation (or often more accurately re-creation) of the *historical* heritage from the *cultural* values and norms it represents. The two are closely interdependent but the distinction, however logically artificial, has a particular significance in many New World societies that are derived from a culturally plural background. In such societies there is not only a demand to re-create architectural styles and technologies from a national past but equally there is a need to rediscover diverse cultural roots and display the 'cultural baggage' that settlers brought with them from their overseas origins. The geographical reality that such pluralist cultures are rooted elsewhere encourages contemporary artifice, relating to historicity, to give them stronger expression in the New World.

In the broadest sense the creation of historicity entails a number of choices concerning the three elements that compose an historic attraction, namely the object, the place and the historic association. Changes in the associations with which an existing object and place are endowed are relatively common in place promotion to a volatile market; the Yorkshire Dales, for example, long interpreted as the 'Brontë Country', are now more likely to be marketed as the 'Herriot Country'. It is physical creativity in the object and its location that are our concern here. Creating the object may involve a clear spectrum of actions that runs through various degrees of *enhancement*, and of *reconstruction*, to *facsimiles*. The artifice of facsimiles itself ranges from the most fanciful theme park, based upon imaginary ideas, to replicas purporting an historical accuracy; reconstruction may be from purely documentary evidence, from existing foundations or from visible ruins; or authentic historic structures may be enhanced with newly created additions. Classic examples of each type of creation are respectively Disneyland (California), Louisbourg (Nova Scotia) and Williamsburg (Virginia); these are considered below in the context of theme parks.

The third element that can be altered is location. Some historic artefacts are essentially mobile, being either transportable or themselves transport. Increasingly, it has proved technically and financially feasible to transport buildings, enabling the resource to be brought to the customer rather than the reverse. The first large-scale project for assembling conserved buildings in a new location was the Hjerl Hede historic village in Jutland, Denmark, which had as its objective not merely the preservation of threatened buildings, but also the maintenance and promotion of rural crafts, customs and ultimately a way of life and a set of values. These social and cultural associations were also fundamental to the establishment of the museum of Welsh rural life at St. Fagan's, near Cardiff. Many other such open-air collections have since been established, such as the Weald and Downland Museum at Singleton in Sussex, and Upper Canada Village (Ontario). Most such collections are specifically rural, but there are some notable assemblies of urban buildings in an urban location, such as Den Gamle By at Aarhus (Denmark), Calgary's Heritage Park, and the most ambitious national architectural collection at the Dutch open-air museum at Arnhem.

The largest example of the second sort of mobile resource, transport itself, is the ship. There is now a long tradition of using preserved ships, whether merchant or warships, as the centre-piece for waterfront conservation developments. Such ships are often berthed in places with which they have historical or name association. The archetype is perhaps *Wasa* (Stockholm), but there are many more, including *Great Britain* (Bristol), *Constitution* (Boston), *Massachusetts* (Fall River), *North Carolina* (Wilmington), *Mary Rose* and *Warrior* (Portsmouth), *Cavalier* (Teeside), *Mikasa* (Yokohama) and *Sackville* (Halifax). However their inherent mobility provides the opportunity of acquiring such resources for their own sake rather than any specific association with the place. The acquiring of the *Queen Mary* by Long Beach, California, is one of the more incongruous of such relocations. The absence of a preserved ship can be rectified by facsimile building, although in many preserved ships, such as *Victory* (Portsmouth), so much of the structure has been replaced that it is difficult to draw too fine a distinction between original and replica. Among the most notable facsimile ships are the *Mayflower* (Plymouth, USA) and *Bluenose II* (Halifax). Ships of all sorts provide catalysts for waterfront revitalisation, which is fundamental to the tourist-historic city and will be discussed later in terms of multifunctional management.

Railway locomotives and carriages are a further manifestation of the transport mobile resource; they are usually exhibited, reused, or still actively used, where they have historical associations, but again may be exploited for their own sake (as in numerous North American restaurants), and in either case they too are often found in or near waterfront locations (eg. Sacramento, California; Savannah, Georgia; Kingston, Ontario).

The creation of historicity has accordingly evolved into a complex phenomenon, many of the variations of which may be found in close juxtaposition. Furthermore it now has a well-established pedigree, with well-known examples extending back fifty years, and has attracted the participation of respected conservation bodies. Thus, although it is ultimately demand-based, it has become part of mainstream conservation technology; since compatible infill and reconstruction of damage (including from earthquakes, fire, etc.) is a necessary part of 'normal' historic conservation, the spectrum has actually become continuous between the extremes of demand-based creation and the resource-based conservation discussed above. Examples examined along this continuum raise the question 'where does authenticity end and fantasy begin?', particularly since tourist-serving conservation must introduce departures from former reality. In the case of Williamsburg, an enhancement involving major re-creation and selective removal, we have noted that many of the reconstructions are themselves now fifty years old and have thereby acquired a secondary historic interest. In the case of more recent creative activity, in North America much has been produced by the highly respected national parks organisations; their concern is often selective reconstruction on archaeologically-identified foundations, perhaps the most famous case being Louisbourg, and in consequence there is again a clear link with historic authenticity.

We reiterate that creation is not restricted to monofunctional centres. Metropolitan examples of both artifice and reconstruction are to be found in Singapore, which has created and re-created various cultural and historical attractions, to stem the damage to its tourist trade caused by rapid redevelopment in the 1970s/80s. Gold Reef City in Johannesburg is an excellent metropolitan illustration of artifice anchored by authenticity; it is an approximate facsimile of early Johannesburg, organised as a theme park, located on off-centre derelict mining land in which an authentic former gold mine complex constitutes the focal attractions. It is a capitalist foundation in which corporations run general attraction, such as a 'Victorian Fun Fair', and sponsor or operate constituent businesses; these control their own replica buildings, museums, authentic historic interior features and trade craft displays, through which they project theme specialist retailing and tourist service provision. Sovereign Hill in Ballarat, Australia, a smaller multifunctional city, is broadly similar. Calgary has assembled a Heritage Park by relocating historic structures from across western Canada to a peripheral location removed from development pressure. The example of downtown Halifax (Nova Scotia), shown in Figure 5.3, illustrates the spectrum from artifice to authenticity typical of many such multifunctional metropolises. Within a restricted area of waterfront can be found preserved pre-Victorian buildings (Historic Properties); preserved Victorian façades incorporated into new building (Founders Square); replica reconstruction of a previous Victorian building (Granville Mall); a modern building housing historic objects (Maritime Museum); and two notable historic ships, namely *Sackville* (preserved) and *Bluenose* (replica) (Heritage Canada, 1987, *et al.*).

The open-air theme park

The conventional theme park is an explicitly demand-based and demand-located recreational development which offers amusement for profit, on the basis of (at least) an admission charge; given the dominance of the capitalist ethic, the scale of the market, the availability of space and the perceived shortage of authentic resources, it is not surprising that it originated in North America. Theme parks, as the name implies, usually combine amusement with education, around some focal theme; this may concern nature or characters from literature (such as fairy tales) but it is commonly cultural/historical. They extend and expand the traditionally rather passive interaction of visitor and site through multi-media presentations (such as the use of holograms in Windsor's 'Royalty and Empire' exhibition), participation in appropriate activities and generally removing the distinction between visitor and visited object. The most famous manifestations are Disneyland (Anaheim, California) and Walt Disney World (Orlando, Florida), which are divided into several different theme 'lands' such as Fantasyland, Tomorrowland and – significantly in our context – Frontierland. Through amusement rides, costumed characters and contrived architecture, these 'lands' play a significant educational role, although compared with that of resource-based attractions this is typically even more simplified and idealised. The powerful impact of Frontierland, in particular, on millions of children's (and adults') perceptions of American culture and history is indisputable; the replicas of historic regional urban architecture – New England, the old South, the West, etc. – not only reflect surviving reality in those areas but sensitise the visitor to a national or regional consensus about the past.

Perhaps the most tangible educational component, from the perspective of the tourist-historic city, is Main Street, USA, the grand entrance to both Disney theme parks. One cannot enjoy these idealisations without a subconscious impulse to look for them in the 'real' world; and this might easily translate into support for 'Main Street' revitalisation, the tourist-historic significance of which we have examined. It should be noted that retailing is a central feature of the Disney parks in general, as of most other theme parks; it is therefore not surprising that shopping centre developers have seen and exploited the theme concept to promote their own ends, and that a heritage theme is increasingly encountered in new shopping centre developments, particularly (but not only) where these relate to inner-city revitalisation (Heritage Canada, 1985).

Relocations While a central characteristic of heritage theme parks is the ability to create attractions free from the constraints of randomly located, fragmentary surviving relics, they have commonly seen the potential of relocating authentic historic structures to support or in place of replicas. In some cases, such theme parks have been resource-based as much as demand-based, in that the relocation of valued structures was the only way to conserve them in the face of urbanisation, flooding or other (usually man-made) environmental changes. A good Canadian example is Upper Canada Village, near Morrisburg, Ontario, which provided a means to rescue heritage structures from flooding and dislocation associated with construction of the St. Lawrence Seaway. Upper Canada Village portrays rural and small-town Ontario life in the nineteenth century, complete with costumed guides and 'hands-on' children's attractions; it forms part of a linear complex of recreational attractions, emphasising rural and small town history in its environmental setting along the Ontario shore of the St. Lawrence. Such heritage theme parks may be commercially or publicly run, but they are usually demand-responsive, strongly marketed to tourists, and concerned to make a profit – in part through retail enterprise. Like other theme parks, they usually charge admission, during limited hours, and are staffed by suitably costumed employees (largely seasonal students in North America); they have no resident population and no organic linkage between their structures other than the museum function; they may also have only limited links with the settlement structure, economy and society in which they are set. Thus they constitute a limited step in the direction of the conventionally evolved tourist-historic city.

Although neither heritage theme parks nor relocated preserved structures are exclusively North American, that continent provides the archetypal examples. However it was European ideas that underlay the early discussion of the social and educational goals that were realised in Hjerl Hede and St. Fagan's. The commercial, rather than educational, success of these pioneers led to many imitators, and the theme park based on relocated collections of buildings is today almost a commonplace of both rural and urban tourism. Apart from its appeal to a profitable market, the idea also has an attraction within the museum and conservation professions, as it has a clear rescue function, as well as being appropriate to current notions of a more interactive relationship between exhibit and visitor. The shift from curatorial and archival roles to informative and entertaining ones favours such developments, illustrated most clearly at the Jorvik Heritage Centre (York, UK) where the methods of presentation owe more to the classical fantasy theme park than traditional archaeology, although of course both the site and the artefacts are genuine.

Two other European reactions to theme park developments in the USA are discernible. The first is the import into Western Europe of the American product, often marginally modified for European tastes, and frequently operated with North American capital, management and methods. There is something incongruous about such imports as Disneyland Paris, in a continent abounding in historic cities; equally bizarre, the largest and most successful European imitator, Legoland (at Billund, Denmark), re-creates in plastic bricks the very historic monuments that are located at Hjerl Hede, or Copenhagen. The second is the perhaps tragic export of historic buildings from Europe as exhibits in overseas heritage theme parks. The relocation of old London Bridge in Arizona is perhaps more comedy than tragedy, but the export of Venetian palazzi to Calgary and Sydney Harbour can only be ultimately at the cost of the historic city itself.

Reconstructions Total reconstructions of historic townscapes, broadly *in situ*, must also be considered in the context of theme parks. They may be either loosely or closely related to the lost heritage; in the first case, such as Plimoth Plantation at Plymouth, Massachusetts and Jamestown Settlement in Virginia, they can more clearly be regarded as theme parks. In the second, they are usually located on and reconstructed with archaeological evidence from foundations; in this case they are a larger step in the direction of the tourist-historic city. Three notable Canadian examples of the second case are L'Anse aux Meadows, Newfoundland,

and Port Royal Habitation and Louisbourg, Nova Scotia, all undertaken by Parks Canada, which has become a world-renowned specialist in this field, and all of major international significance for the conservation of previous structures at these locations. In the case of Louisbourg, a partial reconstruction of the unparalleled eighteenth-century French fortress town is involved, and it relates explicitly to the concept of the tourist-historic city.

Louisbourg Louisbourg (see Figure 7.4; Plates 7.4a and b) exemplifies the demand-based tourist-historic city in which tourist demand is *induced* in order to fulfil a regional development objective. It was originally built as a purely maritime base, to exploit the fishing resource and to provide a strategic bastion against the British colonies to the south, guarding the entrance to the St. Lawrence and New France. It was stormed by New Englanders in 1745 and finally taken and destroyed by the British in 1758–60. Both attacks came initially from the sea; its location on a peripheral peninsula of Cape Breton Island made it inaccessible by land, and remote even today. The decision in 1961 to reconstruct it did not reflect large existing demand for a tourist resource in the locality. It was a federal government decision motivated by the need for a regional development instrument in one of the poorest areas of the country, and specifically to provide work for coal miners laid off through the contraction of the Sydney mines. Since Louisbourg had been a National Historic Site since 1928, the task was entrusted to Parks Canada, and the reconstruction commenced in 1963; it is still continuing, with the objective of rebuilding as realistically as possible one-quarter of the town, some fifty buildings, simultaneously unearthing a wealth of artefacts (Moore, 1984/5). Since some of the unreconstructed foundations have been exposed and marked, and the remainder are still overgrown, the site contains an archaeological-architectural sequence of quite exceptional interest. It is managed to high conservation standards; for example, park entrance facilities and car parking are over a kilometre away and access is by Parks Canada bus only. It could however be regarded as a theme park in that recreation is well catered for, with costumed employees, quasi-traditional taverns and opportunities to purchase heritage-oriented tourist merchandise. The practical limits of 'realism' have perhaps been approached, when unsuspecting visitors are brusquely challenged by 'French' guards whose slovenly dress and undisciplined demeanour is designed to reflect their poor living conditions and deteriorating morale. Visitors' desire for participation in history may fall short of suffering its inconveniences. Priority continues to be given to the provision of local employment; as a regional development instrument it has been successful, for it has become the best-known specific tourist attraction in Cape Breton and generates spin-off for the regional centre, Sydney, which is on the

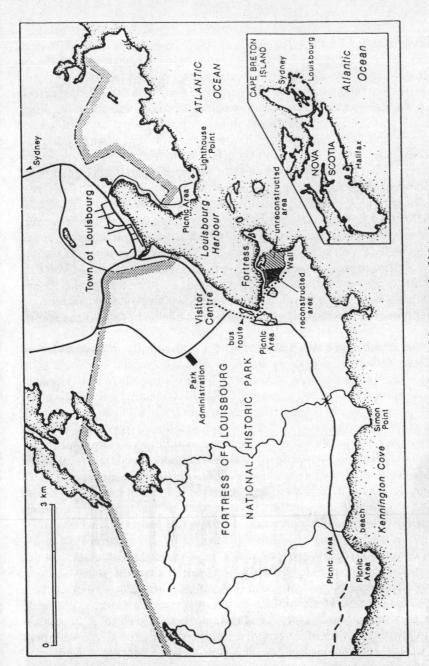

Figure 7.4 *Louisbourg and region. Modern town (shown) 3 km to north of historic fortress town*

Plate 7.4a Louisbourg: King's Bastion and other reconstruction, from unexcavated ruins (JET 1986)

Plate 7.4b Louisbourg: reconstructed main street, towards sea gate (JET 1986)

main access route and contains the majority of the available tourist support facilities.

Enhancement and further variations Given the continuum between created and authentic heritage, their similar tourist marketing, and the strong theme-retailing link, the theme park concept can be more loosely extended even to the least element of heritage creation: *in situ* enhancement. Enhancement usually entails limited modification and infill, as in Victoria, British Columbia, where a genuine British cultural heritage is enhanced by theme facsimiles, attractions (e.g. 'Anne Hathaway's Cottage', 'Royal Wax Museum') and retailing. In some cases, however, it overwhelms the initial heritage component; this is true of Solvang in California, which markets a Danish cultural heritage almost entirely through contrived structures (McGinn, 1986). In such cases the main difference from a conventional theme park is the lack of an admission charge. The retailing component may be so blatant that there is no distinction from a theme shopping centre other than the pre-existing urban location. In fact, some pre-existing towns have adopted totally spurious cultural embellishments, suggested by the local environment, purely for the purpose of turning themselves into successful shopping centres; e.g. Kimberley ('Bavarian') and Osoyoos ('Spanish'), respectively in alpine and arid parts of interior British Columbia (McGinn, 1986). An example of heavy enhancement with a more recognisable historic core is Albuquerque, New Mexico: the original Mexican plaza has been functionally distorted by retailing and surrounded by superficially compatible retail infill development. In other cases there is substantial enhancement, including reconstructions and costumed employees, but focused upon a major historic resource, such as St. Augustine (Florida) and especially Williamsburg; these might still be considered *de facto* theme parks but they are closer on the resource-demand spectrum to the resource-based historic gems, hence consideration of Williamsburg under this heading previously.

   Two further variations on the relationship between historic resources and theme presentations based upon heritage reconstructions can be mentioned. The first can be labelled 'defensive replication', and occurs where the intensity of the heritage demand threatens to damage the historic resource itself. A well-known example is the Vindolanda interpretation centre located near, but not on, Hadrian's Wall in Britain. The pressure of visitors on the wall itself is relieved by offering an interpretation which is a more complete, and therefore realistic, reconstruction of the past than the historic artefact itself. The enormous growth in visitor interest in heritage sites determines that this defensive strategy is likely to become an increasingly popular solution to visitor pressures on key historic sites, such as Stonehenge or the Athens Acropolis; it is well established with respect to specialist heritage interests such as brass-rubbing.

Secondly, the relationship between the original historic site and the subsequent interpretation facilities can become subtly reversed in the historic experience of the visitor. Consider the not untypical case of the battlefield of Waterloo in Belgium. The long-standing and increasing interest in this international heritage has led to the steady accretion of a wide variety of interpretation museums, dioramas, video presentations and the like. More of the visitor's time and attention is now occupied by these entertaining and explanatory facilities than by the much less easily appreciated battlefield itself. The theme park can provide a more realistic heritage experience than the historic site, and in this sense has superseded it. It is predicted that such theme parks, dependent on the historic association of a particular location, will become increasingly common.

The tourist-historic city in the tourist resort region

While demand-based tourist-historic developments may occur wherever the market warrants, their ultimate potential may be greatest in specialised tourist resort regions; it is therefore appropriate to comment specifically on the role of the tourist-historic city in such regions, with the proviso that this is a preliminary statement in a likely growth area of academic and planning interest.

The contemporary scale of tourist resort development world-wide, related particularly to warm beach environments, has generated a demand for the tourist city as a centre for services (see Chapter 3) and also for casual vacation interest trips, thereby creating an opportunity to market urban historic attributes to visitors whose primary motive may be quite different. Since many attractive and rapidly growing resort environments occur in the global 'pleasure peripheries' (Crush, 1983; Husbands, 1986), they tend to contain culturally distinctive pre-industrial cities, relatively untouched by metropolitan development pressures; there is, accordingly, often abundant potential for the demand-led development of the tourist-historic city. To comprehend the global scale and distribution of this potential, it would be necessary to trace the growth of these 'pleasure peripheries' relative to that of metropolitan core regions from which demand primarily emanates. Some are long established, particularly the Mediterranean relative to Northern Europe, and subsequently the Caribbean relative to North America, Southern Africa and the Indian Ocean to South Africa, and the South-west Pacific to Australia and New Zealand. Others are more recent or tentative, notably South-east Asia relative to the Far East, the Middle East and East Africa to the Gulf States, and parts of Latin America to its more developed countries such as Venezuela.

The field of investigation is manifestly very large and very diverse. The common feature relevant to the tourist-historic city is that a recreation-seeking market is available for the consumption of historic tourism resources, if these can be successfully incorporated within the wider tourism package. In addition, from the standpoint of the beach resort region, excursion attractions based on historic cities not only widen the holiday experience but may also aid its deconcentration in space and time. Historic attractions are likely to be less dependent on fine weather and are likely to be located in places other than beach facilities. Thus both holiday season and region can be extended.

The Mediterranean

The Mediterranean, the oldest 'pleasure periphery' on this global scale, is replete with examples of highly developed tourist-historic cities. The most famous (such as Venice, Dubrovnik, Athens, Istanbul, Jerusalem) are clearly resource-based historic cities which can draw tourists in their own right. This raises the question of whether a favourably located tourist-historic city might induce the development of a tourist region in its vicinity, rather than the reverse; this would depend on a coincidence or compatibility in the markets so that visitors attracted to the historic resources of Venice also frequent the Lido, Athens the beaches of South Attica, Istanbul the Black Sea beaches around Kilyos, and so on. The nature of the main heritage tourism market makes this unusual but it indicates once again the spectrum of possibilities that exists, and the difficulty of clearly separating the resource-based from the demand-based case.

The reverse situation, however, is well established on the Mediterranean, namely the incidental use of heritage attractions in historic cities for short excursions during a beach-oriented holiday. The example of the Languedoc coast illustrates the characteristics and variety of such tourist-historic cities. Figure 7.5 shows a resort region stretching from the Rhône Delta to the Pyrenees, composed of a string of beach resorts. Research into excursion behaviour (Ashworth and de Haan, 1987) revealed that almost two-thirds of staying visitors took at least one holiday excursion and the most popular destinations were the inland cities. The variety of historic cities visited on day excursions included major multifunctional regional centres with historic attractions (such as Montpellier, Narbonne and Perpignan), monofunctional preserved historic gem cities (such as Aigues Mortes and Carcassonne) and specialised historic-cultural towns (such as Arles for Van Gogh and St. Maries-de-la-Mer for gypsies).

This functional integration of a variety of historic cities into a beach holiday region is abundantly repeated elsewhere around the Mediterranean coast, including North Africa and islands (e.g. Mdina in Malta). In the

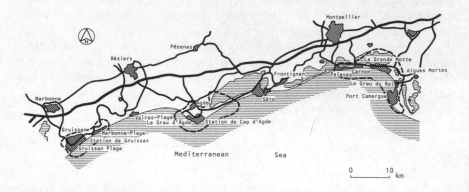

Figure 7.5   *Languedoc coast resort region*

Spanish case, the attempts to link Gerona and Figueras with the Costa Brava, and Malaga and Granada with the Costa del Sol, reflect the policy of moving both up-market and inland, so as to increase the regional economic benefits of tourism. However, a very similar phenomenon can be observed in the use of Ravenna and San Marino by visitors to the Italian Adriatic resorts, without official encouragement.

The Caribbean

The Caribbean illustrates the demand-based case more clearly, since it contains few cities with a pre-existing historic reputation equivalent to the Mediterranean examples cited but many which can be marketed as ancillaries to the development of the area's beach environment. It also illustrates, however, the effect of cultural barriers in retarding the recognition of what would otherwise be resource-based historic gems, until resort development exerts a demand for their historicity. Three very historic Hispanic Caribbean cities, Havana, Santo Domingo and Cartagena (Colombia), were relatively unknown in the English-speaking world until the 1980s tourist discovery of their regional beach attractions, notwithstanding the massive restoration of the old walled city of Santo Domingo (the oldest European settlement in the Americas) by the government of the Dominican Republic in the early 1970s. On the other hand, San Juan (Puerto Rico) has been highly developed as a tourist-historic city as a result of American control; this includes the presence of the National Parks Service at El Morro, its great Spanish fortress.

Most cities of the smaller Caribbean islands are relatively small and offer less obvious potential for tourist-historic exploitation. Those of the Dutch and French islands have a long-standing tourist trade, however, particularly as cruise-ship ports: Philipstad (St. Maarten), Willemstad (Curaçao) and Fort-de-France (Martinique) are notable illustrations. The expansion of the European Community economy has facilitated substantial upgrading of these communities; by 1987 Fort-de-France, the largest (population 97,000 in 1982), had achieved a level of sophistication comparable with that of metropolitan France, visible in substantial physical rehabilitation of its historic city centre accompanied by an extensive range of retail merchandise, and a high level of tourist organisation aimed primarily at the 'captive' market of metropolitan France. While the French islands have an economic bias towards French tourism, their promotion in French-speaking Canada indicates a broader cultural bias in their tourist trade. The Netherlands Antilles, in contrast, have no notable linguistic or market ties with a European 'homeland', and are oriented towards the dominant English-speaking tourist market of the Caribbean.

Paradoxically, few British Caribbean cities have been equipped to take advantage of their intrinsic cultural asset, having suffered a century of benign neglect. Only three cities are both well enough appointed and suitably oriented to attract a large tourist trade: Nassau (Bahamas), Montego Bay (Jamaica) and Bridgetown (Barbados). Of these, only Nassau is a highly developed tourist-historic city, trading on its eighteenth-century heritage including the romantic pirate image, tax-free luxury retail trade, and the proximity to the US market which gives it an outstanding intervening-opportunity location to capture a very large tourist trade arriving by air and sea (cruise ships and private vessels); in all these respects it has more in common with Hamilton and St. George, Bermuda, than with its counterparts to the south. Montego Bay and Bridgetown offer tourist support facilities and more limited historic potential, and are relatively more ancillary to their adjacent beach areas; in addition, Port-of-Spain (Trinidad) has tourist-historic potential which has been retarded by the lack of beach resorts in Trinidad itself, and the oil-industrial base of its economy prior to the late 1980s.

Other urban communities in the British Caribbean are small (except Kingston, Jamaica), unsophisticated and in most cases poor, offering few tourist support facilities beyond banks and native markets; they suffer a dearth of retail facilities and commonly a degree of Third World cultural repulsion to the affluent tourist, notwithstanding their otherwise British cultural affinity. This repulsion is not allayed by the development of historic resources that inevitably stress slavery and colonial domination (Husbands, 1986), which is potentially divisive throughout the Caribbean and Bermuda. However, these poorer communities are particularly interesting cases since they invariably contain tourist-historic potential as ancillaries to the more sophisticated beach resort areas in their vicinity. With the exception of Kingston (Jamaica), which is mostly tourist-repellent because of the scale of its squalor and its crime rate, they are gradually being reclaimed as tourist-historic assets because their absolute concentrations of squalor are manageable or avoidable by a tourist industry seeking historic diversion; and because national governments are usually anxious to siphon off some of the resort-area trade to underemployed urban work-forces, and thereby also reduce the 'leakage' of tourist revenue from the island economy to the overseas business interests which dominate the resort areas. Some are enjoying success as cruise ports, aided by the construction of harbourside duty-free shopping centres removed from the city centre (e.g. Castries, St. Lucia). The negative side of this tourist-urban liaison is the greater opportunity it provides for crime and the selling of illegal goods and services to tourists, of which drugs are now a more prominent concern than prostitution.

Further perspectives on the resort region

The development of the tourist-historic city in small island states (or other microstates) in tourist resort regions carries with it certain implications which are less apparent elsewhere. Given the almost invariable condition of primacy, in which the city (however small) dominates everything else, such territories are effectively city-states and are, in this respect, reminiscent of the most successful European cases such as Monaco, San Marino and Vatican City. This has at least a twofold significance for the present discussion. Firstly, many historic sites in the territory may be only a short ride from the city centre and could be regarded as part of the tourist-historic city; such is the case in St. Kitts, where the great fortress of Brimstone Hill is easily visible and accessible from the capital, Basseterre; or with respect to Fort Rodney and Castries in St. Lucia; or, indeed, many of the colonial forts and plantation houses which abound in the West Indies. Secondly, the tourist industry and its extension into the city are inevitably major socio-economic development issues from the perspective of the nation as a whole.

The potential for development of the tourist-historic city in the tourist resort region is undoubtedly greatest, at the global scale, in the less developed 'pleasure peripheries' serving the world's metropolitan core areas. At the regional scale within the developed core areas, however, there are many longer established tourist-historic cities in the closer, more traditional resort regions. Britain may have the longest such tradition of seaside resorts. It is not surprising therefore that historic attractions have a long history of incorporation into its resort regions. These attractions may be major historic cities serving a range of resorts, such as Canterbury for the Kent coast, Lewes or Chichester for the Sussex coast, or a wide range of historic houses, gardens, museums and sites. One example from many illustrates this variety. Two-thirds of staying visitors at the seaside resort of Great Yarmouth, Norfolk, made at least one excursion to popular destinations including historic cities (Norwich, Cambridge), historic country houses (Sandringham), outdoor museums (Caister) and archaeological sites (Burgh Castle) (de Haan and Ashworth, 1985).

An interesting variant of the development of ancillary historic resources by a British seaside resort is provided by Portsmouth, where visitors at the traditional integral seaside resort of Southsea encouraged the development of heritage-based attractions, usually associated with the naval dockyard at Portsmouth. This phenomenon is relatively common, especially in the South Coast resorts where integral historic attractions and districts add wet-weather diversions and a status background to seaside resorts; the archetype being perhaps Brighton with its Royal Pavilion, 'Lanes' and antique shops. However, in Portsmouth more recently the stress has shifted dramatically in favour of the historic attractions, which are now marketed independently of the resort, and the two sorts of tourism now coexist in neighbouring parts of the same city, with significantly different markets.

Cities in resort regions experience a tourist-historic demand in part because they commonly act as gateway nodes of access, by air or sea particularly; Cairns (below) is a classic illustration. The particular case of the cruise-ship port would repay specific study, since it is the gateway to a limited number of hours ashore in which the tourist-historic motivation is likely to be central, with visitors mostly staying within the confines of the city's attractions and shops. Dubrovnik may be the model tourist-historic cruise port: despite discordances (Carter, 1972; 1981) it has been meticulously restored for a tourist market which is more accessible by sea than by land, and it is spatially packaged (a walled city on a peninsula – Plates 7.5a and b) to fit the time constraints of cruising. While it and some other cruise ports (such as in the Aegean islands) are undoubtedly historic gems, many others again (such as the smaller West Indian cities) are initially cruise ports of convenience (area access, conveniently timed port stops), a function which readily catalyses their tourist-historic development.

In tourist resort regions, whether in core or peripheral countries, it is important to understand the wider geographic role of the tourist-historic city in regional social and economic development. We have noted that it expands both the spatial and temporal foundation of what is otherwise a particularly narrow and usually seasonal economic base. While its regional development value is mostly positive, it may however extend the potential for social friction between the visitors and the visited, and it may provide a particularly effective conductor for the illegal dimensions of tourism (Husbands, 1986). Drug trafficking in Nassau or Montego Bay, for example, has reached

Plate 7.5a Dubrovnik: from city wall (JET 1984)

Plate 7.5b Dubrovnik: cruise tourists entering main street from harbour gate (JET 1984)

serious proportions and threatens a backlash from the US government, in particular.

Finally, it should be borne in mind that the lesser known historic cities, particularly in newly developing resort regions, may be marketed to tourists as part of an overall package of attractions, rather than as an incidental ancillary feature. The schizophrenic Turkish marketing of Mediterranean beaches together with urban classical remains is an obvious example of a recent centrally organised tourism development effort that is based upon the fortunate possession of two quite different resources, namely unspoilt sandy beaches and a plethora of historic relics and associations, relevant to the heritage of the potential West European market. Until recently there was little connection between the two tourism industries, functionally or spatially. The 'heritage' industry accommodated relatively small but high-spending groups of Western visitors in the major historic cities (especially Istanbul, Izmir and Bursa) and regions (such as Cappadocia and Galatia). The more recent beach tourism developments on the Aegean, East Mediterranean and Black Sea coasts are aimed at a market with significantly different age, income and family characteristics. However, although 'heritage' tourists are unlikely to use beach facilities, 'sun' tourists may be induced to use heritage facilities if they are conveniently located for day excursions. Thus, for example, excursions to Ephesus and Miletus are included in beach packages at the central Aegean resorts between Bodrum and Kusadesi; Pergamon and Troy serve the northern Aegean and Dardanelles resorts such as Canalikale, and Perge and Side the Antalya region resorts. Although the historic resources offered are the preserved ruins of entire cities, it is nevertheless clear that in this case they perform only an ancillary function. Similar uses of historic attractions as an ancillary excursion feature in support of the more important climatic and economic advantages can be found in Cyprus, Israel and Egypt.

In all of these cases the fine line between resource-based and demand-based tourist-historicity is particularly difficult to draw, because the same historic resource can simultaneously serve as a secondary attraction to a beach resort and a primary heritage attraction for a separate segment of the tourism market. Thus even the 'monofunctional' historic city can be 'multifunctional' in the sense of performing different tourism functions.

The tourist-historic city and hinterland: the case of the coastal Queensland resort region

The north-central Queensland coast of Australia is a particularly interesting case of the resort region discussed above. Its principal tourist resource is the Great Barrier Reef, a World Heritage Site which is inherently unrelated to the tourist-historic city. Its supporting

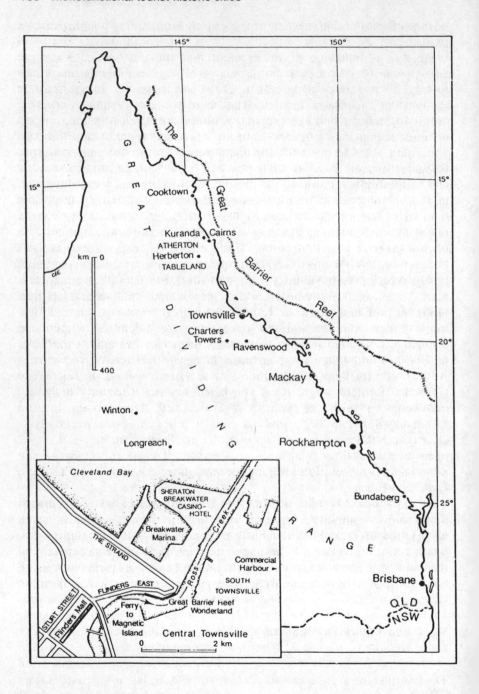

Figure 7.6   *Queensland coast resort region (Townsville inset)*

resources, however, include tourist-historic urban components not only in the ports which are the gateways to the Reef, but more particularly in several hinterland centres which have a close historical interdependence with those ports and are in that sense functional extensions of their tourist-historic cities (see Figure 7.6). This is a further variant on the notion of the dispersed or regional tourist-historic city, and is not unique to Australia.

Access to the Great Barrier Reef is primarily through the coastal ports, of which Cairns and Townsville are the most important. Neither centre projects a prominent tourist-historic image. Both city centres are attractively maintained, contain strong elements of revitalisation and receive significant historic promotion and marketing by local civic and voluntary bodies; but this is clearly ancillary to their prime tourist function as gateways and service centres for offshore marine activities and also for tropical wildlife, national parks and native cultures. They have also become important cultural centres, however, which as we noted in Chapter 5 accords well with historic conservation. Cairns, in particular, through its strategic international airport, is a rapidly growing resort region gateway susceptible to demand-led tourist-historic development.

Both CBDs have attractive pedestrian malls which, given the warm climate, are well placed to remain the focus of commercial activity; they blend elements of historic façade conservation with components of redevelopment to form a substantially historic environment. In Cairns there are traces of a former Chinatown and of Second World War (Coral Sea) heritage nearby. Both CBDs have adjacent waterfront revitalisation. In the case of Cairns, this is the Trinity Wharf tourist retail complex, adjoining the marine terminals and nearby historic 'discard' area, and hotel, office and retail redevelopment. In the case of Townsville, a classic zone of discard (Chapter 4) extends from the mall on Flinders Street to the waterfront on Ross Creek, representing the original port service area, with attractive older buildings inherited from the gold-rush era, now deemed worthy of tourist-oriented adaptive reuse; revitalisation of this Flinders East district is being directly catalysed by waterfront redevelopment expressly concerned with the Reef gateway function and its support services. This is the Great Barrier Reef Wonderland complex, which houses launch terminals, the Marine Park Authority's visitor centre and Aquarium, the associated Queensland National Parks and Wildlife Service, a branch of the Queensland Museum and supportive retailing; the marine-institutional character of the complex reflects the fact that it was primarily funded by all three levels of government as a Bicentennial project. The commercial tourism spin-off for Flinders East was apparent in 1988, partly through the enterprise of its traders' association; although it involves redevelopment of vacant sites (a new waterfront hotel/casino/marina already exists) its overall effect will enhance the tourist-historic city through the restoration of an area conceptually parallel to many in other New World cities (see Chapters 8 and 9).

The tourist-historic city of both Cairns and Townsville is thus significant and growing, though ancillary to their Reef service function. The hinterlands of both ports, however, include tourist-historic components which have developed in close interaction with them and can in varying degrees be regarded as extensions of the ports' own tourist-historic identities. They have to do with hinterland exploitation, notably for gold and other minerals, giving rise to late nineteenth-century boom towns which depended upon and/or stimulated the ports' own growth. The small port of Cooktown, a former gold centre, can itself be seen in this light relative to Cairns. The clearest expressions of the tourist-historic hinterland concept, however, are the Atherton Tableland towns with respect to Cairns, and Charters Towers and Ravenswood with respect to Townsville.

The Atherton Tableland was pioneered in the 1870s as a mining and temperate agricultural area. Its development was seriously impeded, though, by the densely forested steep descent to coastal access points. In the 1880s it became a matter of urgency to link its mining towns, such as Herberton, by rail to the coast; the decision between a variety of difficult alternatives was finally taken in favour of a route to Cairns, and in response to the line's construction Cairns immediately eclipsed other small ports along the coast, reflecting the classic model of colonial port development (Taaffe, Morrill and Gould, 1963). The development of what have subsequently become historic mining and service towns on the Tableland is therefore inseparable from that of Cairns itself. The contemporary tourist marketing of Cairns promotes the rail journey as far as Kuranda as an historic-scenic attraction secondary to the Barrier Reef; the historicity of Cairns in fact centres primarily upon the heritage tourist train that undertakes the journey, and to a degree upon Kuranda itself, which is heavily tourist-oriented with such attractions as a Sunday (craft-oriented) market, related retailing, an early pub and admission-charging amenities.

Charters Towers and Ravenswood may be considered the tourist-historic hinterland of Townsville. They were, once again, mining boom towns; late nineteenth-century prosperity based upon gold left them with a rich Victorian architectural heritage, reflective of the same phenomenon elsewhere in Australia (e.g. Bendigo, Kalgoorlie) and beyond. The National Trust of Queensland has undertaken several restorations in Charters Towers, which is currently a cattle and educational centre; Ravenswood is now a semi-ghost town. Both are economically boosted by historic tourism, and the related attention of film companies; they are well promoted in the coastal centres, access for day trips being primarily from Townsville from which the main rail, road and air links emanate. Further inland, historic resources have been stimulated in a more generalised response to the tourist demand deriving chiefly from Queensland's coastal resorts. These include recent monuments to historic association, in particular the Australian Stockmen's Hall of Fame and Outback Heritage Centre, at

Longreach; and the Jolly Swagman statue at Winton, which commemorates the mythical hero of *Waltzing Matilda*, composed nearby.

More generally, the Queensland coast contains a chain of ports with greater or lesser tourist-historic development, by virtue of its early and long-standing fragmentation into a series of fairly distinct port-hinterland systems, a geographical condition unique among the Australian states. Thus there is a high potential for waterfront and related main street revitalisation, prominently achieved in Rockhampton and Brisbane, in the latter stimulated by riverfront redevelopment for Expo 88. Farther south, Hobart (Tasmania) is a particularly well-developed tourist-historic port city: the Salamanca Place warehouse district was an established focus of historic tourism by 1975, and subsequently of state-led revitalisation of the entire inner harbour. Sydney, however, is by far the most internationally significant case; accordingly it will be considered in Chapter 8 as a prominent example of tourist-historic development in the world metropolis.

Retrospect

This chapter has illustrated the diversity of the resource and demand-based cases of the relatively monofunctional tourist-historic city. It has also illustrated the gradation that exists between them, particularly with reference to the segmentation of the market they may serve; and the range of places and of regional frameworks which might be considered to constitute such tourist-historic cities. The critical interventions discussed in Chapter 6 have been shown to derive from an array of conservation bodies, philanthropists, governments and their agencies, such as national parks, and business interests large and small; the role of key individuals in these interventions is frequently implicit. The complexity of the tourist-historic city, and particularly of its relationship with the city overall, will be seen to intensify as we shift our focus to the larger urban stage.

8 The management of tourist-historic elements in large multifunctional cities

Context

This chapter considers the critical interventions involved in the creation of the tourist-historic city at the largest multifunctional urban scale, which we may broadly term the world metropolis. We will not dwell upon definition; our concern here is essentially with cities of global importance and populations in excess of one million, within which we single out the leading examples for brief specific comment. At this scale, the resource/demand distinction becomes untenable and the tourist-historic city becomes embroiled in much stronger cross-currents of urban development.

As a general rule, the larger the city, the greater the attrition its early historic fabric is likely to have experienced. Although fire remains an indiscriminate leveller of historic cities, the largest cities have additionally been prime strategic objectives of war and civil disturbance and their morphology has borne the brunt of these; this is as true in South Africa or the Middle East today as it has been throughout the generations of conflict in Europe which culminated in the Second World War. More prosaically, in the capitalist world (and historically in the socialist world) a city's importance in the urban hierarchy has been closely matched by the extent of redevelopment pressure to which its inner core has been subjected; this is manifested in the creation of a transport infrastructure as well as in the continuous redevelopment of larger buildings for 'higher and better' uses. On the other hand, the largest cities, particularly political capitals, have been the principal repositories of the ikons of regional and national culture, in all its senses, reflecting the fundamental interaction which has always existed between cities and culture (Holzner, 1967). Thus a geography of the tourist-historic city cannot disregard the largest cities. Even in extreme cases of their destruction, such as in Germany and Poland, greater or lesser attempts have been made to recreate their historicity, essentially because of their symbolic significance to national cultures; Warsaw is the extreme illustration. In addition, redevelopment can provide a windfall opportunity for archaeological discoveries of great interest to tourists. In fact, the larger the city, the higher its profile in the mind of the tourist is likely to be, and the easier its accessibility. Despite inherent difficulties, close attention must therefore be paid to the characteristics of the large metropolis as a tourist-historic city.

A fundamental dichotomy is suggested between 'Old World' and 'New World' metropolises; this is more a matter of their individual history than of their general geographical location. Large cities which possess a major preindustrial heritage notwithstanding the vicissitudes of time (Old World) have tended to follow a different course from the New World cities that do not. The Old World metropolis has tended to deflect its twentieth-century redevelopment pressure away from the congested old city; the tourist-historic potential of the latter has commonly become a factor encouraging this deflection but is not necessarily the root cause. In Europe (and certain North American cities – see Chapter 9) the tourist-historic factor may be most apparent; but in the colonised areas of Africa and Asia the modern-preindustrial dichotomy has typically been institutionalised as a fundamental socio-economic divide between colonisers and subject peoples; the examples of Rabat (Abu Lughod, 1980), Delhi and Tientsin (Western, 1985) were discussed in Chapter 4. In such cases, the modern component itself may acquire a cultural-historic distinction; thus the tourist-historic dimension focuses upon the old city but is not confined to it.

The New World metropolis, on the other hand, has typically evolved on a more spacious initial plan, so that its tourist-historic components have been more readily subject to piecemeal attrition. They may none the less retain substantial tourist-historic interest; this is notably true of many Latin American metropolises, nearly all of which are relatively early preindustrial European foundations. Such New World cities include 'new' foundations in the 'old' continents, for example Cape Town, Singapore and Hong Kong; in the latter two cases recent growth has induced extensive redevelopment at the expense of early structures. Many New World metropolises have, however, conserved elements of their historic fabric in a predictable pattern, and to this extent their tourism geographies may be expected to show significant similarities.

The classic New World metropolis is in a coastal location, where it acted historically as the point of contact with a distant mother country. This emphasises the role of the waterfront in its internal structure. The growth of the city centre inland, away from the constraints of the waterfront, led in time to the waterfront district becoming a zone of discard (Murphy, Vance and Epstein, 1955; Ford, 1979) characterised by early warehouses and other historic structures (cf. Chapter 4); this lateral migration of the core of the central business district has been a fundamental mechanism permitting significant conservation of the original settlement focus, by default. In recent decades there has simultaneously been a decline of waterfront activity, as port functions have relocated (Hoyle, Pinder and Husain, 1988), and a resurgence of interest in historic conservation, even in such cities which had not hitherto perceived themselves to be particularly historic. In consequence the principal tourist-historic focus has become the old city next to the waterfront; a revitalised zone of discard. Notable examples on the scale of the world metropolis are The Rocks, Sydney, Australia, Gastown, Vancouver and Old Montreal in Canada (Nader, 1976; Tunbridge, 1988). These areas offer not only heritage but a human scale; a relief from the concrete canyons which constitute the contemporary New World CBD core. They provide much of the night-life and 'festival market-place' components of the metropolis, for both residents and tourists. None the less, many of the public buildings, monuments and support facilities of interest to tourists will be found in the CBD core. The waterfront as a tourist-historic focus is not exclusively a New World phenomenon; very many Old World metropolises are restoring their waterfronts, which are 'more complexly related to their historic cores, as supplementary tourist-historic components. Neither is the waterfront as a tourist-historic focus purely a metropolitan phenomenon (cf. Townsville, Chapter 7); smaller centres may possess the most historic waterfronts simply because they were the first to be bypassed by the growing scale of maritime technology (Chapter 9). Furthermore, in the New World metropolis not all night-life and related activity focuses on the waterfront zone; some port and inland metropolises have developed alternative off-centre focal points of bohemian activity and cultural/historic distinction, around an early nodal point, or inland zone of discard. Examples are Hillbrow in Johannesburg, Yorkville in Toronto and Kings Cross in Sydney; the latter two are distant from Harbourfront and The Rocks, the respective waterfront nodes.

The New World metropolis has characteristically experienced a period of conspicuous inner-city revitalisation from the 1970s onwards, particularly in North America. In earlier decades the vitality of its inner city was substantially sapped by rapid suburban growth. The reawakening of interest in the inner city resulted from a reappraisal of its cultural, economic and environmental potential for a multiplicity of reasons; this reawakening is not unique to the metropolis but it is most substantial and conspicuous at this urban scale. The revitalisation of the metropolitan inner city has usually been associated with a rediscovery of its tourist-historic potential, but certainly not with this alone; the inner city has been rediscovered as a place to live, work and recreate. The process of revitalisation has most strongly affected cities with buoyant economies and white-collar employment structures, and the New World metropolis typically fits this profile, certainly in the Western societies with which our use of 'New World' is primarily concerned. The renewed competition for access to the perceived amenities of the inner metropolis has put growing pressure on less competitive land-uses, notably low-income housing and facilities; this is less apparent in the USA, with its persistent inner-city social problems (Berry, 1985), than in, for example, Canadian cities (Ley, 1986; 1988). Although the tourist-historic city is now a valued component of the metropolitan economic base, it is, as we noted in Chapter 5, subject to land-use competition; its success is not guaranteed and furthermore may be at the expense of socially desirable objectives (cf. Amsterdam, below). The resolution of such land-use conflict is a particular contemporary problem of many New World metropolises.

We have said relatively little about the Old World case since it usually has a more familiar tourist-historic profile, is less easily typecast and has been much less subject to a reappraisal of its environment and tourist-historic identity in the past twenty years. In general, however, it shares the major competitive pressures within which the tourist-historic city must exist, albeit moderated in most cases by a greater degree of spatial deflection and longer established public intervention in defence of heritage.

The interaction and conflict potential involved in management of the tourist-historic city, discussed in Chapter 6, reach their fullest expression in the large metropolis. All levels of government are likely to play multiple roles in metropolitan management, with varying degrees of dominance and jurisdictional conflict, particularly in the federal systems most characteristic of the New World. For example, in Canada the provinces hold residual power over urban development while in the USA the federal government has greater relative power (Goldberg and Mercer, 1986). The approach to and priorities in metropolitan management, including the tourist-historic dimension, will vary accordingly; variation within a country will be greatest where its central government has the least jurisdiction over urban affairs.

The management of the largest cities in particular, however, cannot be understood without reference to the continuous conflict and compromise taking place between the various public and private players discussed in Chapter 6. Conflict and compromise in urban revitalisation find expression in the location, scale and design of new development and its interface with rehabilitation and conservation; it is thereby fundamental to the evolving shape of the historic, and by extension the tourist-historic, city. Redevelopment and rehabilitation are usually (though not always) in a state of mutual tension; the historic city may be favoured by the latter and the tourist city by either, but the tourist-historic city overall may be a particularly marginal consideration in the revitalisation of the large metropolis and may in fact be disadvantaged by the particular direction it takes. Many examples of conflict and compromise between redevelopment and rehabilitation/conservation (with varying degrees of tourist-historic significance) occur in the large metropolis: the waterfront is one high-profile arena; others are the reuse of redundant or declining inner-city churches, factories and transport facilities, of all of which numerous examples can be found in both Old and New Worlds.

The big league tourist-historic cities

The cities that are the world's principal storehouses of artistic productivity, which have been the stages upon which world-famous historical events and personalities have occurred, and which as a consequence entertain the largest regular flows of heritage tourists, have so far received only passing mention in this book. These are the handful of major metropolises that together form what can be labelled the 'big league' of tourist-historic cities. By definition such cities are just too large to be discussed in detail here but equally they are too important to escape some account of their general characteristics as tourist-historic cities.

The two most obvious and pervasive characteristics of these cities, which in turn largely determine their special quality as tourist-historic centres, are that they are in fact so large in a number of their dimensions as to be significantly different from the cities described so far, and secondly that they form a league, an exclusive grouping of cities bound to each other by links of both co-operation and competition.

The importance of these cities relates not just to their population size, areal extent, capital status, or historical longevity. Most are multimillion cities, which helps to account for the quantity and range of services they offer: almost all are, or were, national or imperial capitals with an accumulation of consequent show-case functions: and most have more than a millennium of historical existence during which they have exercised important influence on a world scale. But possession of one or all of these is insufficient membership qualification. These cities combine this list of superlatives with a contemporary economic, political and cultural importance that results in their being central to world patterns of transport and communications, the location for highest-order service provision for world markets and the centres of international economic, social and political interaction. It is this multifaceted superiority that typifies these cities, and within which the tourist-historic dimension must be placed. Thus if a series of league tables are drawn up of such indicators of tourist-historic importance as foreign tourist visits, art gallery and concert attendance, visits to particular historic monuments, and the like, these would positively correlate with such broader indicators of contemporary importance as international passenger arrivals, numbers of international congresses held, offices of international organisations, societies and commercial firms and many more. The same cities would appear in the leading group on all such tables.

Membership of this league is exclusively European. Many extra-European cities qualify on one or more of the dimensions mentioned. Baghdad has antiquity; Jerusalem and Mecca have international historic symbolism; New York, Tokyo or Moscow have as much world economic or political importance; and Singapore may be as central to world transport networks. But only the spatially clustered group of European cities qualify on all counts. For example, Table 8.1 lists a rank order for foreign visitor nights, numbers of international conferences and a composite index of international 'cultural' features. The sources, weightings and content of any such lists can be questioned but the significance is that much the same group of cities appears in all of them. There is a very real competition between London and Paris for the status of 'world capital', with the former having a consistent edge. Cities such as Brussels, Vienna, Rome, Copenhagen, Munich and Madrid are

Table 8.1 Some rankings in the international big league

(a) Foreign visitor-nights (millions)			(b) International congresses		
Ranking	*Place*	*No. of visits*	*Ranking*	*Place*	*Number*
1	London	*c.* 20	1	Paris	274
2	Paris	16	2	London	238
3	Rome	5.6	3	Brussels	219
4	Madrid	5.5	4	Geneva	212
5	Athens	4.7	5	Vienna	127
6	Vienna	4.6	6	W. Berlin	94
7	Munich	2.6	7	Rome	91
8	Amsterdam	2.5	8	Strasbourg	80
9	Brussels	2.4	9	Copenhagen	71
10	Copenhagen	2.1	10	Amsterdam	47

Source: W.T.O. 1988   *Source*: Labasse, 1984

(c) International 'culture' (composite ranking based on art/culture performances)		(d) Art gallery visits (estimated annual number of visits)		
Ranking	*Place*	*Ranking*	*Museum*	*Place*
1	London	1	National Gallery	(London)
2	Paris	2	Louvre	(Paris)
3	Milan	3	Prado	(Madrid)
4	Madrid	4	Tate	(London)
5	Munich	5	Koninklijke	(Amsterdam)
6	Brussels			

Source: DATAR, 1989   *Source*: CBS, 1987

usually found among the 'top ten' and form a second rank, competing equally fiercely among themselves.

Alongside the undoubted and professionally orchestrated competition, there is equally an element of mutual dependence among these cities, causing them to operate within a network of their peers rather than as the pinnacle of purely national systems. Commodified history and culture are rapidly consumed and the average length of tourist stay, even in these large concentrations of historic resources, is only 2–3 days. Thus a particular tourism trip may include a selection of such cities, or be part of a longer-term 'collection'. Visits to one city encourage rather than exclude visits to others, and conferences, international fairs and similar events essentially migrate between them. Their spatial concentration in one part of the world is therefore both explained by and reinforces their mutual dependence.

The main characteristic of the tourist-historic city within the big league, as we discussed in Chapter 4, is polycentricity. Such cities generally offer many distinct and spatially separate clusters of historic resources, which form part of equally numerous and diverse tourism products. This polycentricity can be explained by the sheer quantity of historic and cultural artefacts and their wide spatial dispersal, the quality of some of them as world leaders in their own right, the historical growth of most of these cities through accretion which has absorbed outlying settlements of distinct historic identity (many of which have experienced recent residential reinvestment of interest to tourists); and from the demand side, the need to satisfy large numbers of visitors in search of variety and novelty. To describe this variety in detail would result in a series of Baedeker's or Michelin's, but a few general characteristics can be noted from a cursory account of two pairs of such cities, namely the leaders, London and Paris, and lower down the league, Brussels and Amsterdam.

London and Paris

Within the polycentric tourist-historic city each individual tourist-historic district is not only distinctive but does not necessarily contribute towards a single consistent aggregate tourist-historic identity for the city as a whole, although it may be one part of the package of experiences assembled by the tourist. Paris for example offers the medieval Ile de la Cité, the seventeenth-century Marais, the nineteenth-century artistic and political associations of Montmartre among its many historic attractions. London offers even less historic or architectural cohesion with its attraction clusters at Westminster, the Tower, St. Paul's and the City, South Kensington museums and many more; they are steadily expanded by a sequence of major archaeological discoveries unearthed during redevelopment, for example Shakespeare's Rose Theatre, and others extensively publicised by the Museum of London (Urban Morphology Newsletter, 1988). The network of attraction clusters is not confined to the central areas of such cities, however extensive, but draws in peripheral sites such as Versailles for Paris, and Greenwich, and more recently Docklands, for London (cf. Aldous, 1979); these may include spectacular new development, such as La Défense in Paris, which will in time acquire a tourist-historic patina, as the Eiffel Tower has done in its first century. Further afield the wider region can be incorporated including Reims or Canterbury among the capital attraction clusters.

Greenwich and Docklands (see Figure 8.1) are an excellent illustration of tourist-historic attractions which are internationally prominent in their own right and which may be visited more or less independently from the rest of London (Page, 1989). The distinction of Greenwich includes the museum ship *Cutty Sark*, the Palace and Observatory, its famous association with the zero meridian of longitude and the traditional tourist means of access from central London by riverbus, through the former tourist barrenness of the dockland districts. It is now further benefiting from juxtaposition to the resurgence of Docklands, the world's largest waterfront revitalisation project. The London Docklands Development Corporation has attracted a scale of reinvestment during the 1980s that is unparalleled, if controversial (Church, 1988). This mostly involves spectacular commercial, leisure and residential redevelopment of derelict areas, but also rehabilitation and compatible infill development in historic waterfront communities such as Wapping, in which private revitalisation of pubs and other services has been stimulated, and conservation of the docks themselves which were historically the main commercial emporium of the British Empire. Tobacco Dock, a rehabilitation/adaptive reuse project, is among the European pioneers of the speciality shopping centre discussed in Boston and Sydney below (Freeman, 1989). The most obviously historic area, St. Katherine's Dock, is adjacent to the Tower precinct and thus easily accessible; but the renown of Docklands preceded its overall linkage to central London, thereby reinforcing its distinctive identity. The Docklands Light Railway does not connect well to the London Underground, and was not well publicised to tourists before 1989; and the sheer scale and progressive eastward thrust of Docklands are likely to reinforce anyway the polycentric tendency of tourist-historic London. Paris has no waterfront revitalisation on this scale relevant to tourism, although the example of London Docklands is prompting, in competitive response, schemes for similar reuse of redundant docklands downstream on the Seine; in the scale of dockland heritage, however, the London–Paris duality breaks down in favour of London's comparison with other Continental cities such as Rotterdam.

Polycentricity is in part a response to changes in the amount or type of visitor demands by the creation of new resources in new areas, but it also offers a flexible opportunity to match these with broader urban planning objectives. New historic cities can be developed to stimulate or exploit existing demand or as part of deconcentration and dispersal strategies. The main problem of polycentricity is the need to link physically the various

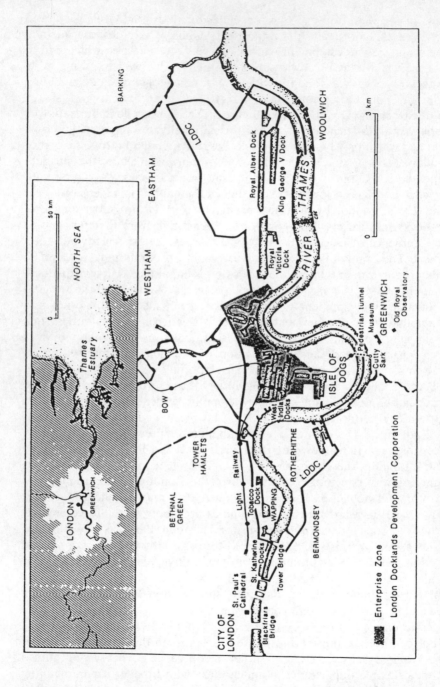

Figure 8.1   *Greenwich and Docklands: London*

clusters. In some cases this is possible by corridors of tourist movement, which thus become themselves linear attractions (such as London's Oxford Street, Regent Street, The Mall, or Paris' Champs-Élysées, Boulevard Saint Michèle). But frequently the distances are too large and clusters are linked by rapid transit systems which may or may not be 'foreigner friendly'; these are usually underground railways, which in turn accentuates the nodality of the clusters, creating networks of nodes with invisible 'dead' links between them. We may logically expect that the characteristics of tourist-historic polycentricity will become more apparent as other great cities world-wide both expand and age.

Amsterdam and Brussels

The comparison of Amsterdam, which has the smallest population and arguably most precarious position in the big league, with Brussels, a relatively successful newcomer, illustrates some of the opportunities and problems of inclusion in it.

The steady weakening of the competitive position of Amsterdam in this respect over the last decade has prompted an examination of its resources, and initiated discussion on both policies necessary to reverse this trend and also on the advantages and disadvantages of membership itself. This debate was brought into the public domain by the unsuccessful bid to host the 1982 Olympic Games. Brussels, by contrast, has risen from relative obscurity to a secure place in the league, single-mindedly pursuing, with official support, the goal of 'capital of Europe' which is fostered by its role in the European Community.

As a tourist-historic city Amsterdam is characterised by a physically compact and thematically cohesive tourist city (see Figure 8.2), composed of an historic node (The Dam) with relatively short axes stretching to the main transport interchange (Central Station along Damrak), to the main entertainment clusters (along Rokin or Kalverstraat to Rembrandtsplein and Leidseplein) and to the 'culture' district (Rijks, Stedeliljk and Van Gogh galleries and Concertgebouw). The tourist-historic resources within this area depend principally upon an urban ensemble from the seventeenth and eighteenth centuries as a whole, rather than spectacular individual buildings, and upon the national show-case functions, supported by entertainment facilities with an international reputation.

The tourist-historic resources of Brussels were until recently those of a medium-sized minor European capital, and in addition a capital whose artistic show-case and symbolic functions were disputed by rival 'capitals' of Belgium's constituent 'nations' such as Antwerp, Brugge, Gent and Liège. A spectacular but small Grand Place and a few surrounding narrow streets form the *Îlot Sacré*, the historic core. The expansion of Brussels as an international government and commercial centre powered

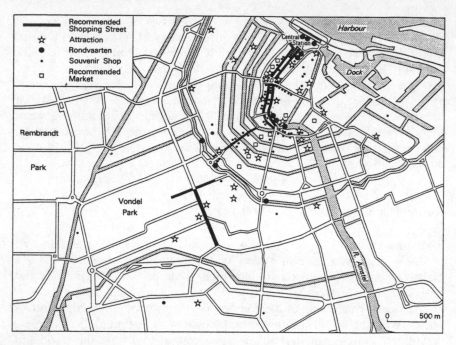

Figure 8.2　*Amsterdam: tourism facilities*

an office development boom, beginning in the 1960s, which both created a demand for tourist-historic facilities but equally threatened to overwhelm the historic city with modern developments. The core was barely saved from redevelopment and is now almost monopolistically occupied by tourism services. To this has been successfully added a series of new historic cities, exploiting existing resources, each offering a different mix of attractions, including the 'Royal City' (Palace, Parliament building, Royal Park), the 'Art City' (the galleries of Kunstberg), and the Marolles, which like London's Docklands or Amsterdam's Jordaans offers an increasingly gentrified 'working-class' city. To these can be added the tourist attractions of the 'shopping city' (Rue Neuve, Place Rogier), 'red-light' city (both sides of the Gare du Nord) and even 'European City' (Berlaymont, Place Schumann). A polycentric tourist-historic city has come into being.

Amsterdam's loss of competitiveness has been ascribed in part to conflict between the tourist-historic function and other urban functions which have acquired, or been accorded, higher priority, and in part to problems of international image (Binnenstad Amsterdam, 1987). The commitment of both the socialist local authority and the national planning agency to the maintenance of a 'living heart' has resulted in a large inner-city resident population with a particular emphasis upon social housing; multifunctionality has prevented the development of either exclusively historic districts or tourism concentrations on the scale or intensity of Brussels' Îlot Sacré.

The perceived image of Amsterdam as a tourist-historic city suffers from two major problems. The first is that the city's image is firmly locked into the urban town design of the early modern period. Visitors, including those from the Netherlands itself, have clear expectations of Vermeer townscapes composed of tightly packed canalside buildings. The commitment to a single period, ignoring the contributions of both earlier and later periods, makes change or diversification, such as occurred in Brussels, difficult. This image in any event does not relate to the Dutch national tourism image (N.B.T., 1987) which is essentially rural ('clogs, windmills, tulips') and water-sport related ('Holland Waterland'). A capital image so discordant with the national projected image has obvious problems. The second is that the current popular image of Amsterdam was formed in the late 1960s and based upon a youth culture of sexual liberalism and narcotic indulgence which has become strongly linked more recently to vandalism, personal insecurity and lack of public order. Amsterdam's image of 'dirt and disorder', compared to Brussels' 'dynamic heart of Europe', has proved a major deterrent to the development of the international functions that support the tourist-historic city.

Many of these deficiencies are beyond the competence of the city authorities to correct, but the policies that have been stressed (V.V.V. Amsterdam, 1987) include integrating the tourist-historic resources of Amsterdam more closely into tourism networks of complementary resources, at the regional (e.g. the neighbouring tourist-historic towns of Hoorn, Enkhuizen, Haarlem), national (e.g. The Hague, Leiden, Delft), or international (e.g. other North-west European capitals such as Brussels, Copenhagen and London) scales. The problems of Brussels, on the other hand, derive from its very success in attracting international attention, which has generated office and residential demands that impose heavy pressures for new development within the historic city. Nevertheless, the most fundamental contrast between the two cities is that in Amsterdam the costs, in terms of urban policy priorities, of being a major international tourism centre are raised in public discussion alongside the undoubted benefits, while in Brussels the value of membership of the international big league and consequent tourist-historic status is not officially questioned.

The second division

Although the big league tourist-historic cities are exclusively European at this time, the 'second division' is by weight of numbers predominantly located elsewhere in the world. We therefore use two New World examples to illustrate the more typical large metropolis, and we discuss them at greater length in view of their comparative unfamiliarity as tourist-historic cities. Note that big league tourist-historic characteristics, particularly polycentricity, are broadly gradational across the size spectrum

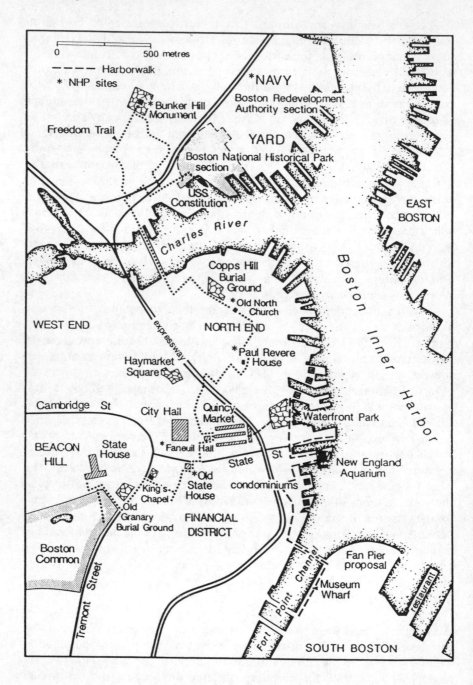

Figure 8.3   *Boston, city centre*

and over time as cities develop, as Brussels illustrates; we should therefore expect that some of our second division will be tending in this direction, and that this may be apparent in physically-fragmented environments such as Sydney, and more so in areas with a network of early settlements, such as Boston – and of course various European examples.

Boston (see Figure 8.3)

The case of Boston, Massachusetts, provides considerable insight into the management issues and problems of the successfully revitalising world metropolis, as these bear upon the tourist-historic city, specifically in a New World federal government context.

Boston is the oldest US metropolis (founded 1630) and the only one with an irregular, quasi 'Old World', city-centre plan. Because of its successful growth as a port and government centre, its congested core peninsula has undergone several cycles of rebuilding, so that little of its pre-Independence fabric survives. However, the distinctive alignment of streets and property lines, plus the Boston area's long tradition as a centre of learning and of urban innovation, have given rise to an architectural distinction in the city's post-Independence development, so that its tourist-historic interest is not restricted to the colonial relics. None the less the catalyst for Boston's present status as a tourist-historic city has undoubtedly been these colonial survivals; as the principal ignition point of the American Revolution the city has remained central to the national foundation mythology of the USA, even through early twentieth-century economic decline, and it parallels Quebec in Canada (Chapter 9) as one of the seeds from which the subsequent national recognition of urban heritage has grown. Most colonial fragments, many specifically associated with the Revolution, were connected in 1974 by the 'Freedom Trail', a line marked along the city's sidewalks which became the focus of its tourist-historic promotion. Subsequent development of the tourist-historic city has been undertaken with clear reference to the sites along the Freedom Trail. Two of these have proved particularly significant to continuing tourist-historic development: Faneuil Hall, a colonial meeting-place which now provides the focus for a famous tourist-oriented market-place; and the USS *Constitution*, which is the focal point of historic interest in the subsequently revitalised Charlestown Navy Yard. Both, along with other Freedom Trail sites such as the Old State House, Bunker Hill battlefield and the home of revolutionary hero Paul Revere, are now administered as components of the Boston National Historical Park.

Some historic components of Boston lying outside the immediate city core are also long-established tourist attractions, and create significant polycentricity. Chief among these are Beacon Hill, an old élite residential area; Harvard University and adjacent central Cambridge; and the many outlying nodes which have particular historical association or amenity, such

Plate 8.1a Boston: Faneuil Hall Marketplace – Quincy Market building to left. Faneuil Hall behind. (JET 1981, reproduced from Hoyle et al, with permission)

as Concord, Lexington (War of Independence), Marblehead and Salem (early ports). The recent growth of the tourist-historic city has created a market for other outlying nodes, including Lowell, a National Historical Park (Chapter 9).

The focus of recent metropolitan tourist-historic growth has, however, been the historic core of Boston, particularly around Faneuil Hall (see Plate 8.1a). Adjacent to Faneuil Hall is Quincy Market, previously the city's chiefly wholesale food market. Local conservation interests prevented its demolition, and the question of adaptive reuse arose during the early 1970s. The city administration actively sought its reuse, in conjunction with its flanking office/warehouse buildings, as a tourist-leisure facility. Quincy Market had at least three major historic assets favouring its development as a new focus of the tourist-historic city: the proximity of Faneuil Hall; the major early nineteenth-century architectural heritage of the market complex itself; and its historic waterfront role. The city promoted its reuse in conjunction with waterfront revitalisation, specifically linking it with a new waterfront park via a 'Walkway to the Sea', thereby restoring the heritage of waterfront access and association even though landfill had in fact distanced it from the present waterfront by over 200 metres.

Following exterior restoration through a federal Historical Preservation Grant, the revitalisation of the Quincy Market complex into the present Faneuil Hall Marketplace was entrusted to the Rouse Company in 1973. Rouse pioneered the concept of the 'festival market-place': a shopping centre not focused upon the traditional suburban anchor tenants (department stores) but upon innovative tourist-leisure oriented shopping anchored by a speciality food complex, in a setting of periodic events and festivities. The Quincy Market building itself provided this food anchor while the flanking buildings were devoted primarily to fashion, gift and related stores; numerous pubs and restaurants were distributed throughout the complex, and a variety of shows and displays were organised on the cobblestone streets. Faneuil Hall Marketplace was heavily promoted for its historic character and waterfront associations; its opening in 1976, the Bicentennial year, when heritage (including maritime themes) was nationally promoted, helped make it an instant success and quickly dispelled doubts that commercial vitality could be restored to the cores of US cities.

The Marketplace immediately became the focus of Boston's tourist-historic city, serving as the central place of refreshment and entertainment, and a point of reference from which most other points of interest, on or off the Freedom Trail, could easily be reached. Its fame and the orientation of its festival events rapidly made it the prime regional meeting place of New England. Furthermore, it immediately set the pattern for other inner-city festival market-places across North America, many of which have developed in waterfront locations, either adaptively reusing historic premises or creating new facilities in otherwise largely historic settings; Harborplace in Baltimore, the Rouse Company's next such venture, was of the latter type. So central and ubiquitous have such festival market-places become to tourist-historic city development in North America that the term 'Rousifying' has lately acquired pejorative overtones, and there has been some move to vary the character of tourist-leisure nodes in revitalised inner-city areas; however, the concept has diffused overseas (for example, London's Tobacco Dock, Canute's Pavilion in Ocean Village, Southampton and pending developments in the 'Waterstad Rotterdam') (Hoyle, Pinder and Husain, 1988). It is of cardinal significance, though, that in the 1980s some variant of the festival market-place has typically become both a principal component of inner-city commercial revitalisation and a principal organising node of the tourist-historic city across North America. In the case of Faneuil Hall Marketplace, the Rouse Company's promotional literature in 1988 claimed that its visitors (local lunch-hour/leisure trade as well as tourists) exceeded one million per month; and many of Boston's biggest events begin and end there.

The present historic quality of Faneuil Hall Marketplace is complex, and arguably declining, notwithstanding the claimed continuity of historic environment, functions and associations. The main structures are 1820s Greek Revival architecture; Faneuil Hall itself, distinct but functionally related, is a Georgian Classical building of the 1740s. However, Quincy Market proper has been modified to provide space for pushcart vendors; and the complex has attracted a variety of new commercial buildings around it, seeking to capitalise upon its success. All of these are subject to stringent planning supervision and most reflect the Marketplace's architectural idioms; one, Marketplace Center, extends the complex towards the waterfront and forms an archway over the Walkway to the Sea. Conversely, individual premises such as pubs have sought to create additional historicity, by, for example, importing interiors from Europe (cf. Chapter 7). The Marketplace management emphasises continuity of historic function; but, as in most such developments, the current shops, services and offices very imperfectly 'echo days gone by'. The fact that they are highly sanitised and expensive compared to their predecessors is evident from the Haymarket, a genuine traditional market nearby that struggles to survive in face of land values largely engendered by the success of Faneuil Hall Marketplace. However, historic continuity of structure and of function is more than sufficient to permit successful marketing based upon its perception; and the tourist centrality of the complex was rapidly secured on the strength of this.

The 'halo' effect of Faneuil Hall Marketplace upon the tourist-historic development of the nearby inner city is unquestionable, but since it is the chief focus of a larger interdependent process of inner-city revitalisation, its specific impact cannot readily be isolated. However, the adjacent historic block containing the Haymarket has been substantially revitalised in the 1980s, and it is apparent that tourists now frequent the pubs on nearby State Street, the centre of the financial district. Retail price levels suggest that tourist-historic Boston has expanded onto State Street but that some core areas, such as the financial district farther south, remain outside the effective tourist-historic city.

The principal growth area of the tourist-historic city is the waterfront, which has interacted with Faneuil Hall Marketplace from its inception. The Freedom Trail is never far from the waterfront: not only are the best-known historic sites proximate to it but the city has now long realised that the heritage of its waterfront structures and activities is fundamental to its identity. In addition, the restoration of historic public access to the waterfront, previously denied by large-scale port facilities, has come to be seen as a heritage issue in its own right. Thus waterfront revitalisation has become the prime focus of inner city revitalisation and a major tourist-historic asset in Boston. The sections of the waterfront which most clearly offer a heritage resource are the original waterfront on the central peninsula, the Charlestown Navy Yard (see Plate 8.1b) and to a lesser extent the warehouse district of South Boston. The most tangible historic fabric, apart from Quincy Market, is the Navy Yard. Like others of its kind (such as Portsmouth and Chatham in England) it offers rare continuity of a distinctive marine industrial heritage. Most of its area is being revitalised by the Boston Redevelopment Authority for residential and commercial uses in which tourist appeal is a limited factor, but the section nearest to the city centre is now the most popular part of the Boston National Historical Park, including the USS *Constitution*, a Second World War destroyer, and a naval museum. The Park section is a prominent

Plate 8.1b Charlestown Navy Yard, with USS *Constitution* and preserved destroyer, from North End (JET 1988)

component of the tourist-historic city, and as the revitalisation of the rest of the Navy Yard is completed, it is expected that tourists will spill over to the retail and other amenities which this offers, along with particular buildings such as the Ropewalk which are subject to strict preservation and will serve a museum function and compatible adaptive reuse. The fuller integration of the Navy Yard into the tourist-historic city is at present inhibited not only by its incompletion but also by vehicular access problems; a water shuttle from the downtown peninsula will alleviate these and itself provide a tourist attraction.

The tourist-historic attraction of revitalised harbourfronts does not however rest purely upon historic structures. Although much waterfront revitalisation in Boston serves residential, office and other non-tourist functions, it is all being provided with a high level of tourist-leisure amenity. By restoring historic waterfront access, this development cannot be separated from historic appeal even where it does not involve historic conservation. Thus the very high profile now being given to the waterfront as part of the tourist city in Boston is in fact inseparable from the tourist-historic city. In Boston most of the waterfront is now encompassed by a unified planning concept known as Harborpark, which is explicitly recreational whatever other functions it incorporates; the amenities provided, including waterfront parks and commercial attractions (such as the New England Aquarium, and marina facilities), are rapidly being connected by the construction of the Harborwalk, to which all waterfront developers must contribute (Boston Redevelopment Authority, 1984). In addition to this pedestrian link, water transport is being developed to serve tourists as well as commuters. In keeping with established practice on other revitalised North American waterfronts, a timetable of events and festivities has been created for mid-summer, under the title of Harborfest; this is an Independence celebration with specific emphasis upon maritime heritage and it augments Boston's status as the principal tourist focus of New England. The fact that the harbour has a serious sewage pollution problem, itself partly attributable to urban revitalisation, does not appear to detract from the tourist perception of Harborpark as the seasonal focus of Boston's leisure activity; neither does the localised continuation of port activity, intermittent friction notwithstanding.

In Boston's Harborpark, as in the tourist-historic city elsewhere, however, the leisure participants cannot be simply equated with tourism. The leisure market includes inner-city gentrifiers, and visitors from elsewhere in the city and region, such as educational visitors to the museums in revitalised Museum Wharf. As we noted in Chapter 5, the spatial distribution of the leisure market is an arbitrarily divisible spectrum which has limited significance to entrepreneurs and is of marginal importance in managing the tourist-historic city.

The management and marketing of the tourist-historic city in Boston reflects characteristics and problems which are broadly comparable to other metropolitan centres, especially those in an advanced stage of revitalisation. Two issues stand out. The first results directly from the revitalisation process: the success of the inner city in selling itself to various economic sectors has generated major socio-economic stresses through the rise in inner-city land values. There is the inevitable displacement of the poor, manifested in the pressure on their traditional facilities, such as the Haymarket, as well as in residential gentrification; the displacement of low-grade uses such as the red-light Combat Zone (Chapter 5); and also the displacement of much of the tourist market itself by the business market in inner-city hotels, except in so far as they offer bargain weekend prices. Many tourists must now travel in – best done by the rail transit system – from accommodation in the suburbs or beyond. Critical intervention has favoured overall inner-city revitalisation, rather than the tourist-historic city as such. As a pioneer in urban innovation, Boston has experienced a long series of critical interventions from government, architects, planners, academics and others; but its revitalisation over the past three decades is essentially the product of determined intervention by the city government and latterly its planning agency, the Boston Redevelopment Authority, to orchestrate economic recovery by co-ordination and conflict resolution between public, private and voluntary sectors at all levels (Brady, 1978). This has involved the adroit manipulation of every conceivable assistance programme available, especially from the federal government. It has also entailed balancing the claims of housing, the maritime economy and all commercial sectors, and compromising between physical conservation and redevelopment.

The second issue partly derives from this central preoccupation but is also unsurprising in a federal political environment: there is no single organisation responsible for the management or the marketing of the tourist-historic city, particularly since the city government closed its tourist and convention bureau. The management of the tourist-historic city is, in effect, primarily in the hands of the Boston Redevelopment Authority, but its mandate is overall revitalisation rather than explicit tourism provision. The City of Boston in the late 1980s pursued a *laissez-faire* attitude to the tourism industry, and was considered by the Boston Preservation Alliance to be slow to recognise the importance of expressly projecting its historic resources to further its tourist trade; this may be the result of a naturally buoyant tourism which does not yet present a perceived management problem. The government organisation with an explicit mandate for tourist-historic development is the federal National Parks Service, which runs the eight-unit Boston National Historical Park and eight other sites within 40 km, and provides advice and technical assistance to conservation activity more generally; it is, however, impaired by limited resources, the fragmentation of its units and more particularly because it does not own most of them, but runs them co-operatively with local conservation interests for which it provides a financial safety net. However, the NHP Visitor Center in State Street does provide a general tourist information facility; and it should be noted that the NPS owns large contiguous tracts in several other cities, notably Philadelphia and St. Louis, in which its tourist-historic management/marketing profile is clearer. Overall, the management and promotion of tourist-historic Boston is a piecemeal affair which is otherwise primarily in the hands of private enterprise (including a metropolitan marketing organisation) and the voluntary conservation sector, in the form of the Boston Preservation Alliance, this groups all local conservation interests, including national bodies such as the NPS and the non-governmental National Trust for Historic Preservation, and through its efforts and dialogue with all levels of government specific historic landmarks (including districts) are preserved and publicised.

Sydney (New South Wales) (see Figure 8.4)

Sydney bears close comparison with Boston, being a metropolis of over three million, a major node of commerce and (state) government and a port with a particularly intricate waterfront which defines the city's character and tourist-historic identity. As the principal focus of Australia's Bicentennial celebrations it assumed an exceptional international tourist-historic profile in 1988.

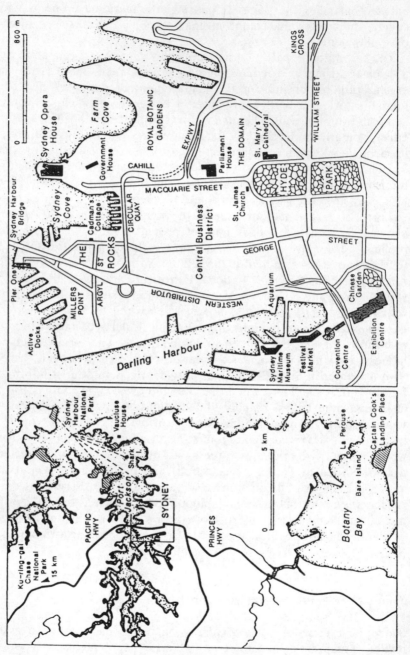

Figure 8.4 *Sydney*

Sydney is not only the original focus of white settlement in Australia but has also succeeded in preserving more material heritage from its early decades than might be expected in a metropolis of its size. This is in part the legacy of the site itself: the choice of site, an inner cove of Port Jackson rather than the intended Botany Bay, has been fundamental to the character of subsequent urban evolution. Port Jackson has provided an unusually protective environment for early waterfront heritage by virtue of its extent and intricacy. Sydney Cove itself has fostered historic survival through the familiar process of retreat by a growing CBD away from the spatial constraint of the waterfront: early Sydney survives in The Rocks, on Sydney Cove, and adjacent Millers Point. There are also various survivals of early settlement in other coves of Port Jackson, particularly at Parramatta in the inland reaches and on its more low-lying southern shore; these early waterfront communities, such as Camp Cove (site of the first British encampment) and Watson's Bay, were soon absorbed by the growing city, but preserve a distinctively intricate morphology suggestive of European coastal villages. Vaucluse House, an early nineteenth-century mansion and estate, is a National Parks Historic Site in one such cove. Some historic structures also remain on Botany Bay, at the entrance of which is Captain Cook's landing place (1770), an open area now preserved as a National Historic Site; the paucity of early development on Botany Bay is counterbalanced by the late arrival of contemporary development (airport, container port, marine industry), which fostered its survival. Furthermore the southern edge of Broken Bay, north of Port Jackson, is conserved in Ku-ring-gai National Park; although this is natural conservation, it is obliquely relevant to the tourist-historic city because of the insight it provides into the environment the First Fleet would have encountered in Port Jackson, which shaped Sydney's early development. Fragments of this environment are directly conserved, however, with historic fortifications and other structures, in Sydney Harbour National Park on Port Jackson.

The contemporary CBD of Sydney also contains many historic structures, from the late nineteenth century. Recent high-rise redevelopment has thus far been less detrimental to middle-aged commercial structures than in the more congested peninsula site of Boston, an illustration of the site factor noted in Chapter 6. This relative site expansiveness is a background factor in the surviving architectural distinction of for example George Street, the principal retail focus. Human factors in the city's evolution have also fostered substantial historic survival, however. The government-institutional character of Macquarie Street has preserved some of the finest Georgian and later architecture, particularly the New South Wales legislature and government buildings, the early military barracks, St. James' Church, St. Mary's Cathedral and the royal monuments, against the open setting of Hyde Park and the Royal Botanical Gardens. The Macquarie Street–Hyde Park axis more generally conserves the indelible imprint of British cultural heritage. Beyond historical development patterns, however, the survival and development of the tourist-historic city centres upon contemporary management policy. To this end the State Department of Planning and the City Council have jointly prepared a Central Sydney Strategy, with considerable conservation emphasis.

Sydney, like most Australian cities, used the occasion of the Bicentennial to bring already well-developed tourist-historic promotion into sharper focus. Efforts to accentuate its 'tourist-historicity', as well as historic conservation and publicity, include the marking by historic plaques of extant and former structures, in particular along Macquarie Street, and the illumination of historic buildings. The Harbour Bridge (1932) and the Opera House (1973) are, however, an important reminder that the most spectacular structures marketed to tourists, even in an historic city, may be promoted for their scenic landmark value in the cityscape rather than for their heritage significance, which may not yet be generally perceived; these two structures dominate Sydney Harbour and thus the overall cityscape, and they are central symbols in Australia's international tourist promotion effort.

Among the factors which have fostered the survival of early Sydney is its relatively poor land transport system: the city's nodes and districts have consequently developed a clearer local identity and have so far largely preserved it from the ravages of freeway construction and associated redevelopment. It is doubtful if Paddington, a gentrified inner-city district famous for its Victorian terrace houses, would have survived or retained its tranquil environment in many US and some Canadian cities.

Three components of Sydney's tourist-historic city merit more detailed discussion, being prominent examples of more generally characteristic features of the tourist-historic metropolis; the foremost is The Rocks, the zone of discard adjacent to Sydney Cove. This is regarded as the birthplace of the nation and is accordingly of great significance, but its general evolution and recent revitalisation are none the less similar to comparable environments elsewhere, especially in New World seaports. While the early Sydney Town was subsequently laid out to a grand design, this first area of settlement was too rocky to permit orderly development and rapidly evolved into a 'sailortown' of humble residences, dubious business activities and waterfront warehouses threaded by dangerous alleyways; above it, however, were located more élite homes, occupied by various prominent national and local figures, whose presence promoted some architectural distinction and continuing social significance in the wider vicinity. Notwithstanding, the heart of The Rocks was infested with lawlessness and eventually plague, the focus of which 'lay in the squalid slums and warehouses of this harbourside refuge for rats' (Sydney Cove Redevelopment Authority, 1984, p.7). This resulted, after 1900, in government acquisition of the area for the purpose of substantial demolition and some redevelopment, which was furthered in the 1930s for the construction of the Harbour Bridge, and in the 1960s for the construction of the connecting Cahill Expressway. A proposal at that time to sell much of the remainder for private redevelopment did not, however, proceed and in 1968 the State Government accepted the concept of revitalisation, in the Sydney Cove Redevelopment Authority Act. The executive Authority was formed in 1970 and took over The Rocks in a condition of decay and rapid population decline; 'vacant land, derelict buildings and various makeshift land uses such as car parking showed little to remind Australians that this was the spot chosen by Captain Phillip to be their nation's birthplace' (Sydney Cove Redevelopment Authority, 1984, p.7).

The Authority's approach to revitalisation substantially paralleled evolving contemporary thought overseas; however, in the early 1970s it required an environmental 'Green Ban' on development by the building labourers' union, a critical intervention possibly unique to Australia, to enforce the degree of historic continuity now manifest. The objective has been to rehabilitate the remaining older buildings deemed historically significant, whilst redeveloping much vacant land and some housing considered to be of slum quality. The initial strategy was to identify flexible 'envelopes with options' which defined the general height, area and bulk, and specified range of uses, of development within three designated sections of The Rocks; the plan detail was refined in 1982–3, in the light of evolving circumstance and consultation with the National Trust, and substantially completed in the 1980s. The Authority is bound to retain the land in public ownership, however, and envisages a continuous management of tenancies and use of premises. The development controls ensure height and design compatibility with existing historic buildings, keep new buildings away from the shoreline and generally ensure that larger new buildings are confined to the south of the area, where they blend with the CBD core; each development site is subject to a detailed approval process. Land-uses are primarily mixed residential, commercial and open space, emphasising the area's continuing role as home and workplace as well as its new tourist-leisure identity; this entails both continuity of use and adaptive reuse of rehabilitated structures. As elsewhere, festival market retailing and services occupy both adaptively reused buildings (such as the Argyle Stores warehouse) and small purpose-built complexes. It is noteworthy that the southern zone which blends with the CBD core contains, in addition to office buildings and high-income apartments, high-rise hotels which serve The Rocks and thereby fit the tourist-accommodation transition zone in our model (Chapter 3); this zone is now providing the income permitting both improvements to the tourist-historic focus and the return of a profit to the State treasury. The residential function has been, predictably, sensitive: the revitalisation programme met resistance in 1971 from residents fearing displacement. Although the Authority was bound to allocate 35 per cent of housing at subsidised rental, to ensure the right of existing residents to remain in the area, it was empowered to clear what it perceived as slums and also obliged to finance itself primarily from rental revenues; both grounds for contention, but in practice greatly reduced by the

Plate 8.2a Sydney: The Rocks – tourist-retail conversion of terrace houses; Harbour Bridge, in background (JET 1988)

substantial replacement of residence by commercial activity, all at market rental (Sydney Cove Redevelopment Authority, 1984; 1989).

By 1975 the Authority's work had already established The Rocks as the main tourist-historic focus of Sydney (see Plate 8.2a). Since that time, while the conservation of older structures has continued, selective redevelopment has become more prominent and has allowed an intensification of tourist shops, and creation of spaces for activities; these include outdoor theatre and other educational events, helping to give The Rocks a profile in the national foundation mythology akin to that of central Boston. Redevelopment is also contributing to the tourist-historic resource through now mandatory archaeological site digs. A 'halo' effect has appeared beyond the designated area: waterfront warehouse revitalisation for restaurants within The Rocks has been broadly paralleled west of the Harbour Bridge by the refurbishment of Pier One as a market-restaurant complex, and there has been piecemeal revitalisation of Millers Point. The tourist-historic role of The Rocks and of its 'halo' is facilitated by the Authority's Visitors Centre, which offers similar publicity, interpretation and audiovisual facilities to those offered by National Parks visitor centres, in Australia and elsewhere; this association is enhanced by the proximity of Cadman's Cottage, the oldest surviving residence in Sydney, now a National Parks-run Historic Site, the most significant historic landmark in the revitalisation of The Rocks.

Plate 8.2b Sydney: Darling Harbour – museum ships and Harbourside festival market-place (JET 1988)

The 'halo' effect in Millers Point may intensify since this area is now located between two nodes of major revitalisation, The Rocks and Darling Harbour. Millers Point contains several historic landmarks such as the colonial Garrison Church and the oldest hotel in Sydney, and numerous Victorian terrace houses. Market demand for both residence and tourist provision in Millers Point is constrained, however, by the predominance there of low-income public housing.

Darling Harbour (Plate 8.2b) is radically different from The Rocks but is equally similar to waterfront tourist developments elsewhere in the world. This is not surprising since, although it is run by a State Authority, it is largely the product of an Australian development company (Merlin International) which drew its expertise from the US Rouse Company (see Boston above) and has since used its success in Darling Harbour as a springboard to further contracts in North America and Europe, such as Rotterdam. Darling Harbour is a combined festival market-place, exhibition centre, recreation and convention centre opened during the Bicentennial year. Together with Sydney Maritime Museum and Aquarium, it represents a total redevelopment of the inner part of Darling Harbour, the principal dock area in this century which, like very many others world-wide, underwent a contraction in maritime usage, chiefly in favour of Botany Bay, as port congestion increased (Proudfoot, 1982). The Darling Harbour redevelopment is very large scale, clearly draws (like others) the inspiration for its festival market-place from Harborplace in Baltimore and limits historic conservation to some warehouse restoration and restored ships on its waterfront; it does, however, make cultural reference to its environment through the creation of Chinese gardens adjacent to the pre-existing Chinatown at the head of the harbour. Its overall leisure appeal is one of modernity, emphasised by a monorail which links it to the CBD. Although it is a Bicentennial novelty, its size and enormous popularity in 1988 (250,000 per weekend) indicate that it will remain a central focus of the tourist city of Sydney, but historic mainly in the minimal sense of revitalising and restoring access to a traditional waterfront, the original character of which has been essentially displaced. The interesting question arises as to whether this largely placeless development will in the long term draw tourists at the expense of Sydney's tourist-historic city, or provide an extraneous tourist magnet from which the latter will derive additional benefit; this will be influenced by the character of further dockland revitalisation planned in Sydney. It should be noted that the Kings Cross entertainment/night-life district is a much longer established tourist node for which a residual historic identity is also comparatively incidental. The question of whether tourist-non-historic facilities support or compete with tourist-historic counterparts was discussed in Chapter 3, but is particularly relevant in the diversified world metropolis which Sydney exemplifies. The short-term evidence here is that Darling Harbour now dominates local leisure trade but that overseas tourists prefer The Rocks, for its atmosphere and human scale (Sydney Cove Redevelopment Authority, 1989).

The third component of the tourist-historic city meriting specific comment is Old Sydney Town. This is a totally artificial theme park located near the Pacific Highway 88 km north of Sydney. This distance is an interesting illustration of the potential reach of tourist-historic features purporting to relate directly to the world metropolis, rather than to satellites; apart from the cost advantage of a 'greenfield' site, such features can be marketed as day excursions, in this case by rail or road. Old Sydney Town is a researched 'authentic' facsimile of Sydney Cove in the early 1800s; apart from the buildings, it projects non-stop 'street theatre' in the form of activities based upon events of the time, and crafts are portrayed as usual in historic theme parks (Chapter 7). Such enterprises not only draw directly upon the tourist-historic market, but also play an important role in sensitising children in particular to be future consumers of the 'real thing'. Like zone-of-discard reclamation and dockland revitalisation, historic theme parks are now a standard component of tourist-historicity likely to be encountered as one of the assemblage of 'standards' which now substantially comprises the typical tourist-historic metropolis (cf. Calgary and Johannesburg, Chapter 7).

Sydney's tourist-historic city contains not only components but also causative patterns of critical intervention which bear close comparison with large multifunctional cities elsewhere. In comparison with Boston, critical intervention appears more widely distributed among the variety of possible sources; however, there is a clear preponderance of one level of authority involved, namely the State of New South Wales. The focus of the tourist-historic city, The Rocks, has been controlled by the state government for many decades and is now, like Darling Harbour, in the hands of a state-created authority which has, *inter alia*, built the State Archives in The Rocks. The state Department of Environment and Planning is an active collaborator in the conservation and marketing of tourist-historic locations elsewhere in the city. The National Parks and Wildlife Service is a major participant, managing an inner-city fragmented national park and historic sites broadly comparable to Boston's, and a range of natural and historic locations within and outside the metropolis; it too, however, is an agent of state government as elsewhere in Australia. Similarly the National Trust, which plays a major advisory and participatory role in urban conservation, is organised at the state level though independent of government; so is the Historic Houses Trust, which owns Vaucluse House and is active in The Rocks. A state commission is also prominent in tourism promotion, though supported by a city agency and a federal commission, based in Sydney. This preponderance of state-level critical intervention is in marked contrast to Boston (also a state capital) in which the interplay between local and federal initiative has predominated; the Canadian case is intermediate, and other jurisdictions, federal or otherwise, distinctively influence the prevailing patterns of tourist-historic intervention within them. A further comparison with Boston concerns the overall profile of inner-city revitalisation, which is a less urgent focus of attention in Sydney than it has typically been in American cases; it is, none the less, a wider concern than the tourist-historic city.

The large multifunctional city: convergence

The case studies serve to illustrate the recurrence of essentially standard themes and components, even though variously assembled by different agents of critical intervention in each large city. The larger the metropolis, the greater the tendency for these 'standards' to appear earlier and in larger formats and numbers. The uniqueness of place, which is so fundamental to the logic and ultimately to the commercial success of the tourist-historic city, depends increasingly on how these recurrent features are assembled, and how much sensitivity is shown to local distinctiveness in the development and marketing of each. As we portended in Chapter 6, such is the interconnectivity of tourist-historic urban management around the capitalist world that an ever-present danger exists that standardisation will submerge local identity; this interconnectivity includes the international involvement of developers, architects and planners and the continuous sharing of knowledge through conferences and professional literature. Hence the 'Rousification' which has engendered a reaction in the United

States, as noted above, if not yet in Europe or Australia. This phenomenon is not confined to the large metropolis but, given its range of development opportunities and its centrality to the information network, it is most clearly apparent there; considering that the large metropolis has in any case experienced the greatest erosion of its original cultural identity, this is especially threatening. Some of the recurrent elements are tourist-non-historic, and the accord or discord that may exist between them and the tourist-historic city, a particularly prominent question in metropolitan centres, is thus also susceptible to repetitive scenarios.

By an intriguing irony, disinvestment from South Africa has provided that country's major cities with a windfall opportunity to moderate the standardisation of their tourist-historic development: an example is The Workshop in Durban, a revitalised railway workshop financed by South African capital, in which the festival market retailing displays a purely South African identity, although international enterprise was involved in the redesign process. Even here, however, plans for waterfront revitalisation on Durban Harbour and The Point (adjacent seafront) project global concepts of reuse, and conflicts with still-incumbent maritime functions.

There are, none the less, dimensions of divergence remaining more generally between large metropolises, and these focus primarily upon the Old World/New World dichotomy identified earlier. Beyond this, local site characteristics, histories of development and contemporary policies of intervention may all inject elements of distinctiveness into the tourist-historic evolution of different major cities. It might be argued that the longer history of development experienced by Old World cities has endowed them, even at the large multifunctional scale, with a distinctiveness of architectural form, building materials, historical association and symbolism largely denied to New World cities whose rapid development has occurred during a more internationally interactive age. Certainly the 'Englishness' of London, or 'Frenchness' of Paris, are important promoted assets. However, as argued earlier, the tourist-historic city is essentially a modern phenomenon despite its dependence on resources from the past. Therefore its requirements for facilities, investment and management are likely to be increasingly similar whether in Brussels and Amsterdam or Boston and Sydney. Indeed, so strong is the metropolitan convergence of actors, methods and goals that increasingly individual distinctiveness is a deliberately contrived ingredient added at a late stage of the promotion of the tourist-historic city.

In the final analysis, however, in all large multifunctional cities these issues of tourist-historic development will be subordinated to larger issues of urban management and, in particular, of inner-city revitalisation.

9 The management of tourist-historic elements in medium-sized multifunctional cities

General characteristics

Our title implies an intermediate category of city (broadly, 100,000 to one million population) which hardly lends itself to simple categorisation, still less to precise demarcation. Our examples will include some which are high-level administrative centres with strong metropolitan characteristics and some with central cores which are historic gems equal in tourist significance to any considered in Chapter 7; in two cases (Quebec, Pietermaritzburg) these apparent extremes coexist. There is no unifying set of characteristics and problems except the very diversity implicit in multifunctionality, and the management approaches appropriate to this broad group range across the possibilities described in Chapter 6. Since they are defined neither by general central significance nor by a simple historical specialism, they will not necessarily be patronised by tourists. The degree to which they are tourist centres will be strongly influenced by the extent of their inner-city revitalisation, in turn normally a function of the degree to which their economy rests upon white-collar activities (Lipton, 1977, Ley, 1988). It is not therefore surprising that the most successful tourist-historic cities among them are typically formerly small historic centres which have grown through the attraction of quaternary activity, or administrative/research centres which have found it expedient to foster a formerly latent historicity.

In such centres, the imposition of explicit conservation controls across the entire city will not usually be possible; on the other hand, environmental conservation sentiment from public and voluntary sectors alike will usually be strong. In New World cases, this is likely to mean controls on CBD high-rise redevelopment comparable to those which are often attained at the large metropolitan level in the old world; in cities which are 'core-gems' this will probably involve lateral deflection of high-rise development (e.g. Quebec, Charleston), whilst in others some degree of visual control over the CBD is likely to be enforced (such as the 'view-planes' to major landmarks in Ottawa, Montreal and Halifax, Nova Scotia). In cities with a commercial heritage, this does not preclude a more explicit control and revitalisation of zones of discard (e.g. Ottawa, Quebec, Charleston), as in larger centres, and impressive examples of waterfront revitalisation may be encountered (Halifax, Quebec, Savannah, Victoria BC). A management policy strongly geared to white-collar and tourist markets can, however, cause a problem of social displacement proportionately greater than that of the large metropolis: all of the New World examples noted have experienced more or less severe pressures for gentrification and related revitalisation in recent years, in the American cases at the expense particularly of the black ghettos.

Both of our Old World examples are rich in tourist-historic resources but illustrate the disparity that may exist, particularly in Europe, in the degree to which they are exploited (cf. Chapter 6); Norwich is an unequivocal core-gem while Groningen remains a relatively latent tourist-historic city. Among the New World cases, three are outstanding examples of essentially resource-led core-gems, namely Charleston, Savannah and Quebec; Ottawa illustrates the case of a national capital painstakingly nurtured to major tourist-historic status largely in response to demand; and Pietermaritzburg, considered comparatively with Harare and other Southern African cities, illustrates tourist-historicity in an environment of racial and related political constraint. These examples provide much comparative illumination but do not pretend to identify all parameters of tourist-historicity in a group of cities defined, in the broadest context, only by its 'intermediacy'. Our apparently disproportionate attention to New World cases reflects our continuing quest for global illustrations of, and less familiar perspectives on, the tourist-historic phenomenon.

The chapter continues with a broader consideration of the relationship between urban revitalisation, in various manifestations including the waterfront, and tourist-historic development; in this our concern is primarily but not exclusively with medium-sized multifunctional cities.

European regional capitals: Norwich (UK) and Groningen (Netherlands)

Such medium-sized, multifunctional, self-standing, regional capitals as these are typical of many cities which are the home of most Europeans. These two examples are ostensibly very similar in many respects: they contain populations of 100,000 and 160,000 respectively but both are the uncontested service centres for regional populations of around half a million; both are located sufficiently far from major national conurbations to be relatively isolated until recently from the mainstream of economic and social change, and their regions remained dominantly rural; both developed a wide range of industrial, commercial and public service functions without any one becoming dominant.

Despite these basic similarities their stage of development of the tourist-historic city is markedly different. This difference is difficult to explain in terms of the availability of historic resources. Both have a thousand years of experience of urban settlement and have enjoyed periods of commercial prosperity, political importance and cultural fertility that have left a legacy of buildings, street patterns, associations with historical characters and events, and local artistic productivity. Yet Norwich has a long-established world-wide reputation as a heritage city (earning the coveted three stars in the Michelin *Guide*) attracting, mostly through its heritage, more than one million visitors annually; while Groningen has no such international, or even national reputation, and attracts less than 250,000 visitors, only a minority of whom are heritage tourists.

Norwich early recognised the value of its surviving artefacts. Local sentiment was reflected by the Civic Trust proposing area conservation measures in 1958, a plan for historic building preservation was in operation by 1962, the first local land-use and traffic plan was adopted in 1967 and a comprehensive conservation plan for the entire inner city in 1969. Thus the combination of a local popular consensus and statutory planning measures from the local authority, which more often than not had a ruling Labour majority, played a central role. Consequently Norwich can claim a number of national 'firsts': first pedestrian precinct, London Street 1962; first conservation area, Elm Hill 1967; first ring-and-loop traffic scheme 1969. The main motivation was not originally or dominantly tourism development, but a mixture of civic pride and a caretaker responsibility for a nationally recognised asset. The high priority accorded to conservation, the restrictions placed on other urban functions, together with the relatively extensive central area within the line of the walls, encouraged the development of a modern commercial district outside the main monument clusters, which were thus left to develop the character of historic districts (see Figure 2.5).

The economic and architectural history of Groningen has been similar in a number of ways. The existence of 369 nationally listed monuments, and more than 1,400 locally listed buildings, dominantly of the seventeenth and eighteenth centuries and almost all located in the central area (see Figure 9.1), testify to both the rich history of the city and its exploitation of the existing legislative framework for building conservation. However, Groningen has neither Norwich's international reputation nor self-image as a heritage city, and attracts only a fraction of the tourism revenues. Its planning history has been quite different. The compact inner city (see Figure 9.2) within the *grachten* (defensive waterways) has continued to serve as the main shopping and entertainment centre as well as accommodating major government, educational, transport and residential functions, often in modern purpose-built structures. Despite the existence of enabling area planning instruments, a rigorous traffic separation and circulation system, and an expenditure on the restoration

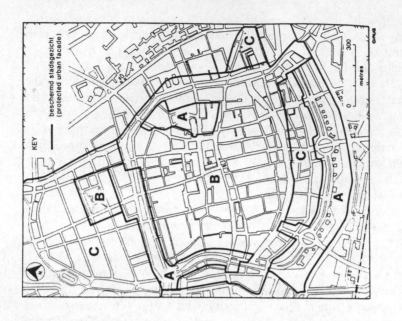

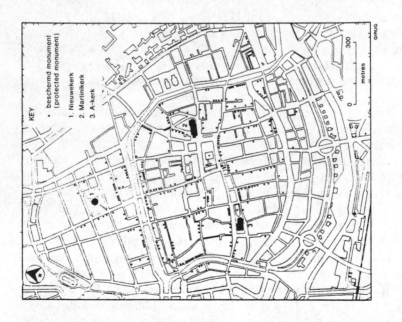

Figure 9.1   *Groningen: listed buildings and designated areas*

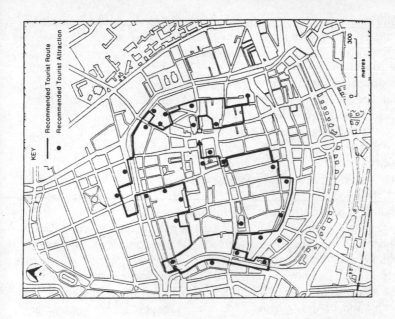

KEY

Recommended Tourist Route

• Recommended Tourist Attraction

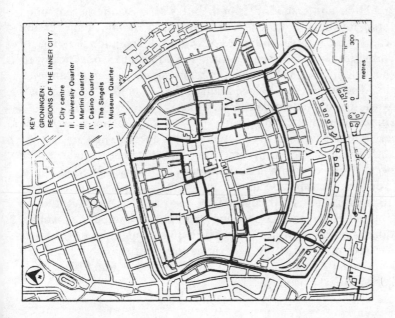

KEY

GRONINGEN:
REGIONS OF THE INNER CITY

I. City centre
II. University Quarter
III. Martini Quarter
IV. Casino Quarter
V. The Singels
VI. Museum Quarter

Figure 9.2 *Groningen: functional areas of the inner city*

of individual monuments at least as large as in Norwich, an historic city as a morphological entity with a clear image has not emerged.

The explanation lies partly in the local political will to maintain the traditional multifunctionality of the inner city and consequent resistance to the deconcentration of many services, so that no separate modern commercial centre has emerged, and partly in the absence of a well developed heritage tourism product appropriate to the historic resources. Although both building conservation and tourism are accorded attention in recent plans (Gemeente Groningen, 1988), neither receive the same priority as in Norwich.

Compare the Elm Hill conservation area in Norwich, described in Chapter 5, with Groningen's Martinikerkhof. The first developed in the 1960s, as a reconstruction of late medieval façades and street design, to become a much photographed tourist attraction and location for appropriate leisure shopping functions. The second was a deliberate creation of city planning in the 1970s, linking a number of major monuments around an open green and including pedestrianisation, the removal of discordant street furniture, expensive stone surfacing and the reintroduction of gas lighting. The area serves a representative and symbolic function for the city, accommodating the provincial government, local radio station and cathedral church but with a strong accent upon the residential function. It is a tourism attraction, as the main feature on the local tourist route, and does serve the recreational needs of residents and visitors for open space. Although adjacent to, it is, however, morphologically quite separate from, the main commercial entertainment and shopping districts of the city (see Figure 9.2) and neither contains, nor would be permitted to contain, such premises.

Thus a combination of the timing and intentions of planning intervention and the possibilities and priorities perceived by decision-makers has led to quite different historic cities emerging in otherwise similar urban circumstances. Norwich, with internationally renowned heritage in a physically distinct setting, occupies an important place in a wider circuit of such cities and is self-consciously historic. Groningen, although preserving buildings and even conserving small areas, maintains a compact multifunctional central city which cannot be explicitly identified as historic, has no clear self-image of being a heritage city and sees tourism as an additional and minor function to be accommodated within the existing functional and spatial structure.

'Core-gems': Quebec City, Charleston, Savannah

These cities had metropolitan populations of 603,000, 376,000 and 142,000 respectively in the mid-1980s. They are too physically and functionally diverse to be considered exclusively as historic gems.

Notwithstanding, in the New World context, they belong to a handful of cities of such exceptional historic interest that their tourist value was, in the first two cases at least, appreciated well before contemporary mass tourism; with their few peers, such as New Orleans, they acted as beacons to the concept of the tourist-historic urban economy in North America. Realisation of the economic base that tourism could provide, particularly when augmented by festival events such as Quebec's Winter Carnival, diffused from these archetypes to other cities during the 1970s; this coincided with the widening definition of heritage, and was promoted by the conservation lobby as the prime lever of commercial investment in the historic city. Publicity given to the tourist-historic receipts of Quebec's economy undoubtedly furthered the growth of both public and private investment in tourism across Canadian cities (Galt, 1976). The paradoxical result of this economic promotion is that the disparity in tourist-historic orientation observed in the above European examples is no longer as likely to be encountered in their comparatively resource-poor New World counterparts.

Quebec City (see Figure 9.3) Quebec's recognition as a World Heritage Site by UNESCO attests to its international stature as an historic gem (Ross, 1984; Leahy, 1986/7). Its core is the only remaining walled city in North America, the cradle of French civilisation there, and the oldest city proper in Canada, with a compact morphology and an irregular street network reflective of its pre-industrial European origin (and with the accompanying constraints on activity and movement). Founded in 1608 at a defensive site controlling navigation on the St. Lawrence River, it became the capital and largest city of New France (Nader, 1976); accordingly it was endowed with a wealth of public buildings and cultural institutions, many of which still survive alongside a substantial heritage of early residences. It grew from the initial seventeenth-century waterfront location (Basse Ville), which remained its commercial centre, to its eighteenth-century political/military focus on the overlooking bluff; this occasioned Wolfe's historical ascent to the nearby Plains of Abraham to effect the British conquest of Quebec in 1759. The British conquest is a major event in Western history and endowed the city with secondary heritage characteristics of major tourist significance; these include the Citadel, the present walls and the Victorian Dufferin Terrace, a promenade overlooking the St. Lawrence. The nineteenth and early twentieth-century evolution of the city as a major Canadian port further endowed Quebec with a waterfront heritage in Basse Ville which, with recent outward recession of port activities, has added to the historic interest of the lower town area (Tunbridge, 1988).

By the twentieth century the lower Basse Ville had become a classic run-down maritime zone of discard, whereas the upper walled Haute Ville retained much of its early character; this resulted from the city's relatively

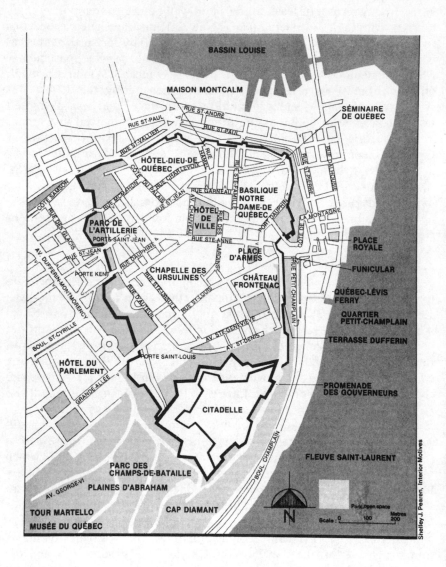

Figure 9.3 *Old Quebec. Tourist map (from Canadian Heritage, 14, 4, Winter 1988–89, courtesy S. J. Pearen and Heritage Canada). Haute Ville = walled city; Basse Ville = riverfront area, including Museum of Civilization and Vieux Port; active port to north and south of map*

slow growth, in losing competition with Montreal. Thus the initial nucleus of tourist-historic Quebec was Haute Ville; though notwithstanding its survival, conflict between the constraints of a historic townscape and continuing urban development arose by the inter-war years (Dalibard, 1988/9; Lemoine, 1987). The creation of an historic district in 1963 prevented substantially incompatible physical development within the city walls; before this, protection depended on the efforts of concerned citizens, from the nineteenth century on, including prominent English Canadians (Lemoine, 1987). The city's growth has been deflected primarily northwards and westwards since the nineteenth century, when the constraints of the walled city first became apparent (Nader, 1976). Since the provincial legislature (hotel du parlement, Figure 9.3) had already followed the westward trend in 1878, the development of the government bureaucracy west of the walled city occurred naturally, as did the main commercial/office district; and rapid suburban commercial and industrial growth has recently proceeded farther west, in the direction of Montreal. Meanwhile Haute Ville has become the retail/service district catering primarily to tourist and leisure business, a role which maintains an uneasy equilibrium with continuing institutional, specialist office and residential functions, of which the latter is increasingly dominated by gentrification (reflecting the white-collar economy) (Mendel, 1988/9). However, the tourist-historic city has included from its inception the Citadel (1820s), the provincial legislature and, above all, the Plains of Abraham immediately west of the walled town. Note also that modern tourism can be dated from the opening of the Canadian Pacific Railway's Château Frontenac hotel in 1893 (which now dominates the historic townscape); but tourist-historic interest in Quebec has been recorded since 1830 (Nader, 1976).

In the early 1970s the tourist-historic city was effectively extended to include Basse Ville. The provincial Ministry of Cultural Affairs rehabilitated Place Royale, the earliest focus of Quebec, close to the St. Lawrence waterfront; the survival of the early church, Notre Dame des Victoires, provided a centre-piece for this museum, visitor centre and tourist-retail project (Ross, 1984). The project both enhanced the tourism economy and spread it more widely, thus easing pressure on Haute Ville; as with other zones of discard, it was relatively easy to acquire property for rehabilitation and for archaeological excavation (Ross, 1984). The success of this provincial scheme encouraged a further spread of the tourist-historic city to include the adjacent waterfront and warehouses extending round to Bassin Louise; in this case the federal government, as one of several such projects on its harbour property across the country, undertook to revitalise redundant port facilities in time to mark the 450th anniversary in 1984 of Cartier's voyage of discovery. This included the creation of waterfront leisure facilities, such as a market and theatre, and the adaptive reuse of space and some structures to serve varied tourist and local needs. This 'Vieux Port' project further stimulated private market revitalisation, both residential and commercial, in Basse Ville. The subsequent construction of the new Museum of Civilization (1988) near Place Royale is a further major cultural contribution by the provincial government which is aimed largely at historic tourism (but in French, a problem discussed below); it is an important illustration of the use of a new building to enhance tourist-oriented historicity, through blending form and function with historic buildings and incorporating the two within it. Heritage Canada (cf. Chapter 7) has also stimulated private reinvestment in Basse Ville through a co-operative venture in warehouse revitalisation with private developers and the provincial and municipal governments (Ross, 1984). The overall reclamation of Basse Ville into the tourist-historic city, with its accompanying overtones of local gentrification, has not however occurred without significant social costs of displacement and conflict over reuse priorities (Tunbridge, 1988).

Tourist mobility and provincial marketing have, as elsewhere, promoted the further extension of Quebec's tourist-historic city into its surrounding region. In Quebec's case, however, this is enhanced both by the importance of the outlying heritage (particularly the villages of Île d'Orléans, some 10 km downstream), and by the provincial tourism emphasis upon French-style '*pays*' of marked regional character and cohesion.

Management of tourist-historic Quebec has posed planning problems for the city government comparable to those encountered in European historic gems, particularly where these now constitute the cores of significant metropolises. The tourist dollar has not been won without conflicts, opportunity cost and substantial investment, but of course the amenity created does not serve the tourism economy alone (Nader, 1976). Zoning and development controls on height and view-planes (not always adhered to — Duchesne, 1975) have been applied to protect the morphological character of the walled city, and to maintain a functional balance there between local and tourist needs (e.g. for hotel accommodation versus housing, cf. Chapter 5); protecting the social character from gentrification has not been a realistic possibility. Also, environmental management problems of traffic circulation and parking in the narrow streets of the old city result directly from its contemporary economic base, particularly as this conflicts with continuing residential and other local needs.

Critical intervention in developing and promoting the tourist-historic city has come from the voluntary and private enterprise sectors, as well as from the public sector at all three government levels. Private architectural firms have helped to stimulate the reclamation of neglected areas, sometimes in partnerships with voluntary sector interests such as Heritage Canada, and have in the process contributed to the evolution of conservation practice in the dominant public sector (Leahy, 1986/7). The city government gave little attention to conservation outside the walled precinct until legislation in the late 1970s (Duchesne, 1975; Dalibard, 1988/9), hence the Grande Allée which developed to the west in the 1830s has been invaded by the modern high-rise CBD; civic perspectives widened in the 1980s, however, and many revitalisation projects were accelerated for the Cartier anniversary (Ross, 1984). In its first comprehensive management plan, the city government is seeking to balance diversified residential and service employment growth in the old city with a co-ordinating role in public/private heritage protection and tourism provision. The latter includes restoration, research, interpretation, archaeology, attention to circulation and parking and expansion of accommodation (Ville de Quebec, 1988). The provincial Ministry of Cultural Affairs similarly broadened its approach in the 1980s, moving from a costly and destructive 'pickling'/original reconstruction approach to more flexible conservation and reuse in the Place Royale area; nearby warehouse revitalisation by another Quebec government corporation, in private partnership, hastened this change (Leahy, 1986/7). The federal government has played a much longer-standing role than its recent waterfront initiative, primarily through Parks Canada (cf. Halifax in Chapter 5), which owns the walls and a large part of the intramural city (Dalibard, 1988/9), and the Plains of Abraham which have been a National Battlefields Park since 1908 (MacRae, 1988/9); the federal government constructed the Governor's Walk from the Citadel to Dufferin Terrace in the 1950s (Nader, 1976), and the Citadel, although a major tourist-historic resource, remains under federal military control. Parks Canada's recent initiatives include archaeology and the redevelopment of eighteenth-century cuisine for the benefit of tourism (Walker, 1988/9); and it was instrumental (with Heritage Canada) in the World Heritage nomination. Notwithstanding the range of tourist-historic agents, and perhaps because of their imperfect co-ordination, Quebec's heritage resource remains under potential redevelopment pressure (Dalibard, 1988/9).

Quebec is, furthermore, a notable illustration of political tension over 'whose heritage?', reflecting French Canadian nationalism. Cultural sensitivity over the heritage that Quebec (now approximately 90 per cent Francophone) projects to both residents and tourists is heightened by the nature of its society and economy: although a major port, its economic base in the late twentieth century is primarily that of a provincial government and tourism centre. Thus it is simultaneously the focus of Francophone Canada's cultural aspirations and of its tourist industry, which creates unusual sensitivity in the matter of heritage interpretation. An early manifestation of French-English tension was the blowing up of the Wolfe memorial on the Plains of Abraham by nationalists in 1963 (later reconstructed), notwithstanding the generous marking accorded to his opponent Montcalm (MacRae, 1988/9). Local tensions over the validity of Anglophone heritage are matched by periodic intergovernmental conflicts, particularly during the Parti Québecois government (1976–84) when the federal government sought to promote bilingual cultural balance and to demonstrate its own relevance\in the face of the provincial denial of it: the federal Vieux Port revitalisation provided an ideal opportunity to attain both ends, since its focus was culturally neutral yet timed to mark an event of seminal significance to French Canada. The Francophone identity of Quebec in the late 1980s is secure enough for the city to maintain a tourism economy projected largely at an Anglophone market; but province-wide hostility of a Francophone minority against the use of any English street signs creates a communication problem with the main tourism market, the United States. The 'whose heritage?' brake upon the tourist-historic economy may thus extend to the means as well as the substance of communication. In any event, the management of tourist-historic Quebec may be viewed as a process of creative tension between its leading extra-provincial and intra-provincial agents, in government, voluntary and private enterprise sectors, rather than as the product of a single agent or level of critical intervention. It has advanced in a sometimes brittle tit-for-tat manner which has brought the benefit of lavish investment at the cost of more than usual intermittent conflict. Such a scenario may be anticipated elsewhere if the heritage projected to tourists is the focus of cultural discord.

Charleston (see Figure 9.4) Charleston, South Carolina, is the 'earliest and most complete attempt to preserve an entire historic city ambience' in the United States, and both in its innate character and extent of conservation is the closest American equivalent to the European historic city; so comprehensive has been its core revitalisation that it is perceived as 'returning to a classic pre-industrial city in form, character and structure', with (*inter alia*) the clear implication of élite dominance of the city centre (Ford, 1979, pp. 213–4). It is one of only three US cities of metropolitan size with most of their central areas in preservation districts, and thus the most viable contenders for the present notion of historic core-gems; the others are Savannah and Santa Fe. Like Quebec, Charleston possesses a service-dominated economy which both supports and results from its historic conservation: tourism is second only to the adjacent naval base, and it is also a major commercial port; the city lacks the governmental function of Quebec but none the less has a strong white-collar component oriented to conservation.

Charleston's evolution has in general been very favourable to the development and retention of what is now seen as historic. The original English colony was established on the Ashley River in 1670; it was moved in 1680 to the present inner-city site, a seafront peninsula between the Ashley and Cooper River estuaries, and was fortified in 1704. As one of the main ports of the southern plantation economy, it flourished

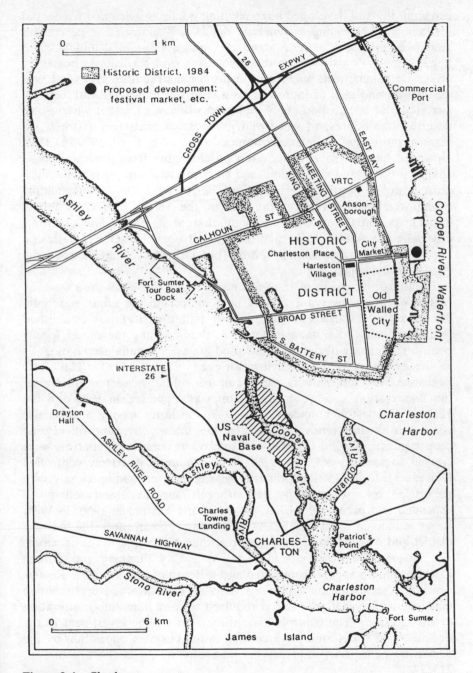

Figure 9.4 *Charleston*

economically and developed a largely high quality service and residential environment, providing commercial needs and seasonal or permanent residences for the plantation aristocracy and a substantial middle class; it was America's sixth city in the early 1800s and accordingly possessed important commercial, public and institutional structures. But Civil War destruction and lack of industrial growth in the late nineteenth century left a city 'of vacant houses, of widowed women, of rotted wharves, of deserted warehouses, of weed-wild gardens, of grass-grown streets, of acres of pitiful and voiceless barrenness' (quoted in Ford, 1979, p. 213). However, 'poverty saved Charleston's architecture from modification by changing tastes and demolition' and 'left the city with an architectural purity rare in North America' (Ford, 1979, p. 213), notwithstanding further damage from an earthquake in the 1880s. The city's innate heritage potential was augmented by that of its immediate environs, especially the Ashley River plantations and Fort Sumter in Charleston Harbor, where by an initially bitter (but ultimately fruitful) irony the Civil War had begun.

The tourist discovery of historic Charleston in the 1920s prompted the realisation that conservation could help to reclaim the urban economy. The Old City District (800 acres, over half the city) was established in 1931, much earlier than in Quebec, thus creating the oldest legally constituted historic district in the United States, a seminal step nationally in the evolution of the tourist-historic city (Datel, 1990). This early beginning was substantially the result of voluntary sector enterprise: the Preservation Society of Charleston was organised in 1920 and the Historic Charleston Foundation in 1947, the latter having a particular concern with the renovation and resale under covenant of historic properties. In the Old City District significant demolition controls were applied to 'century-old structures', and a more restrictively controlled Old and Historic District (primarily residential), coinciding closely with the original colony, was designated within it. This was subsequently much expanded and became the Charleston Historic District in 1966; in 1976, it was redoubled to include nearly all of central Charleston (the business district and over 6,000 houses) under stringent preservation restrictions. The Historic District is administered by a City Planning and Zoning Commission, an appeals committee and a Board of Architectural Review which oversees exterior alterations, new construction and even routine maintenance; special approval is required for any demolition, alteration or construction. 'The controls have stimulated a huge investment in the quaintness of Charleston', overcoming initial business opposition by the demonstrated capacity of preservation to generate profit (Ford, 1979, pp. 213, 215).

Charleston (like Savannah but unlike Quebec) is unusual in North America at this urban scale in that its entire city centre is within the historic district and 'conforms in every way to the architectural sense of

Plate 9.1a Charleston: Broad Street – 'Four Corners of Law' (St Michael's Church, Federal Court, County Court, City Hall) at Meeting Street, middle distance (JET 1980)

Plate 9.1b Charleston: Meeting Street – St Michael's Church, typical narrow side street and sideways house facade (right) (JET 1973)

place of the city' (Ford, 1979, p. 215); its morphology retains the symbolism of a pre-industrial city, dominated by churches, civic buildings and markets, most particularly at the traditionally central 'Four Corners of Law' at Broad and Meeting Streets (Plates 9.1a and 9.1b). The architectural controls are complemented by a 90-foot height limit downtown surrounded by a 50-foot limit in residential areas adjacent, to preserve the city's scale. As in Quebec, this has been made possible by enforcing the natural tendency for modern commercial activity, particularly office buildings, to decentralise out of the congested original peninsula location, in this case primarily north-westward along the interstate freeway inland, but also across the Ashley and Cooper Rivers. The traditional shopping streets are essential to the tourist city for parking and provisioning and because the carriage companies (the most appropriate means of touring the historic city) are based there; thus the revitalisation of their retail environment into an explicitly tourist-historic component has been a recent priority.

The contemporary tourist-historic development of Charleston is probably unsurpassed in the New World; its 2.7 million tourist visits in 1987 (Department of Planning and Urban Development, 1987), development and marketing are consistent with its core-gem status. This has been achieved through further critical intervention, fifty years after the first which secured the initial consolidation and upgrading of the historic 'product', designed to capture the greatly expanded tourist-historic market in a climate of growing competition for it. In this second stage of intervention, the voluntary sector has been joined by more comprehensive municipal involvement and by a plethora of other government and private agencies. Both preservation bodies remain active entrepreneurs, operating information centres, shops, tours, house museums, seminars, an affiliated reproductions business and various events. The Charleston Museum operates other house museums, and the National Trust for Historic Preservation runs Drayton Hall, an eighteenth-century plantation house on the Ashley River. The City is responsible for planning the balance of tourist-historic and other urban components. Charleston County has a wider responsibility for recreation and tourism; and State agencies run outlying heritage attractions, and activities upon which the tourist-historic city impinges such as the Port of Charleston. The federal government is (as in Boston) a vital agent, as supplier of matching grants for various tourist-historic initiatives, through the National Parks Service which (*inter alia*) runs Fort Sumter as a National Monument, and because of the pervasive tangential presence of the US Naval Base. In the private sector the regional Convention and Visitors Bureau and major private developers have contributed support to the tourist-historic city. The promotion of Charleston has been in the hands of a private marketing agency since 1975.

Charleston has been described as a tourist centre in the mid-development phase, with a widening catchment area and range of attractions, but visitor surveys reveal that the historic city remains the dominant focus of attraction (Stough, 1988, after Butler, 1980). Familiar North American themes, such as bed-and-breakfast in historic homes and periodic festivals, are well developed. The Festival of Houses gives tourists access to historic homes, and the annual Spoleto Festival U.S.A. exemplifies the confluence of tourism, the arts and the historic city discussed in Chapter 5. This is paralleled by the city-run Piccolo Spoleto, for which 'the entire city of Charleston becomes a stage as historic churches, parks, schools, streets, restaurants and even boats in the harbor are the non-traditional performance spaces' (Charleston Gateway, Inc., 1987, p. 22); this reflects similar tourist-leisure uses of historic cities elsewhere. The historic city's retail and service business has become heavily biased towards restaurants, antique shops, boutiques and related specialist activities, reinforced by Charleston Place, a compatible new retail/conference/hotel development linking the King Street antique district to the Market. The Market, which was almost entirely tourist-oriented by 1989, is being further reinforced by adjacent waterfront revitalisation. The port on the Cooper River remains very active, but some recession has freed warehouses for tourist-historic adaptive reuses, such as restaurants, and space for a planned major redevelopment including a Rouse Company festival market-place (Barrineau and Sullivan, 1985). While the historic peninsula is the essential core-gem, the regional historic attractions of Charleston have been augmented by outlying State initiatives, a re-creation of the first colony on the Ashley and a naval ship museum on the Cooper River. The wider region also contains vital components of the tourist city, particularly overspill accommodation and service facilities inland along Interstate 26, beach/sports resorts on coastal islands and harbour cruises including to Fort Sumter and the Naval Base. All are co-marketed and largely co-managed with the historic city, and are clearly ancillary to it (cf. Chapter 7, resort regions).

This comprehensive development of the tourist-historic city based upon central Charleston has not been attained without cost. Black faces are hardly visible in its promotional literature, and black, and low-income white, residents have been displaced to ghetto housing north of the historic core, although used as essential low-wage labour and visible (as in the Market) where culturally appropriate. Again, though in a different context from Quebec, we must ask whose heritage is being primarily conserved and marketed, and who is paying; the benefit-cost equation is heavily imbalanced at the expense of the black population. '"Gentrification" is occurring on a massive scale as the central city has become the most desirable residential location in the metropolitan area' (Ford, 1979, p. 214).

Other problems reminiscent of European historic cities arise: traffic and parking, the integration of contemporary functions into a largely frozen historic landscape, environmental pressure and invasion of privacy and the artificiality of a city-core economy based upon boutiques and restaurants. By 1978 the need to manage the historic resource base, to remain competitive yet minimise costs such as environmental stress, social friction and possible stifling of a high-technology growth industry, had generated a tourism study (Charleston County, Park, Recreation and Tourist Commission, 1978). Among its chief recommendations were stricter traffic and parking controls in the congested southern peninsula, combined with provision of shuttle bus services; a new Visitor Reception and Transportation Center at the northern gateway of the historic district; new nodes of attraction; and publicity for lesser known parts of the historic city. By 1989 these objectives had been largely attained: in particular, the City and Chamber of Commerce, using federal assistance, had constructed the VRTC, and a major hotel and parking garage had been built at the site; the King Street-Charleston Place-Market-Waterfront retail/leisure axis was well advanced; and the historic Harleston Village and Ansonborough localities were better publicised. These geographical strategies to protect and enhance the tourist-historic resource closely reflect our comments in Chapter 5; in addition, the quest for better education of external tourist agents and for closer co-ordination between the many internal tourist-historic agents strikes a familiar chord. In the final analysis, in North American historic cities at least, the investment stimulated by tourist-historic success is essential to the funding of revitalisation, as well as invaluable to city revenues and employment generation. In return for its social and environmental costs and the public expenditure needed to combat them, Charleston has obtained an economic and morphological core-gem which is quite atypical but commonly envied among American cities (despite periodic environmental setbacks such as hurricane damage in 1989).

Savannah (see Figure 9.5) Savannah, 160 km south of Charleston, has many similarities with it in environment, evolution and tourist-historic development; accordingly this discussion will focus upon its significant differences. It was a British military foundation of 1733 laid out in a rectangular grid, systematically punctuated by some twenty-four squares; its physical plan is thus unique in North America and resembles the formal planning found in various European Georgian cities. Its architecture is largely Georgian and subsequent neo-classical, with Victorian southward extension, framed by subtropical live oaks; it reflects the city's prosperity, as the main Southern cotton port, up to the Civil War (Plate 9.2a). The survival of its tourist-historic potential depended primarily upon two historical circumstances: first, the Union General Sherman, who captured it during his march through Georgia in 1864, was so enchanted by it that he spared it from destruction (cf. Rothenburg and Heidelberg, Chapter 7); and second, the collapse of the cotton price in the late nineteenth century

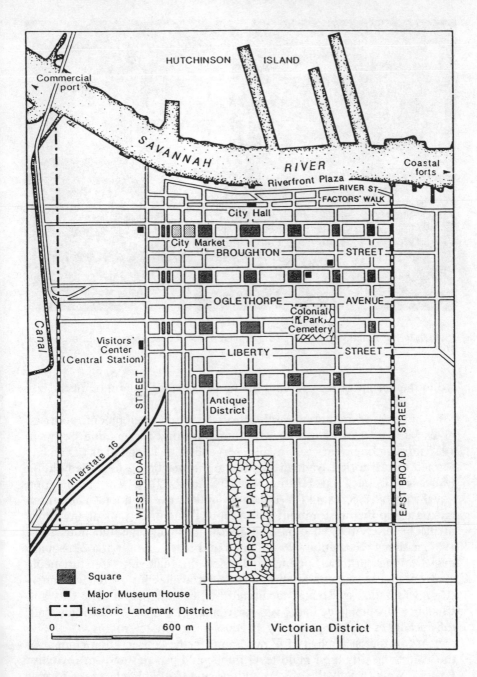

Figure 9.5 *Savannah, city centre*

Plate 9.2a Savannah: typical square, with Georgian house (now restaurant) (JET 1973)

led to the decline of the port and the undisturbed degeneration of the city thereafter.

Savannah's revitalisation and tourist-historic development occurred much later than in Charleston. Its tourist-historic reclamation began in 1955 through one clear-cut critical intervention: leading ladies of the city formed the Historic Savannah Foundation in reaction against demolition (Advisory Council on Historic Preservation, 1979). The Foundation bought up old houses and resold them under covenants that committed purchasers to their restoration; it also lobbied and undertook an inventory of the historic city, and other initiatives, including museum houses. In 1967, national recognition was obtained in the designation of a 2½-square mile National Historic Landmark District, the relatively late start being compensated by the continuous subsequent availability of federal inner-city revitalisation assistance, facilitated by this designation. The City and Chamber of Commerce had given early support to the Foundation's lead, the incentives including sharing a state tax on hotel rooms. A steady increase in tourist publicity followed and, in the conservation climate of the 1970s, the City used multi-level public and private funds to revitalise Factors' Walk (chiefly the office buildings and Cotton Exchange of former cotton merchants), and the adjoining waterfront warehouses and plaza on River Street, creating a festival market retail complex which is physically quite unique to Savannah (Plate 9.2b) (Carpenter, 1977). It has been

Plate 9.2b Savannah: Factor's Walk, showing pedestrian bridges over access lanes to riverfront (behind); City Hall in distance (JET 1973)

complemented by landscaping along the Savannah River, a maritime museum and a waterfront hotel redevelopment; overall it has become the central landmark in the tourist-historic image of Savannah, enhanced by festival events organised by the waterfront merchants' association. More generally, the tourist-historic city has developed parallel to Charleston in the 1980s; for example, the Historic Savannah Foundation maintains an active tourist role in information, guided tours and provision for specialist visits and events. The Savannah Visitor Center occupies a gateway location analogous to that of Charleston, and is heavily promoted as an intercepting attraction in itself, being an historic railway station adaptively reused for various tourist amenities. A characteristic tourist function is restaurants serving regional (Low Country) cuisine, in some of the most historic buildings. Tourist-historic marketing includes outliers such as the nineteenth-century coastal forts (one being under National Parks Service control, cf. Fort Sumter) and extends to inherently non-historic harbour cruises and coastal resorts. A major waterfront redevelopment scheme is planned for Hutchinson Island, across the Savannah River, although this remains uncertain in view of continued port and industrial development upstream and funding questions. As in Charleston, expansion of contemporary commercial uses has been accommodated primarily by lateral deflection to inland suburban growth, near the interstate freeway access points; in Savannah, however, the combined effect of suburbanisation and the diversion of tourist trade to discrete locations (Factors' Walk, antique district) has left the CBD core blighted, except for the limited City Market retail revitalisation.

The problem aspects of tourist-historic development in Savannah are similar to those of Charleston and more generally reflect those in core-gem cities elsewhere. Gentrification, though less pronounced, has locally reduced social diversity by driving blacks and poor whites out of parts of the inner city, into the decayed Victorian District where revitalisation remains tentative; traffic problems have increased, albeit moderated by the regularity and width of the street system. As in Charleston, however, it is difficult to see how the economy of the city could be revitalising without its commitment to tourist-historic development and the related growth of white-collar activity and a leisure-oriented residential élite; unlike Quebec, neither city has enjoyed the long-term stability of white-collar employment associated with major government functions. In any case, Savannah's tourist-historic development remains incomplete; Historic Savannah Foundation's critical intervention continues with a survey and coalition action plan for further improvement to the Historic District, especially its neglected fringes (Historic Savannah Foundation, 1988). The Savannah Area Convention and Visitors' Bureau, responsible for marketing the tourist-historic city, has commissioned a report on how best to develop it further and competitively defend its market (Davidson-Peterson Associates, Inc., 1988).

Nurtured tourist-historicity: Ottawa (see Figure 9.6)

Our earlier dichotomy (Chapter 7) between resource and demand-based small tourist-historic centres is too simple to encompass medium or large cities. The above core-gem examples are implicitly resource-tending, however, while other medium cities may be demand-tending. Ottawa illustrates the case of political capitals in which such demand may lead to a specific nurturing of tourist-historicity (cf. 'invention of tradition' discussed by Taylor, 1989); similarities could be found in other capitals, such as Washington and (in time) newer cities such as Canberra and Brasilia. More extreme cases of nurturing, to overcome negative images and economies, are considered later in this chapter.

Ottawa (metropolitan Ottawa-Hull, 820,000 in 1986) is a medium-sized city of moderate historical interest by national standards, but with a status (as federal capital of Canada) and socio-economic character which have permitted progressive improvement of its environmental quality; to this end it has capitalised heavily upon its historic attributes in recent years. This historic exploitation has been directed at two markets, mutually supportive in a broad sense but not necessarily compatible in detail: the national/international tourism market of a capital city, and the local

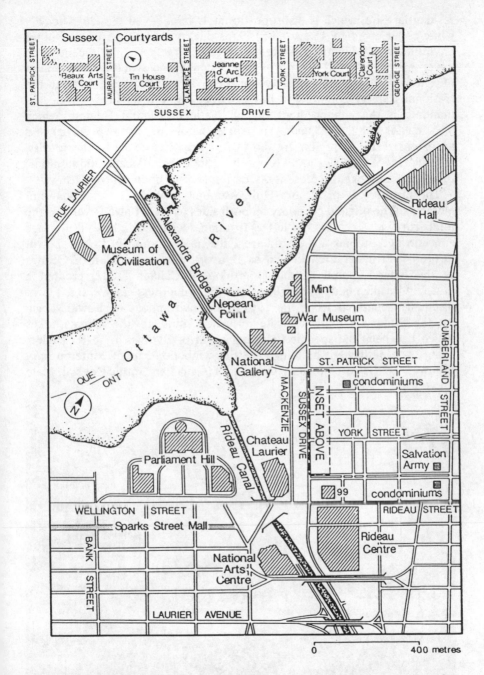

Figure 9.6 *Ottawa, city centre. Byward Market, historic focus of Lower Town, is between York and Rideau Streets; Hull north of Ottawa River*

residential élite, which is disproportionately large given the city's heavily white-collar economy (Ley, 1988). This duality is characteristic of other environmentally favoured white-collar cities, but particularly centres of government. However, the role of government agencies in the development of Ottawa's tourist-historic city has been unusually large, in that the National Capital Commission has provided the critical intervention: its mandate is the enhancement of the National Capital Region, which also includes Hull (in Quebec province, across the Ottawa River) and an extensive fringe region around both cities. Reference to the tourist-historic city of Ottawa should properly include the adjacent communities, therefore, although the present discussion focuses upon central Ottawa.

The historic city of Ottawa-Hull essentially comprises two discordant elements. The original economy on both sides of the Ottawa River was the lumbering industry; this has left a 'frontier' social and industrial heritage concentrated around the Chaudiere Falls, in Hull, and in Lower Town, Ottawa, which was then known as Bytown. The designation of Ottawa as the federal capital of the Dominion of Canada (1867) created a much more dignified 'Westminster in the wilderness' in Centre Town, discreetly separated from the roisterous environment of Lower Town by the Rideau Canal, a strategic water route to the Great Lakes which had been the specific founding agent of Bytown in 1828 (Taylor, 1986). The parliament buildings are the symbolic focus of contemporary Ottawa, and their architectural distinction (Canadian Gothic Revival, Plate

Plate 9.3a Ottawa: Parliament from National Gallery, Sussex Drive (JET 1990)

9.3a), on a limestone bluff overlooking the Ottawa River, enhances their nodal significance for tourist-historic Ottawa-Hull. From this initial focus, however, the tourist is chiefly drawn east across the Rideau Canal to Lower Town West and the Byward Market area, which is Ottawa's principal concentration of historic conservation and tourist-oriented activity. Lower Town West projects a traditionally lower class multi-ethnic (primarily French/Irish) cultural identity in a physical setting of uneven quality; it was originally an imperial military reserve on which short-term leases discouraged quality construction (Taylor, 1986; Newton, 1980) but it does contain many locally distinctive heritage buildings of limestone or log construction.

Lower Town slipped into a classic zone of discard character after the shifting of the city's focus of power to Centre Town. It had always included the red-light district and became increasingly a warehouse-industrial environment, intermixed with the market complex and lower-class accommodation (Tunbridge, 1986a). Notwithstanding various federal bodies concerned with Ottawa's beautification since the early twentieth century (Taylor, 1986), no official attention was given to the heritage potential of Lower Town until the early 1960s. This was, none the less, a relatively early date for systematic cultivation of the historic city; the National Capital Commission provided the catalyst for its progressive revitalisation by the decision to acquire and rehabilitate the limestone buildings of Sussex Drive, a strategic 'Mile of History' connecting Parliament with the residences of the Prime Minister and Governor General (Rideau Hall) (Bond, 1961). The NCC rehabilitated the commercial eastern frontage of Sussex Drive by the Centennial year, 1967, and by 1970 this frontage had become tenanted largely by retail/service activities of a distinctively 'contemporary' nature, geared to the historic milieu and its exploitation to serve new élite residential and tourist markets. In the process, older commercial functions were mostly displaced; these included retail/service activities of either a low grade or a nondescript specialist character, and also wholesale/warehouse activities, of which over sixty had been located in Lower Town West in the 1950s (Tunbridge, 1986a). The retail/service transition was discussed in Chapter 5 and is summarised in Table 9.1.

From the NCC's initial catalyst, Lower Town West has become the essential core of Ottawa's tourist-historic city, through the agency of various public and private entrepreneurs; its revitalisation gathered momentum in the late 1970s and has continued to intensify and diffuse east and north. The City of Ottawa furthered the NCC's initiative by its revitalisation of the Byward Market building, which is the focus of the traditional retail complex, by area landscaping associated with construction of the adjacent Rideau Centre and, subsequently, by efforts to create a Heritage Conservation District which would extend limited heritage zoning by enforcing appropriate design controls. Increasingly, however,

Table 9.1 Change in services in Lower Town West, Ottawa, 1965–85

Principal business of establishment		Number of establishments					
		1965	1969	1973	1977	1981	1985
Retailing: food,	Total	38	40	40	32	36	40
drink, tobacco	Contemp.	–	–	1	2	5	6
Retailing: clothing,	Total	26	34	28	24	30*	39*
footwear	Contemp.	–	1	5	5	16*	31*
Retailing: other	Total	55	65	72	78	84*	74*
goods, general	Contemp.	–	3	8	14	29*	35*
Restaurants, bars,	Total	25	22	23	27	47	79
entertainment	Contemp.	–	1	2	7	29	68
Other consumer	Total	58	60	50	59	68	70
services	Contemp.	–	–	–	–	1	5
Automotive	Total	9	10	8	6	5	5
Overall total, commercial consumer services		211	231	221	226	270*	307*
***'Contemporary' business total.		–	5	16	28	80*	145*

** 1989: Total 180*. Intensified specialisms in all categories
* Market stalls excluded (mainly 'other goods')
'Contemporary' definition problem: see Tunbridge (1987a)

Source: Tunbridge (1987a), modified.

the momentum of revitalisation has been transferred to the private sector as land values have risen; while this removes a burden from the public purse it also creates the inevitable displacements of lower-income stores and residences, and conflicts between conservation and intensification-redevelopment interests, which have also impeded acceptance of a formal Heritage Conservation District.

Specific public policy decisions not directly focused upon the area at issue may be identified as further key influences upon the pattern and pace of tourist-historic revitalisation; this is commonly true elsewhere. Two stand out in the case of tourist-historic Ottawa: first, relaxation of Ontario's drinking laws in 1973 created overnight the possibility of both outdoor and Sunday drinking, thereby opening up the leisure exploitation of historic environments to a hitherto unprecedented extent; and second, the building of the nearby shopping/convention Rideau Centre and closing of Rideau Street to cars in the early 1980s required a major civic effort to reorient traffic patterns and link this redevelopment with adjacent land-uses, as an integrated Rideau Area Project, which provided a major stimulus to speculative investment in Lower Town West and particularly the adjacent Byward Market (Gilmore, 1984). This is closely parallel to many similar historic-redevelopment juxtapositions in North American city centres; while not necessarily co-ordinated or highly successful, they are a high-profile indicator that the historic city, and its tourist market, are interrelated with a larger entity (cf. Chapter 5).

While it is not possible to identify precisely which public intervention caused how much growth in area land values, the cumulative effect of public nurturing, combined with a growing fashion for leisure exploitation of historic areas, has generated a frenetic market for the provision of retail, service and residential premises, the latter in the form of both hotels and 'gentrified' living space (largely condominium apartments). The positive aspect of this is that the potential of a comparatively scarce tourist-historic resource is being very fully exploited; the problem encountered in Europe of a resource in excess of demand no longer arises. The negative aspect, however, is that management policies nurturing the tourist-historic city in a favourable socio-economic environment may stimulate speculative overcommercialisation by the private sector, which creates the need for counteractive management intervention not originally envisaged, to control such consequences as socio-economic displacement and conflict between conservation and land-use intensification through incompatible redevelopment. The case of Lower Town West indicates that the former problem requires close examination: on the one hand, the displacement of the low-income population is unquestionably occurring through commercial redevelopment of former residences, including the loss of above-store apartments and the progressive attrition of housing in favour of parking space; on the other hand, the displacement of lower-grade commercial activities does not necessarily mean the displacement of their entrepreneurs, since these have typically been small Jewish landowners who have often retained the premises and retired on the high rents that conversion to the new boutique/restaurant environment has generated (Tunbridge, 1986b). Furthermore, the pressure which revitalisation activity creates upon low-grade incumbent land-uses does not automatically result in their displacement: the Salvation Army has successfully fought the threat created by high-rise condominiums erected opposite by building an adjacent hostel in association with the City's public housing authority, thereby reinforcing its locational inertia. The conservation/tourist development problem, alluded to in Chapter 3, is manifested by a recent attempt to erect a seventeen-storey hotel overlooking the Byward Market and connected to the Rideau Centre. This threatened both the historic ambience of the Market and its hours of winter sunlight, a critical consideration in Ottawa's severe climate; after municipal vacillation it was overturned by the provincial review board, in response to opposition by a conservationist coalition. Victory for conservation of the historic resource in one battle does not, however, guarantee its survival in a protracted war against speculative redevelopment interests, quite apart from the loss of tourist amenities which such victories may entail.

In 1986 a survey of the contemporary retail/service businesses in Lower Town West was undertaken, to establish to what extent their location had been influenced by the heritage quality of the area or of the buildings they occupied (Tunbridge, 1987a). While some were chains (e.g. larger restaurants), most were independent local decision-makers, subject to uncertainty and idiosyncrasy. It was found that the heritage appeal was for the most part secondary in a perception of the area as 'the place to be', its momentum supported by factors such as Sunday opening. Since this perception is ultimately derived from heritage-based promotion, it can be regarded to a large extent as an unwitting indirect response to the heritage factor. However, there was a clear distinction between heritage perception and behavioural motivation: some merchants with an active perception, and even a limited heritage area motivation, either avoided or protested the costs and constraints of occupying a heritage building; an example is youth-oriented pubs. Also, while the nurtured historic city is the ultimate mainspring of the area's commercial revival, merchants' comments about both area and building produced a dozen other reasons for their locational choice which further cloud the significance of heritage (see Tables 9.2 and 9.3); some of these (e.g. positive externalities of the area, access/size/floor level characteristics of the building) may have no significant link with historicity, while others, including the ultimate non-choice reason, 'all I could get' in the area, are to varying degrees unconscious admissions of it. Our discussion in Chapter 5 of the intricate way the historic city is used, initially derived from European experience, is clearly reflected and extended in this New World case study. In Ottawa, as Tables 9.2 and 9.3 indicate, there is a functional variable in historic orientation: a few functions, notably quality restaurants and ladies' clothiers, are very sensitive to heritage. How far this reflects the personalities of particular Ottawa merchants, or a functional distinction of national or wider significance for the tourist-historic city, remains to be determined; it is however anticipated that functional distinctions will commonly arise in the 'highest and best' use of the historic amenity, as of commercial location attributes more generally.

The survey did not systematically assess tourism orientation, but most merchants were asked how far they were dependent upon tourists. It was apparent that a spectrum exists: some functions are heavily tourist-dependent (e.g. many restaurants and luxury good dealers) while others either avoid the casual tourist market specifically or shun the peak land values associated with it (e.g. some galleries, high-fashion retailers). While a functional spectrum could also be identified in historic orientation, there was no evidence of detailed correlation between strong historic and strong tourist orientation; rather, the entire area is in general terms the focus of the tourist-historic city and in detail the two dimensions vary independently,

Table 9.2 Locational (area) choice: Lower Town West, Ottawa, 1986 (Survey of 'contemporary' businesses)

	Clothing	Other goods	Restaurants, bars, entertainment	Other services	Total
Total respondents (1–5 motivations each).	39	46	43	11	139
Motivations for area choice:					
Area centrality					
Central/focal/high traffic etc.	26	27	38	11	103
Focal for specific groups (e.g. tourists)	18	25	29	9	81
Focal for specific function	1	3	–	–	4
Anticipated development potential	6	3	8	2	19
Lack of competition	–	1	–	1	2
Area environmental					
Heritage/historic area	1	1	2	–	4
'Trendy', 'In', 'Place to be'	6	11	5	3	25
Artistic/culture/craft compatible	1	1	–	–	2
'Classy', quality-clientele and stores	6	4	–	1	11
Positive business mix, variety	5	–	6	1	12
Life, activity, dynamism	4	1	2	–	7
Good staff environment	1	–	–	–	1
Not shopping centre/mall	12	2	2	–	16
Sub-area factors					
Market association (specific)	1	–	3	–	4
Street-specific image associations	1	3	–	–	4
Adjacent attractive business (espec. Rideau Centre)	2	–	1	1	4
Interactive non-business focuses (gov't., instit'n.)	1	1	–	–	2
Personal factors					
Specific liking (atmosphere, amenities)	7	7	6	1	21
Proximate living	3	2	1	1	7
Existing associations (personal or business)	1	1	–	–	2
Inherited location (i.e. premises)	1	–	1	3	5
Other factors					
Available/affordable at time	2	1	1	1	5
Commercial information *re* availability	1	–	–	–	1
Forced move (from outside)	–	1	2	1	4
Sunday opening/brunch crowd	3	1	3	–	7
Building-premises needs determined area	2	–	–	–	2
Miscellaneous (property investment, inertia, etc.)	8	7	5	1	21

Source: Tunbridge (1987a), modified

Table 9.3   Building choice: Lower Town West, Ottawa, 1986 (Survey of 'contemporary' businesses) *Source*: Tunbridge (1987a), modified

	Health and other food	Ladies' clothing	Men's clothing	Children's clothing	Specialist boutiques	Furnishings/furniture	Arts and crafts	Gifts/toys	Sports/outdoors	Other retail	Restaurants	Bars/nightclubs	Cafes	Other services	Total
Total respondents (1.5 motivations each)	2	25	5	2	7	11	8	2	2	21	31	4	8	11	139
Motv'ns for building choice															
Site/immed. environment															
Good traffic/site visibility	1	7	3	1	2	3	2	1	2	5	9	2	2	4	44
Proximate attractions (non.bus.)	1									1	3	1			6
Proximate attractive business		4	1		1		1	2		1	1			3	14
Anticipated proximate development				1	1										2
Not a shopping centre	1	6	1											1	9
Avoidance compet'n, negative business										1					1
Building quality															
Heritage – prime		8	1				1	1			6		1	1	19
Heritage – secondary	1	6	1	4	1	2	1	1		4	2			1	24
Form, character, etc.		9	2	4	1	1	1			3	2	1	2	4	30
Condition		4	2	1						1	4	4	1		17
Size and expandability	1	4				3	4	1	2	5	5			3	28
Level (street or otherwise)				1				1	1					2	5
Existing specialist facilities											3	1	1		5
Appropriate for function	1							2			1	3			7
Freedom to do what wanted	1													1	2
Building obtainability															
Affordability/'right price'		7	1		1	6	3		1	5	11	2	1	1	39
Availability at time	1	12	3		3	7	7		1	10	12	2	5	3	66
Commercial info. (and connections)	1	2		1							3	1		1	9
Favourable deal (with owners)		3					1			1	2	1		3	11
Other personal															
P/bus. links with property							1	1			2				4
P./empl./family links nearby	1										4		1		6
Other															
Inertial or inherited location; other							1	2			1	3	1	1	9

the degree to which individual merchants relate to them being a matter of personal idiosyncrasy as well as of functional type. (It was also apparent, however, that personality and merchandise themselves are significantly related, in a sphere of business which emphasises individual predilection and often craft-related skills.) The responses clearly indicated, however, that the intensity of tourist use of the historic area is uneven and subject to distance decay: in 1986, tourists came essentially from one direction (the south-west corner, Parliament and the Rideau Centre), tourist dependence was extremely strong around George Street, but there was a marked fall-off in tourist perception and commercial orientation north of Clarence Street, and to the east. Local residents, workers and students, however – particularly those now choosing to live in Lower Town and nearby gentrified areas – enjoy a wider cognition of the area's potential. Of course, the manner in which the tourist-historic city is perceived, and the patterns of its usage by consumers and by commercial interests, have profound significance for its overall management. A particularly critical question will be how to enforce restraints on the design and scale of redevelopment, as in the Market hotel conflict, when the commercial sector displays only a limited orientation to historicity and, commonly in North America, is adept at circumventing development controls.

Since the survey was conducted, significant modification has occurred to the tourist attractions in the vicinity, the consequent movements of pedestrian tourists and the precise tourist-historic geography of Lower Town West. While the specific case is unique to Ottawa, it clearly demonstrates the impact of tangential changes in the tourist city upon the pattern of use of the historic city. The specific changes are the opening of the new National Gallery and Canadian Museum of Civilization in 1988/9; these are very impressive national investments in the tourist city of Ottawa and they are being marketed accordingly. They serve to draw the tourist towards the Ottawa River waterfront, being connected by a pedestrian route across a bridge, and in so doing they also create a united tourist city of Ottawa-Hull more visibly than hitherto; this will be reinforced by the proposed national ceremonial route which passes both. Furthermore, the National Gallery links Parliament and Lower Town West, both architecturally and in terms of new pedestrian movement patterns. The Gallery thus increases tourist flows on and near Sussex Drive north of Clarence Street (especially since it reinforces the nearby Canadian War Museum and Royal Canadian Mint) to the obvious benefit of pubs, restaurants and boutiques in that area. It is, in addition, boosting the value of its vicinity for gentrification, as illustrated by the Gallery Court condominiums (Murray Street) which provide a resident market for tourist-oriented business and have in their ground floor expanded the businesses potentially available to tourists. The proximity of the National Gallery and the redevelopment opportunity of this condominium complex have enabled the National Capital Commission to create an attractive courtyard behind the adjacent reconstructed Sussex Drive frontage. The courtyard completes a chain of four extending behind Sussex Drive. They are a prominent part of the NCC's nurturing contribution and are a prime focus for indoor and outdoor pub and restaurant space, and for periodic festivities; they now provide an alternative tourist corridor between the National Gallery and the Byward Market. The three older courtyards are the result of selective preservation and clearance of old warehouse walls (Plate 9.3b); this technique for the creation of pedestrian spaces in the tourist-historic city is not unique to Ottawa, another example being Unwins Courtyards in The Rocks, Sydney.

The National Gallery of Canada in itself is an unusually effective illustration of the problem of defining components of the historic city.

Plate 9.3b Ottawa: Tin House Court, Lower Town West; subsequent construction of further courtyard towards Catholic cathedral, background (JET 1982)

Although a new building, it projects and enhances the historic identity in a variety of respects and can therefore be claimed as part of both the historic and tourist city. In the first place it is a modern rendering of Gothic Revival architecture, specifically designed to balance the Library of Parliament on the opposite side of the Rideau Canal, as well as adjacent heritage buildings in Lower Town. Secondly, it is designed to provide a panoramic view of the Parliament buildings, and also of the Ottawa River waterfront which has powerful historic associations with the origin of the city as well as some residual heritage buildings. Thirdly, it contains within it two heritage reconstructions, of which the Rideau Chapel is nationally prominent, retrieved from an Ottawa convent demolition in 1972. Fourthly, its prime function is as a compatible receptacle for some of the country's prime heritage artefacts. Finally, the perspective that it is a prime focus of the historic city is specifically promoted in the tourism literature, which it dominates. In these respects the National Gallery is, like the Museum of Civilization in Quebec, a particularly prominent illustration of the manifold strategic role which a contemporary institutional building may play in the tourist-historic city. The Canadian Museum of Civilization in Hull plays a broadly similar role, containing in addition historic streetscape reconstructions. Jointly they provide, through both displays and entertainment activities, a cultural focus parallel to the role of high-culture institutions in the tourist-historic city (cf. Chapter 5), and echo similar developments in major capitals elsewhere.

In Chapter 3 the point was made that the tourist city functions as part of a wider network of tourism centres, a point already illustrated in other contexts. Ottawa's tourist city, and more specifically tourist-historic city, is focused upon the inner city, which is capable of drawing tourists independently; however, it is primarily marketed as a regional entity, including various outlying museums, open-air attractions and historic features; and beyond this it is also marketed as part of a wider macro-regional network of centres. Regional marketing is accomplished by the NCC, the metropolitan regional authorities, the City of Ottawa and other individual municipalities, as well as by private enterprise. The organising bodies for the wider network of tourist centres are principally Ontario and Quebec provincial ministries, which promote their provinces' tourist attractions in this way, primarily for the US market; more generally, state and provincial tourism agencies across North America are actively engaged in promoting such regional networks, over and above local promotion for which they commonly provide umbrella distribution systems. Even in the case of a medium-sized city, therefore, the question arises as to how narrowly its tourist-historic city may be defined, and how distinctively it functions and is projected within the more generalised tourist package at both urban and different regional levels. The historic city which is subsumed within this package is itself strongly shaped in Canada by provincial government agencies: in Ontario, the provincial Planning and Heritage Acts set the legal framework within which historic conservation takes place; and the Local Advisory Committees on Architectural Conservation (LACACs), answerable to the Ministry of Culture and Communications, are empowered to recommend buildings and areas to be conserved.

Ottawa therefore stands out as a special case of federally-nurtured tourist-historicity within a provincial and local framework which is more generally conducive to its development and regionally-based promotion. The role of the National Capital Commission, in stimulating conservation and in promoting/managing numerous tourist activities, largely integrates Ottawa and Hull into a single tourist-historic entity, notwithstanding provincial management environments which would otherwise be mutually exclusive.

Constrained tourist-historicity: Pietermaritzburg (Figure 9.7)

The case of Pietermaritzburg in Natal, South Africa, illustrates the quasi-Western historic core-gem functioning under a dual constraint: apartheid, and the external sanctions which have recently resulted from it. It is a white settler city (population 170,000, including 60,000 whites) which is now the *de facto* hub of a multiracial metropolitan area of over 450,000 (1988).

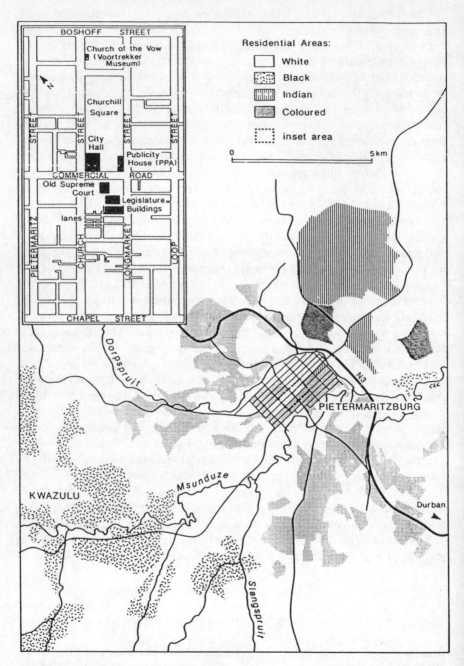

Figure 9.7 *Pietermaritzburg. Historic landmarks include Publicity House*

Pietermaritzburg's historic resource consists of some of the finest British colonial Victorian heritage in existence (Daniel and Brusse, 1977), grafted onto an originally Boer Voortrekker plan. It is an exceptional illustration of the European historic city developed in an alien cultural environment, and the constraints surrounding its recent development and contemporary tourist status are a direct reflection of this environmental discordance. The dual constraint is a specific result of the efforts of South Africa's white rulers to retain the European identity of their cities. A measure of their success is the fact that residents and tourists alike can still immerse themselves in a pervasive transplanted urban environment and remain largely oblivious to its rapidly growing black appendages, which mostly remain part of the homeland of Kwazulu. The discordance between the reassuring European heritage and the surrounding African reality has negative implications, for it must necessarily retard the political adjustment of its white residents and mislead the unwary tourist as to the nature of South Africa. This discordance is, however, lessening in response to recent changes discussed below.

The origins of Pietermaritzburg are intimately linked with the concept of European supremacy. Its most famous building is the Church of the Vow, constructed by the first Boer settlers in 1838 in fulfilment of the covenant with God which, they believed, had brought them victory over the Zulus at Blood River. Little else from the Boer origins survives, except street names and the street-plan, laid out in an expansive grid with water conduits permitting irrigated agriculture, characteristic of the Voortrekker *dorp* (Haswell, 1984). The advent of British control in 1843 caused the withdrawal of most Boers, but the British retained Pietermaritzburg as the capital of Natal; this has remained the city's basic function to the present time, which has been highly conducive to its orderly evolution and ultimately to its conservation. Pietermaritzburg thus developed as a colonial administrative centre; the Voortrekker grid was fragmented in the central area by the addition of passageways more conducive to urban activity, and the city core developed as an intimate and homogeneously Victorian urban environment (Plates 9.4a and 9.4b). The passageways, or 'Lanes', are fundamental to the ambience and tourist appeal of the city core, the architectural gems of which include the City Hall and Legislature and old Supreme Court of Natal, i.e. the symbols of political power. An integral part of the Victorian ambience is also the monuments, which reflect the application of that power in various colonial wars with the surrounding tribes. The answer to the question 'whose heritage?' is obvious, but by virtue of this the city retains its pre-eminence as colonial urban heritage and is actively promoted to tourists, within the prevailing constraints.

The fundamental constraints to the tourist-historic city in Pietermaritzburg are those of apartheid. The Group Areas Act restricts most of the inner city to white residence; a limited area removed from the main CBD is designated for Indian residence and businesses. While there is no racial

Plate 9.4a Pietermaritzburg: colonial legislature, Longmarket Street (JET 1978)

Plate 9.4b Pietermaritzburg: Victorian City Hall and retail facades, Church Street; semi-pedestrianised in 1980s (JET 1988)

restriction on movement (at least by day), the effective tourist-historic city for white South Africans and most foreign visitors is focused upon the well maintained white area. Apartheid has also served to restrict the market for the tourist-historic city, however: for non-white South Africans, economic limitations, restaurant and hotel restrictions and the questionable relevance of an essentially white heritage have all inhibited tourism. Apartheid has recently induced externally imposed constraints in the form of international economic pressure on South Africa (corporate disinvestment, etc.) and the significant curtailment both of air links and, more subtly, of incentive fares and advertising on those routes which remain. These factors have reduced both the real disposable income of South African whites and the influx of foreign tourists, causing a slump in hotel occupancy in the mid-1980s. In consequence, notwithstanding its low costs, the potential of Pietermaritzburg's tourist-historic city has not been fully realised in the 1980s, although it is the object of sophisticated management and marketing as discussed below.

Change presently occurring in the national and local environments of Pietermaritzburg, however, bears strongly upon the evolution of the tourist-historic city. The scale of unrest in the surrounding black townships in the late 1980s has had little effect on the inner city but has heightened white consciousness of its discordance with the metropolitan reality. The encroachment of black informal retailing into the white 'sacred space' (Western, 1981) of the city centre has met with growing acceptance by the city's white population. Local government policy, liberal by South African standards, is eroding the constraints of 'petty' apartheid: public facilities have been desegregated and public transport is now run by Kwazulu, while the Legislature (redundant as such) has acquired a multiracial identity as the seat of the incipient Natal–Kwazulu Joint Executive Authority. National government policy has been more resistant to change; nevertheless, it has opened the CBD to non-white ownership and permitted the desegregation of restaurants and hotels, which in the relatively progressive local environment have significantly enhanced the non-white profile in the city's economy (the President of the Chamber of Commerce in 1988 was black). The potential for non-white tourism has been augmented by this desegregation, particularly as entrepreneurs have realised that a growing proportion of stagnant consumer spending power is in non-white hands; how the new tourists will relate to the tourist-historic city remains to be seen, but they are likely to respond to the subtle changes it is now undergoing and, in fact, to give momentum to them. Prominent among these changes is the growing recognition of the heritage, and tourist, value of ethnic diversity in cities. Haswell (1984) has argued for the recognition of the Indian contribution to Natal's urban heritage, and in the past decade several National Monuments of Indian origin have been recognised. In Durban the particularly conspicuous Indian heritage is a well recognised tourist attraction, as is the Cape

Malay district of Cape Town. The acceptance of the black African role in the tourist-historic city is more problematical: although it was largely built by black hands it essentially excludes black identity, an exclusion made more explicit by black influx control legislation from the 1920s, which peaked under formal apartheid with the attempt to deny permanent status even to the limited black townships permitted within urban boundaries. Extensive demolition of black and even long-established Coloured districts has occurred (Western, 1981). Since the 1970s the national government has reluctantly acknowledged black permanence in urban areas and has ostensibly abandoned influx control in the late 1980s; but recognition of black urban heritage, as against sufferance, requires a leap of imagination apparently beyond it. However, Pietermaritzburg has reached its 150th anniversary (1988) confronted with changing political and economic reality, and is attempting that leap of imagination: it has produced a planning blueprint which will further revitalise its central area around a pedestrian-oriented Civic Square in which the multiracial character of the tourist-historic city will for the first time be explicitly acknowledged. The plan calls, among 'other things, for the creation of mosaic pavement in which the historical role of the black population will be portrayed. Multiracial evolution of this white 'sacred space' is, in fact, already in progress through the changes noted above and through minor retreat from group area rigidity. Beyond these developments, planning for post-apartheid Pietermaritzburg, and the blending of its tourist-historic city with the forces of socio-economic change, is already in progress (Wills *et al.*, 1987).

The tourist-historic organisation of Pietermaritzburg is relatively sophisticated: management and more particularly marketing are parallel to that in the Western world, reflecting its continuing predominantly 'first-world' identity. The role of the national government, which is unitary rather than federal, is primarily the periodic designation of buildings as protected National Monuments. There are currently 24, of limited value for area conservation and vernacular heritage, and thus inevitably biased against 'non-white' structures. This inadequate protective base has been accompanied by a limited popular conservation ethic (Haswell, 1984). However, the city planning authorities have latterly proposed conservation districts and listed historic buildings, albeit still mainly 'white', with a high degree of public control over their conservation (City of Pietermaritzburg, 1986). Also, extensive rehabilitation of the main Victorian heritage has occurred, through public and private agencies, and major excesses of incompatible redevelopment have been avoided. Local academics were early actors both in the political processes of conservation and in tourist-historic promotion. Despite the relative lateness of historic resource management, the Pietermaritzburg Publicity Association, a non-profit organisation formed by local business, citizens and the City Council in 1931, is unusually prominent by Western comparisons in tourism and general marketing activity; this includes tours, gift retailing, local distribution of literature, and national and international promotions of the 'City of Beauty and History' (Jones, 1988). It is a prominent example of similar associations in Durban and elsewhere in South Africa, illustrating the blending of public and private interests in marketing referred to in Chapter 6. International promotion is focused upon Western Europe and the few politically friendly countries, such as Taiwan; as racial distortions slowly diminish, the prospects for overseas market penetration may be expected to improve, although for the immediate future they will continue to be constrained by the stigma of the city's national identity. Satour, the national tourist marketing organisation, greatly assists its marketing efforts; its overseas constraints have been partly offset by its recent success in encouraging internal tourism, as the depressed currency has held most South Africans to domestic travel (Jones, 1988). A visitor survey in early 1988 indicated a predominance of South African and UK visitors to Pietermaritzburg, and the predominance of architecture, history and museums in attracting visitors in general (Pietermaritzburg Publicity Association, 1988); like Victoria, BC, and peers elsewhere, it trades heavily upon the imperial past. Themes familiar from tourist-historic marketing in the Western world include Pietermaritzburg's successful promotion as a conference centre, and as the Gateway City to the regional scenic and historic attractions of Natal, initiating a 'battlefields excursion' to the historic sites of Zulu-Boer-British conflict. Within the city, modest publicity is given to Indian sites (Hindu temple and mosque) and to Sobantu, an internal black township, where cultural crafts are publicised. In 1988, however, the 150th anniversary provided the focus for marketing (as in Durban, Chapter 8, in 1985), and in its honour the city centre was decorated with banners which provided a backcloth for a series of parades and special events.

Notwithstanding, the forces of change in Pietermaritzburg raise the question of what future may realistically be expected for this well articulated tourist-historic city in an environment of post-colonial liberation: can it achieve political reconciliation, or at least acceptance for its economic benefits, whilst avoiding demographic suffocation by Third World urbanisation pressures? Western (1985) has argued, with particular reference to Cape Town, that the colonial identity will become increasingly submerged and irrelevant even though its structures may linger on; whether this need be so in a medium-sized historic city merits further comment, particularly in relation to Harare.

Harare Harare, Zimbabwe (metropolitan population *c.* 900,000, 1983) was founded as Salisbury, the capital of the new British colony of Rhodesia, in 1890; its central square, until 1988 Cecil Square, is coextensive with the original Fort Salisbury set up by Rhodes' Pioneer Column, and is unquestionably 'sacred space' to the white population of Zimbabwe. The city is of particular interest to the present discussion because it achieved majority rule, nationally and municipally, only in 1980; the subsequent fate of its tourist-historic identity can be monitored, with an eye to the fact that its centennial is in 1990. During its ninety years of white minority rule, growth was a higher priority than the conservation of its physical fabric, which was not generally perceived in heritage terms (Kay and Smout, 1977); none the less, Cecil Square, the adjacent Parliament and Cathedral, the British South Africa Company's first office building and a number of other buildings, monuments and historic markers represented an anchor of social identity to the settler population and a rudimentary tourist-historic city, which was augmented by the creation of the First Street Mall and some conservation of the early commercial streetscape in the 1970s (Tunbridge, 1984) (Plates 9.5a and 9.5b). Since majority rule in 1980, the settler heritage has been treated fairly gently, although statues of Rhodes quickly disappeared and a minority of the city's streets were renamed from white pioneers to black African nationalist leaders. The government's urban preoccupation, however, has been the control and development of the black townships which are rapidly expanding on the edge of Harare; it has also built monuments on the edge of the city (the Heroes' Acre war memorial, and national stadium) which have initiated an alternative nationalist urban heritage. Thus while the settler heritage continues to exist, it is subject to relative neglect, increasing marginalisation and periodic specific displacement; a pattern somewhat suggestive of the British heritage in French Canada. In 1988, the colonial panorama monument on the Kopje, overlooking the inner city, was intact but in some disrepair; but Cecil Square was renamed Africa Unity Square, so that its fundamental heritage significance was no longer marked, although it remained indelible to the tourist with background knowledge. It appears that the focus of white Zimbabwean activity and identity is subtly shifting from the city centre to focal points in the still predominantly white northern suburbs; the district centre of Borrowdale, in particular, projects a quasi-English village atmosphere which preserves a familiar ambience in its shops and cafés and is also relatively immune from the petty crime which besets the city centre as its Third World identity gradually increases. Concern for both white sensitivity and tourist-historic identity in Harare is now a secondary priority at best, and the city's impending centennial, in marked contrast to Pietermaritzburg's and others (Chapter 2), is politically contentious; government is taking no action, and the university's 1990 conference is not directly linked because of overtones of colonialism.

Other Southern African insights The prevailing climate of tolerance but marginalisation in Zimbabwe is not necessarily mirrored by the attitude of other Southern African states to their settler heritage, and to the tourist-historic identity which derives from it. In Swaziland and Lesotho, for

Plate 9.5a Harare: former Pioneer Column memorial from former Cecil Square; both now commemorate Organisation of Africa Unity.

Plate 9.5b Harare: St Mary's Cathedral, continuing repository of colonial heritage; from Africa Unity (Cecil) Square (JET 1982, reproduced from *The Canadian Geographer*, 1984, with permission)

example, generally conservative governments have maintained the limited settler urban heritage that they possess. More conspicuously, Malawi has identified a number of its older colonial structures as National Monuments, and more generally has not marginalised the colonial heritage; this is particularly apparent in Blantyre and Zomba, and elsewhere in the context of mission stations and the suppression of slavery. The urban heritage of British Southern Africa, however, aside from South Africa and from Harare and Bulawayo in Zimbabwe, is essentially one of small cities with quite limited white settler heritage and comparatively little contemporary pressure from rural-urban migration; this limits the insight they can offer for potential change of the tourist-historic city in a mid-sized South African city. Existing study (Wills *et al.*, 1987) of post-apartheid transition in Mafikeng (ex-Mafeking, Bophuthatswana, South African homeland) and Windhoek (Namibia) is similarly of limited value because these cases are respectively small and tentative. If there is a lesson to be drawn for Pietermaritzburg from these comparative examples, however, it must surely be that the best chance for the survival of a tourist-historic city based primarily upon minority settler heritage lies in the absence of racial hostility; reconciliation came perilously late in Zimbabwe and is, for Pietermaritzburg, currently the focus of frequently anguished local debate against a tense and unpromising national background. It may be noted that Pietermaritzburg's status as a 'Rhodesia in exile' for a significant number of former Rhodesian whites is unlikely to ease its transition into a reconciled post-apartheid future.

Pietermaritzburg: future constraints The planners of post-apartheid Pietermaritzburg are already addressing the likely impact of reform upon its historic continuity (Wills *et al.*, 1987). Drawing insight from the case of Harare and those noted above, they point to an intensification of residential and commercial pressure upon the city centre when the Group Areas Act is repealed; they argue that the historic city will be partly protected by anticipated enclaves of high-income, essentially white, gentrification, but that otherwise there will be a major planning problem of reconciling intensification pressures with environmental quality, in which the conservation of specific heritage buildings will likely depend upon their designation as National Monuments. Whether the national government of the day would be motivated to enact such designation is, of course, an open question; which brings us back to the importance of racial reconciliation to the substantial survival of the tourist-historic city under majority rule.

The constrained tourist-historicity of Pietermaritzburg is not therefore simply the direct and indirect result of apartheid at the present time; it is likely to continue beyond the end of apartheid in a different form, namely a struggle for survival against inundation by an indifferent (if not hostile) majority population. Its prospects for overcoming this ultimate constraint depend in particular upon racial reconciliation, a modification of the heritage identity in a multiracial direction and a general awareness of the economic rewards of marketing the tourist-historic city. Fortunately for the city, there are some grounds for cautious optimism on all three counts, notwithstanding township violence during its 150th year.

The significance of Pietermaritzburg for our general theme extends beyond the specifics of South Africa, however: it reflects the much wider vexed question of minority heritage (particularly but by no means only a problem of Third World tourist-historic cities) which is likely to create greater or lesser constraints both for its conservation and for its economic exploitation. Jerusalem and Bethlehem during the Palestinian *intifada* are a further, if more complex, illustration. The question of 'whose heritage?' may very well prove to be the most pervasive constraint to the full development of the tourist-historic city (Tunbridge, 1984). It may be most in evidence between the scale of the world metropolis, in which cultural plurality is usually difficult to deny, and the small city, in which cultural singularity is both most likely and least contentious. In the case of South Africa, smaller and more local historic gems such as Graaf Reinet and Matjesfontein in the Cape, and Pilgrims Rest in the Transvaal, are less encumbered by the constraints on minority heritage which beset a regional administrative centre such as Pietermaritzburg.

Urban revitalisation: socio-economic motivations and the tourist-historic city

We noted in the context of the large metropolis (Chapter 8) that a process of revitalisation has strongly affected the inner cities of the Western world in the past two decades, with particularly dramatic significance in the New World. Its interface with the tourist-historic city is so important that it requires further consideration, and since most beneficiaries are medium-sized cities, it is appropriate to refine this interface here.

Inner-city revitalisation is a complex process involving change in many socio-economic aspects and resulting from a variety of causative influences, which vary locally but are generally considered to include changing demographic structure, affordability of housing, cost of energy and fashion; these are typically interwoven with revaluation of the inner city as a heritage resource and, for this and other reasons, as a location possessing desired environmental amenity. The revitalisation process has generated an extensive literature which has tended to emphasise the socio-economic aspects of internal residential change, and to neglect the tourist-historic dimension—notwithstanding the fact that the tourist-historic city is manifestly part of the revitalisation process, is based upon essentially the same heritage resource and must interrelate with socio-economic changes affecting the city's own population.

Inner-city revitalisation in Canada, as one representative illustration, has been extensively discussed in terms of internal socio-economic forces. It has been established that upgrading residential areas relate to factors such as proximity to existing élite residential districts, cultural institutions, environmental amenities and heritage architecture (Ley, 1988). The relationship of residential gentrification to the growing provision of specialist, élite-oriented retail and service amenities has received tangential attention but little direct examination (see however Jones, 1984; Tunbridge, 1986a and b, 1987a). The significance of both the upgraded residential areas and retail/service amenities to the tourist-historic city has, to date, been largely a matter of implicit assumption. As we noted in Chapter 5, the degree to which the tourist-historic function abets, or possibly conflicts with, the development of amenities for the local population requires exploration. Perhaps the closest approach to a balanced discussion of revitalisation in both local and tourist contexts is the specific case of waterfront revitalisation, which has become a focus of academic study in its own right and which is widely understood to have major significance for both internal and external consumers of the city's amenities (Hoyle, Pinder and Husain, 1988).

It is well established (Lipton, 1977; Ley, 1988; *et al.*) that urban revitalisation in general is most highly developed in white-collar cities possessing a high level of amenity, or the potential to reclaim it, and least in blue-collar and/or poorer communities. In the former (such as Ottawa, Halifax, Vancouver and Toronto in the Canadian context) it is quite clear that the development of the tourist-historic city cannot be understood without reference to the wider process of socio-economic revitalisation centred upon the city's own population. The reverse, however, may also be true, as is evident in the case of Ottawa/Hull's National Gallery and Museum of Civilization; but this remains to be investigated. It is easy to identify the reciprocity between general urban revitalisation and the tourist-historic city in cases where both are well advanced, although tracing how their interlinkage has evolved is an altogether more daunting prospect.

In blue-collar and/or poorer cities this interlinkage acquires a very particular interest. This is because development of the tourist-historic city may be the *sole* key to more general urban revitalisation, with all the socio-economic significance this implies. Accordingly, the development and marketing of the tourist-historic city as a means of overcoming negative urban images, and levering wider revitalisation, will now be considered.

Negative images: marketing the tourist-historic city to promote revitalisation

The attempted stimulation of tourist-historicity to boost otherwise limited urban economies has now become commonplace. In both Europe and North America, however, there are dramatic recent examples of depressed early industrial communities which have succeeded in promoting their tourist-historic attributes and substantially reviving their economies thereby (Soyez, 1986). A prerequisite for this success has been the extension of the market perception of heritage to include industrial structures and technology, and more generally Victoriana; prime illustrations are the revitalisation of Robert Owen's New Lanark (Scotland), and the recognition of Ironbridge Gorge (Shropshire, England) by UNESCO as a World Heritage Site, marketed as the 'birthplace of the Industrial Revolution' by the local authority (National Trust, 1988; West, 1988). This heritage dimension is commonly blended with other regional attributes, whether architectural, historic or literary.

A notable national-scale illustration was the establishment in 1987 of a marketing consortium, under the auspices of the English Tourist Board, to promote 13 mainly medium-sized multifunctional cities. This 'Great English Cities Promotion' is remarkable in that the places included were not historic gems, but generally declining industrial 'coke-towns', with negative, tourist-repellent, images. Conversional marketing (see Chapter 6) chose not to ignore the industrial image but to capitalise upon it. The nineteenth-century textile mills of Bradford, Leeds and Manchester, the potteries of Stoke, the docks of Plymouth, Newcastle and especially Liverpool were revalued as 'industrial archaeology', cleaned up and packaged as world economic heritage, combined with Victorian literary romanticism that had already secured a world market thanks to the spread of the English language and specifically British literature, and sold with resounding success. The Brontës, Bennett, Dickens, Victorian Music Hall and a succession of film and television costume dramas created a world market for a heritage that these towns could produce in abundance. The internal and external urban markets were mutually reinforcing. The very multifunctionality of these towns and their copious provision of urban services was a major selling point to visitors, while the presence of visitors added much needed economic support to these services, and provided a boost to local self-esteem and civic pride. Some effort is being made, for example in Bradford, to include recent ethnic minority culture in the marketing package, with what long-term success remains to be seen (see Chapter 10).

The most noteworthy North American illustration of an industrial town turning an extremely negative image into tourist-historic success is Lowell, Massachusetts. While Lowell is exceptional, what is critically important is that innumerable industrial towns in the largely depressed north-eastern United States seek to emulate its success. Given the limited market and the reality that a specific tourist-historic theme cannot be infinitely duplicated, many will fail to do so; but Lowell has established a geographical pattern of *aspiration* in the quest for economic revitalisation of faltering industial towns (Fleming, 1981).

Lowell has a specific claim to fame in that it is regarded as the first industrial town in the USA, having been founded by mercantile enterprise and capital from nearby Boston in the 1820s, thus initiating an American industrial revolution which closely followed that in Lancashire and was largely based upon derivative technology (Vance, 1977). As in Lancashire, it was founded as a textile manufacturing centre, but based upon water power as well as water transport. The multi-storey mills, similar to those of northern England, are thus set in an environment of canal waterfronts, a factor which has materially assisted their subsequent promotion to tourists. Following a long industrial decline, by the 1960s most of the mills had closed and Lowell's physical and economic condition had become degraded; this projected a totally negative image of unemployment and deprivation, again paralleling the Northern English pattern.

Stimulation of the tourist-historic city resulted, characteristically, from the persistence of a small number of local boosters. They succeeded in generating Congressional pressure for the National Parks Service to create a novel urban-industrial National Historical Park in Lowell (Quasten and Soyez, 1987). The National Historical Park was created in 1978 as an unprecedented co-operative venture between the National Parks Service, which has acquired limited parcels of land and acts as overall co-ordinator, promoter and interpreter, and the state and municipal governments (Karabatsos, 1980). There is an explicit intent to 'spin off' a wider economic renaissance from the success of the tourist-historic city, and this has been significantly achieved with the attraction of several major high-technology employers to the city.

The National Historical Park and Heritage State Park are focused on the Visitor Center, which occupies space along with a variety of commercial, retail and office tenants in a restored textile mill (Plates 9.6a and 9.6b), and provides historical interpretive material. The NPS also conducts tours, both on foot and by water, of the mills, workers' boarding houses, canals and associated industrial heritage, which is gradually being rehabilitated and reused. In addition, the NPS plays an advisory role in matters such as revitalisation of the main street.

Through its prestige and resources, the National Parks Service has been the ideal, and probably indispensable, medium to reverse Lowell's image and create its tourist-historic city. Its role, however, raises questions concerning the wider viability of this type of rescue operation. Under no circumstances could the level of NPS expertise and funding committed to Lowell be freely repeated elsewhere. Furthermore, recent conservative US administrations have opposed such enterprise, which is peripheral to the core commitments of the NPS. Apart from its intrinsic value, however, the NPS is mindful of the practical conservation value of what we term the tourist-historic city in relieving pressure on the overused rural/wilderness sections of the national parks system. This is a point of global conservation significance to which we shall return in Chapter 10.

The success of cities such as Bradford and Lowell in overcoming negative images is therefore important in demonstrating both socio-economic

Plate 9.6a Lowell: NPS ranger-led tour by canalside industrial exhibit; City Hall in background (JET 1982)

Plate 9.6b Lowell: adaptively reused mill, containing National Historical Park Visitor Center (JET 1982)

revitalisation and environmental benefits which might be gained by similar tourist-historic stimulation elsewhere. Further beneficiaries must, however, be geographically selective in face of resource and market realities.

Waterfront revitalisation as tourist-historic stimulant

We have established that waterfront revitalisation has become closely interwoven with the development of the tourist-historic city, since it is now a leading edge of urban revitalisation more generally. At this point it is appropriate to review the waterfront phenomenon, specifically to illustrate the extreme importance it may have to the development of a tourist-historic city in otherwise marginal situations, with particular reference to the case of Portsmouth, England.

The process of systematic waterfront revitalisation began in the United States, where by the 1960s the need to reclaim derelict inner cities had become more urgent than elsewhere in the Western world and where the market potential of underused, centrally located land was quickly perceived by the most enterprising communities (e.g. San Francisco, Boston). The phenomenon has now diffused throughout the Western world and, with qualifications, to some cities beyond it, for example Hong Kong, Cape Town and various Third World tourist cities (Hoyle, Pinder and Husain, 1988). Its global relevance to the tourist-historic city may be most apparent outside of Europe, given the widespread and relatively recent dependence of New World cities on some kind of river, lake or seafront for communication and/or industrial activity.

Waterfront revitalisation is typically predicated upon the decline of port and related commercial and industrial waterfront land-uses, and perceived environmental needs to correct the blight thus engendered and reduce water pollution. Traditional inner-city port locations have declined for a number of reasons, but most fundamentally because of changing technology favouring new, scale-efficient urban periphery locations with space to expand and freedom from friction with contemporary inner-city land-uses. These factors are more fully discussed in Hoyle, Pinder and Husain (1988). They have broadly coincided with the more general move to revitalise the inner city, which has led to the realisation that the waterfront represents a classic zone of discard containing major revitalisation opportunities (Chapter 8). Once the negative image of waterfront proximity had been reversed, which in North America occurred with significant clean-up operations on the Great Lakes and elsewhere in the early 1970s, the waterfront became the leading edge of inner-city revitalisation: specifically, it was perceived as a 'windfall' resource of redevelopment land, an amenity to which public access (long denied or discouraged) should be restored, and a major heritage resource since the oldest structures in the city are commonly found there and their maritime and sometimes naval links are phasing into a past legacy to be remembered. Potential incompatibilities between these resource evaluations, and the resulting conflict resolution between multiplicity of agents, have been considered elsewhere by Tunbridge (1988).

From our present perspective the tourist-leisure dimension, which draws chiefly upon the amenity and heritage resources, is a major contender for prime waterfront space but not in every case ultimately dominant. Furthermore, tourist-leisure uses do not always directly utilise the historic environment (as in Quincy Market, Boston), but invariably do so indirectly in that they provide a foil for adjacent heritage buildings or at the very least bring back a popular awareness of the historic waterfront (as in Harborplace, Baltimore).

The general contribution of the waterfront to the tourist-historic city has been extensively illustrated in Chapters 7–9. There are, however, cases where waterfront revitalisation has played a quite disproportionate role in its development, in otherwise marginal situations. In some cases the waterfront has provided the indispensable catalyst to the tourist-historic city, in poorer cities in which the latter has provided the sole momentum for revitalisation; despite its complexity as a large city, this is substantially true of Liverpool, where the Albert Dock is a globally prominent illustration (Hoyle, Pinder and Husain, 1988; Freeman, 1989). We noted that the waterfront element has been an important asset in Lowell, where external forces were enlisted as critical intervention for the city's tourist-historic-based reclamation. In Saint John, New Brunswick, which lacked such external support, waterfront revitalisation has virtually alone created an effective tourist-historic city and stimulated some wider urban revitalisation. Saint John is an industrial port with little white-collar employment, relatively high unemployment and until recently a quite run-down urban environment. Seeing tourist potential in its impending bicentennial (1984), and the nationalist associations of its founding (by the United Empire Loyalists), it revitalised Market Slip, the central waterfront at which the Loyalists had landed, while a private developer built the adjacent Market Square, a festival market centre incorporating waterfront warehouses with new construction; a library, convention centre and first-class hotel were integrated on the adjacent waterfront, and the whole complex was operating by 1984 (Lindgren, 1984). It has subsequently become the *de facto* city centre, attracting major international meetings and hosting royal visits, and a noted stop on the tourist circuit of the Maritime provinces. Subsequently there has been significant upgrading of conservation and tourism in the adjacent inner city and increased evidence of revitalisation activity there.

Portsmouth (See Figure 9.8) The case of Portsmouth is of exceptional interest in that it has developed a major tourist-historic identity, largely

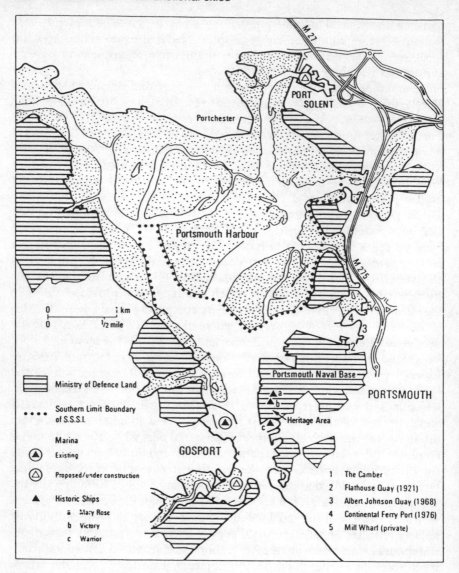

Figure 9.8 *Portsmouth; courtesy Hoyle et al, 1988, R. Riley and Portsmouth Polytechnic Department of Geography. Harbour area; Southsea and other coastal tourist attractions 1–2 km to south–east*

during the 1980s, almost entirely on the basis of its waterfront and immediately adjacent areas. Its historic role as a naval base and dockyard town declined sharply, and in the inner city there has been a need both to replace the lost employment and to reuse waterfront facilities vacated by the navy. The city's tourist role was traditionally based upon the seaside resort district of Southsea, with a limited tourist-historic component focused upon HMS *Victory* just inside the naval base, Southsea Castle and Old

Portsmouth. The development of the tourist-historic city was impaired by Portsmouth's lack of a clear image, single focus or legible structure, by the severity of wartime bombing in destroying much of its historic fabric and by difficulties of access to and within the island site.

However, recent civic-co-ordinated enterprise has successfully built up a major tourist-historic profile from this limited base. Reawakened interest in the nineteenth-century city has helped by bringing the distinctive 'village' ambience of Southsea into the tourist-historic city, and more recently the demolition of a power station has permitted the further infill enhancement of Old Portsmouth. But the prime tourist attractions are on the waterfront. The D-Day Museum, containing the 'Overlord' Tapestry, was added to the Southsea seafront in 1983, and the historic role of Portsmouth as the D-Day command centre has thereby been promoted through an entirely new structure. The recovery of the sixteenth-century warship *Mary Rose* from the seabed in 1982, and its subsequent presentation with a museum inside the naval base, has provided an equivalent tourist magnet. In 1988 the restored nineteenth-century battleship HMS *Warrior* was added, permitting the marketing of a three-ship/museum historical sequence in the Portsmouth Naval Heritage Project. Furthermore, the Royal Navy Submarine Museum at Gosport has added a museum ship in the 1980s, and is linked to other waterfront attractions by water transport. Also, waterfront revitalisation for residences and commercial use is continuing around the Camber Dock (Old Portsmouth), the original medieval harbour, and may increase its tourist accessibility as against the preceding marine industries. In addition, marina facilities have been constructed at several locations inside Portsmouth Harbour, and elsewhere, including part of a new waterfront development at Port Solent (Riley and Shurmer-Smith, 1988).

The city's promotion with slogans such as 'Flagship of Maritime England' and 'Birthplace of Australia' (commemorating the sailing of the First Fleet from Portsmouth in 1787) have provided strong mental images to add to its tangible heritage. Its success in drawing tourists is particularly attibutable to skilful improvement and exploitation of its accessibility: it is the main port, hence intervening opportunity, *en route* to the Isle of Wight and Channel Islands, and has displaced Southampton as the regional passenger port for the Continent (Riley and Shurmer-Smith, 1988), which provides both an opportunity to break the journey to advantage and a spectacular view of the naval base and attractions of Portsmouth Harbour from the decks of ferries. In 1989, it exploited its new-found tourist centrality as the focus of a regional 'Defence of the Realm' heritage promotion.

A problem area is the effective incorporation of the outstanding naval base heritage into the tourist-historic city: despite the navy's reduced space requirements its sensitivity over security has hampered public access to most of its historic buildings and delayed their profitable adaptive reuse, although by 1988 a heritage area was recognised around the *Victory*, *Mary Rose* and *Warrior* by agreement with the city and conservation interests (Riley, 1987;

Riley and Shurmer-Smith, 1988). In the long run, Portsmouth must benefit more fully from the exceptional tourist-historic appeal of naval waterfronts, already being demonstrated elsewhere (e.g. Chatham, Boston, Bermuda, Pearl Harbor) (Tunbridge, 1987b).

Riley and Shurmer-Smith (1988) point out that Portsmouth, like other successful centres of waterfront revitalisation, represents a fusion of positive 'bottom-up' local enterprise with favourable 'top-down' international and national factors, of which the naval evolution is generally one.

Overall, Portsmouth demonstrates waterfront development and revitalisation which is heavily and successfully tourist-dependent, in part through the unusual extension of the port function to meet tourist needs. Furthermore the waterfront and its immediate environs are virtually coextensive with the tourist-historic city. Naturally, the city's long-standing links with the sea and with seaside visitors would tend to bias it thus, even without the strength and successful promotion of recent waterfront developments; as we noted in Chapter 5, however, some market segmentation exists between seaside and historic tourists. Portsmouth is, none the less, a powerful statement of the role the waterfront can play in the development of the tourist-historic city, specifically one of medium size. It may also be a powerful statement of the ideological sentiments, in this case imperialist and militarist according to Bradbeer and Moon (1987), upon which contemporary heritage marketing is based; to this we shall return in Chapter 10.

The medium-sized multifunctional city: a synthesis

The above examples, including those introduced in specific contexts of revitalisation, have attempted to illuminate the characteristics and problems of tourist-historicity in medium-sized multifunctional cities. While they cannot provide a comprehensive image of what is, in any case, a very broad urban type, they do suggest some recurrent tendencies in tourist-historic development among cities of this scale. They are small enough to have a good chance of substantial historical survival, in some cases containing within them some of the most notable tourist-historic gems. They are, however, large enough to experience political pressure in either a favourable or unfavourable direction; to experience social and intercultural tensions relating to whose heritage is being purveyed and who benefits and pays in the process; and to experience substantial environmental costs, notably in traffic and parking pressures, from tourist-historic patronage.

We have attempted to convey something of the range of tourist-historic conditions occurring within this broad urban type, from resource to demand-tending cases, with different degrees of emphasis upon the development of tourist-historicity. We have noted that the range includes some cases such as Norwich or Charleston which became major centres almost unconsciously, others such as Ottawa or Groningen favoured by degrees of nurturing, and yet others handicapped by constraints; although it is implicit that these are net assessments of more complex processes operating within them. These processes of tourist-historic development evolve over time, at varying paces according to resource endowment, capacity and will to exploit it, and the vagaries of tourist fashion. Individual cases, such as Norwich, Charleston and Ottawa, may shift from stimulation to defensive strategies (cf. Chapter 6) as success breeds pressures. Within the range of tourist-historic conditions, medium-sized cities are commonly engaged in wider aspects of urban revitalisation; and at this scale tourist-historic development may very well, as in Lowell or Portsmouth, constitute its leading edge.

The case studies have elaborated further the sources of critical intervention, and the combinations in which they can occur in tourist-historic development. In addition to the various governmental, commercial and institutional agents, the enterprise of individual citizens must never be overlooked. Direct enterprise by academics, such as geographers in Pietermaritzburg, St. Johns (Newfoundland) or Victoria (BC), and numerous others elsewhere, is an important indication that academic involvement extends beyond the dispassionate evaluation attempted by the present authors. Intervention by various combinations of these factors has fulfilled three recurring roles: that of 'catalyst', providing the critical stimulus to others at the critical moment; that of 'concierge', protecting not only the fabric of the historic city but equally the heritage of all its citizens; and finally that of 'referee' when choice between tourist-historic and other urban functions is necessary. The very success of the tourist-historic function will often require further intervention if it is not to threaten the multifunctionality of medium-sized cities.

10 Conclusions

Values, contentious issues and the present perspective

Throughout this volume we have alluded to the impact of tourist-historic development on different facets of human geography. Attention has been drawn to some of the tensions and the opportunities in our society which this phenomenon has brought into focus. While our perspective has been as far as possible that of dispassionate observers and interpreters of its significance, nevertheless value judgements are sometimes implicit in our words. The preceding chapters were not written in order to promote the historic city, its conservation, or packaging as heritage; nor to encourage the development of tourism, despite our dependence for subject matter on the products of those who have preserved the past and marketed it to tourists. This book should not, therefore, be side-tracked by debate as to what should exist; our prime objective has been to elucidate what does exist and must be seen in clearer focus by geographers of all persuasions, and by urban practitioners at large, because of its often major impingement, welcome or not, upon their own concerns. In the process, of course, we may have helped to clarify the perspectives of those who do choose to take explicit value positions on our subject matter. The conclusion of our mandate none the less requires us to comment more extensively on the problems and potential which, depending on value positions, could be identified with a phenomenon as geographically potent as the tourist-historic city; and to confront some of the inevitably contentious issues that have arisen from the preceding analysis. These issues are generally as interconnected as the many other strands in the geographical web, but it is useful to group them under socio-political, cultural, economic and environmental headings.

Socio-political issues

The central socio-political issue of the tourist-historic city has two facets: whose heritage is being conserved and marketed, and to whom do the consequent benefits and costs accrue? These have been persistent threads throughout the preceding chapters. At this point we are concerned primarily with social class and its political ramifications; the cultural dimension is interrelated but involves further aspects which require its separate consideration.

Ideology Debate concerning the political ideological assumptions and intentions of heritage is not new. The deliberate destruction of surviving artefacts from the past has been a feature of most political revolutions, as equally has been the preservation of such objects by conservative regimes. It is not surprising therefore that the very success of the conservation movement, and its manifestation in the tourist-historic city, should have resulted in a sharp questioning of the socio-political messages inherent in the heritage industry. It is clear from the examples described in this book that the tourist-historic city can be motivated by, and itself propagate, ideas that may be described as imperialist, capitalist, racist, nationalist, separatist, socialist, militarist, sexist, pacifist, or indeed almost any other set of political dogmas. The existence of this possibility is not in itself the problem, at least once the idea of a neutral, value-free heritage is abandoned as unrealistic, and the implications of this to the tourist-historic city are appreciated. The central questions to be addressed are, first, which socio-political assumptions and messages, determined by whom, are to be encouraged, tolerated or discouraged by a particular tourist-historic development; and secondly, are particular ideologies implicit in the basic concept of the tourist-historic city, as described?

The authors are convinced that the answers to both questions can be found pragmatically. The second they would dismiss with a curt 'no'. Despite the success of Horne (1984), Hardy (1988) and others in finding clear cases where the tourist-historic city has been shaped in the service of a particular political ideology, other diametrically opposed ideologies can be found among the cases considered above. The tourist-historic city is not value-free but it need not express any particular set of values. The answers to the first, and more taxing, question are most likely to be found by examining the practical results of tourist-historic development in terms of the distribution of its costs and its benefits through society. Regardless of the answers that emerge, the development of the tourist-historic city will not be arrested nor will the need to study it be reduced; only the tranquillity and the direction of its evolution will be at issue.

In any event, the socio-political messages conveyed by heritage interpretation have been shown in Chapter 2 to be in practice extremely varied, generally mixed and capable of variable reception. It has been suggested that the social climate in different societies, such as Canada and the UK, may be variously predisposed to judge similar heritage as, for example, militaristic or nationalistic in a negative sense (Tunbridge, 1989).

Residential gentrification An important vehicle of social tension over residential heritage is of course gentrification, which needs no further comment regarding its well-known cost to poorer social classes (in the West European context see the discussion in Burtenshaw *et al.*, 1981). Note, however, the paradox that the recognition of vernacular residential heritage is directly inimical to its retention by poorer occupants, who accordingly bear the cost of recognition rather than benefit fairly from it. While tourist-historic development is not of course the principal cause of gentrification, it is commonly an accessory before, during or after the fact.

The issues however are more fundamental than the simplistic view that conservation necessarily results in deportation and repopulation. The two central difficulties in this respect to emerge from the cases above are, first, that different social groups place different valuation on conserved buildings and areas; and second, that if private finance is to support the creation of the tourist-historic city, then constraints on the operation of free-market profit-making will be difficult to enforce. These two dilemmas have confounded attempts of social democratic (as in Sheffield, UK) or communist (as in Bologna, Italy) city governments actively to promote urban conservation while committed to preventing its gentrification effects.

Employment A less clear-cut social issue is that of employment. There is well-articulated concern about the nature of employment in inner-city/waterfront revitalisation areas such as London's Docklands (Church, 1988), but this involves a displacement of blue-collar by white-collar opportunities in which tourist-historic development (although commonly an accessory factor) is not the main focus of concern. It would be appropriate, however, to look more closely at employment generation by the latter. Since, like tourism in general, it is a personal service industry it will commonly be non-unionised, minimum-wage, seasonal or ephemeral in nature and thus, arguably, encouraging an undesirable exploitation of economically marginal groups. Some of it, even in Western urban economies and most certainly elsewhere, is in the informal sector. Differences occur between jurisdictions in degree of labour protection; in 1988 that in New South Wales was clearly stronger than that in Ontario and most Canadian provinces, for example. None the less, a social focus of investigation and, for some, bone of contention exists in the employment structure of the tourist-historic city; irrespective of whose heritage is being marketed, there is a potential issue of social equity in the distribution of the rewards which could affect its continuing development. In tourist economies based upon seasonal student labour this issue may be masked, but not necessarily indefinitely.

The general issue, which relates equally to other service industries, is whether the sort of employment primarily generated encourages the maintenance of a pool of disadvantaged and exploited labour, distinguished by income, race or gender, or is a welcome employment opportunity, often the only realistic option for such groups, especially in the inner city. Note, however, that the restoration work intrinsic to tourist-historic development is often highly skilled and labour-intensive; quality employment generated in Hartlepool, where it was sorely needed, by refitting HMS *Warrior* for display in Portsmouth, has been extensively replicated elsewhere.

Access to benefits A further potential social issue is the affordability of tourist-historic services to many of the local population. This is only a reflection of the more generally recognised problem of unequal access to urban benefits and costs. The tourist-historic city conveys a wide variety of priced and unpriced services; some, such as environmental amenity, are public goods available free of charge. Again, the general issue is whether such benefits, and the concomitant public costs, such as physical congestion, pollution, litter and the like, are evenly spread through all social groups. The creation of the tourist-historic city alters the pattern of priced goods, including many services and land values. This distributes benefits to some and costs to others. Perhaps the most visible index is the increased cost of eating and drinking establishments, but less obvious will be rises in rent levels, and the disappearance of many providers of cheaper goods and services in response to these increases. The impact of the tourist-historic city in these respects is once again entangled with that of wider revitalisation forces.

Further perspectives While the social overtones of the tourist-historic city can be problematic, it would be unreasonable to deny that, in the absence of severe social tension, the development of an image which is saleable to the outside world could be a socially unifying source of local pride in a heritage not previously perceived. Such a notion might be regarded with suspicion in radical circles but this does not make it unworthy of investigation; it has been actively promoted by Soyez (1986), with particular reference to the German Saarland, a declining industrial area.

Finally, it should be noted that in Third World cities tourist-historic employment, in itself, can only be considered a desirable option, particularly since so many opportunities (legal and otherwise) are afforded to informal enterprise; Third World tourist-historicity does, however, invoke wider tourism issues of cultural conflict extending beyond our immediate concerns. Cultural tensions specific to tourist-historic development are considered next.

Cultural issues

The complication of social class tensions by the presence of perceived cultural distinctions, as in plural societies, raises parallel, and frequently linked, aspects of the 'whose heritage?' and 'whose benefit?' issues, which present further complications for the development of the tourist-historic city. We have considered the common case of minorities who do not relate to mainstream heritage values; we must further note the phenomenon of adaptive heritage in which immigrant minorities remould pre-existing homes, shops etc. in their own cultural image and thereby present the larger society with the need to modify its heritage perception to include elements which may be wildly discordant with conventional wisdom (and, for that matter, planning policy). This is widespread, particularly well manifested in Toronto (Weier, 1986), and had become a central conservation issue in Canada by 1989. Social tact requires that the promotion of the tourist-historic city in plural societies include reference to both the original and adaptive structures considered to be heritage by the minority concerned; fortunately its value in adding an exotic spice to tourist-historic marketing is usually well recognised in the 'New World', even in South Africa, but the willingness of the long-established European societies to acknowledge and promote the heritage of their immigrant minorities, other than through a few acceptable and 'colourful' elements such as ethnic restaurants, is less clear.

The issue here is again broader than heritage alone; deeper social and cultural problems (cf. Carter, 1989, on Welsh cities) are merely reflected or exacerbated by the tourist-historic city rather than caused by it. A society committed to cultural assimilation of minorities, or their marginalisation, will fail to conserve or project their heritage, while one equally committed to cultural pluralism should translate this commitment into its tourist-historic city.

This issue is likely to be critical over the next few decades in the test-beds of West European cities with substantial established cultural minorities. The extent to which the values of the Indian subcontinent in Bradford, Turkey in the Ruhr, Morocco in the Dutch Randstad, and many others, can be successfully grafted onto the existing heritage, will be interesting to observe. Periodic cultural misunderstandings and expressions of value differences, such as those between Western liberalism and Islamic fundamentalism in early 1989, are cause for some pessimism over the acceptance of the concept of a plural heritage for a plural society.

We have also noted the interesting case of majority alienation from existing tourist-historic development. We must reassert the great importance of achieving a stable *modus vivendi* over this issue for tourist-historic development in many former colonial cities, particularly those of Africa, and in some which have experienced internal colonialism, as in the southern

USA; Williamsburg, Charleston and Savannah have all been reticent, until recently, in relating their heritage to slavery.

Beyond this there is the equally intractable dilemma caused by a total misfit between heritage and population, which results from the vicissitudes of international relations. Slater (1988) has noted the interesting problem of Silesian cities, which have been allowed to decay to the extent that their heritage is unacceptably alien to the Polish culture which now occupies them. Wroclaw (Breslau) was severely damaged during the final German stand in 1945 and is still in process of restoration; more particularly the strongly German towns of Lower Silesia have been neglected or insensitively rebuilt, e.g. Jelenia Gora (Hirschberg). This contrasts sharply, of course, with the enormous efforts to restore the war-damaged cultural heartlands of both Poland (Carter, 1981) and contemporary Germany. In the formerly Germanic world, the relationship between contemporary tourism, historic survival and culturally-compatible reconstruction is very distorted, given the massive war damage but very different economies and political perspectives in West Germany, East Germany and Poland, and the strong survival but again differing perspectives in Switzerland, Austria and Czechoslovakia. A major complicating factor is that Germans provide the most lucrative tourism market for this region and therefore Germanic heritage is saleable; the political ferment at the time of writing portends increasing exploitation of this market for the heritage of, for example, old Prague (Carter, 1981).

The problem of conserving, let alone reconstructing, alien heritage in conquered territory is politically intractable, and clearly detrimental to disinterested tourist-historic development: many historic gems lie neglected or little patronised while their peers elsewhere may suffer tourist inundation. The corollary of this reluctance to restore alien heritage is the projection of nationalism in the restoration of one's own, with the attendant temptation to ignore or underplay the contributions of those elements perceived as alien. Many references have already been made to the potential conflict between heritage used for nationalist purposes and that marketable to tourists. The cities of Africa, the Caribbean and even the 'colonies of settlement' are all confronted to varying degrees by this problem. A less starkly contrasted example is the neglect of Georgian Dublin (Kearns, 1982), or for that matter nineteenth-century Montreal, because they are perceived as alien to the current separatist ideologies of their jurisdictions.

Tourist-historicity may be an instrument of national unity and pride or a vehicle for repressive cultural chauvinism. As we observed in the context of South Africa, the cultural and hence political significance of what is deemed to be urban heritage is profound and its promotion through tourist marketing can only serve to accentuate this fact. This surely merits geographical monitoring. The concepts of cultural disadvantage and heritage dispossession deserve examination if particular social groups are not to be written out of the script of history by a confiscation of their past.

Economic issues

The fact that tourist-historic promotion offers a 'windfall' economic gain is obviously central to the success of the contemporary tourist-historic city and is thus a *sine qua non* of this book. Its positive economic potential is so large and so obvious as to be almost irrefutable. This is not the place to reiterate the economic arguments for tourism but the case for the tourist-historic city in particular rests upon three generally applicable axioms:

1. that heritage tourism capitalises upon the already existing resource of the historic city;
2. that tourism use of the infrastructure and services of the city will incur only marginal cost to existing facilities;
3. that in terms of employment generation a small investment, relative to that required in other economic sectors, will create employment in urban areas with few alternatives.

In addition, cities have become the recipients of incoming tourism flows even without any positive stimulational action. Much urban tourism planning has been a reaction to a situation over which urban governments felt they had little direct control, therefore it was only sensible to profit from what could not be prevented.

However, that is not to argue that any development of the tourist-historic city, to any extent, in every situation, will produce a positive economic balance of costs and benefits. Hewison (1987) alleges that the 'heritage industry' is consuming a growing quantity of resources, is replacing 'real' productive industry and is growing in an inverse relationship with economic growth. These allegations beg too many questions concerning the nature of resources, industry and economic decline to be lightly accepted; in criticism, one need only point to the great environmental value of cultural resources as relatively inexhaustible alternatives to the consumption of material resources, a matter which we will shortly pursue. But the challenge is a salutary check to indiscriminate tourist-historic development.

A strong case could be made for geographical discrimination in where and to what extent a tourist-historic economy should be promoted. Some cities clearly have less economic need than Lowell or Bradford, which face few economic alternatives, and more occasion to fear the distortion of healthy commercial structures by the competition of tourist-city uses, especially for land and labour, to say nothing of the indirect economic costs that may arise through traffic congestion and competitive pressure on the residential environment. Some cities are far better located than others to compete successfully for the ultimately finite 'tourist mark/dollar': those with best market proximity and/or most diverse supporting regional attractions will be most likely to succeed. This is not to dispute the importance of local enterprise in generating tourist interest, particularly to the extent that the tourist-historic 'product' can be differentiated from competition; but the market is not infinitely elastic, and is particularly prone to shifts in consumer preferences. Tourism demand is large and expanding, but it is clear from the variety of cases discussed above that so also is the supply of historic cities to satisfy it.

There is a clear need for geographical analysis of the appropriateness and viability of a tourist-historic economy, relative to the larger economy of the community and the wider tourist appeal of its regional setting.

Environmental issues

There are very significant environmental issues intrinsic to the tourist-historic city that invite close attention in general, but particularly from geography as an established environmental discipline. The problems are well recognised, and include traffic and human congestion, with the short-term blight, refuse etc. and long-term environmental damage caused by both; the Acropolis in Athens and Anne Hathaway's Cottage near Stratford-upon-Avon are famous illustrations of the eroding effect of constant pressure from tourist hands and feet. The British National Trusts' policies to limit tourist flows to their properties are motivated by long-term preservation imperatives (Lloyd, 1989; Tunbridge, 1981). More subtly, the capitalist tendency to over-inflate tourist-historic development, particularly in New World situations, creates not only economic distortions but also untoward morphological change which can erode the historic environmental resource upon which tourist commercial exploitation is based. There is a clear case for geographical discrimination in the development of a tourist-historic identity on environmental as well as economic grounds.

The nature of the tourist-historic city as defined in this book offers solutions to this problem. If heritage does not exist in fixed quantities at predetermined locations but is shaped and managed, then the solutions to the problems of excess demand lie in judicious increase in supply or in better management. It would perhaps be difficult, although not impossible, to build a new Acropolis, but the environmental capacity of the existing site could be increased through management or the creation of alternative interpretive centres.

Notwithstanding environmental problems, tourist-historic development offers very positive environmental potential. Heritage tourism has played an important role in justifying conservation and influencing the general climate of opinion in its favour. In addition cultural attributes have a value as sustainable resources: the more mankind can be persuaded to 'consume' cultural resources in lieu of material goods, the better its chances of sustaining the global environment indefinitely. The cultural resource of the tourist-historic city cannot be taken for granted, but given appropriate management it can be sustained to a degree that many material resources cannot. Far from denigrating its value, therefore, a strong case can be made for the imperative of its development.

Recreational resources in general, derived from the physical and the cultural environment, can be sustained. However, they are under pressure from tourism to the extent that locally they cannot indefinitely meet the demands placed upon them. It is here that the environmental potential of the tourist-historic city is most explicit: with judicious management, the tourist-historic city can relieve tourist pressure on rural and wilderness resources and thereby promote the sustenance of recreational resources overall. Of course Lowell National Historical Park will not directly relieve tourist pressure upon Yellowstone or Yosemite National Parks, but by chain reaction it can make a significant indirect contribution. The environmentalist might suggest that we should be rather less preoccupied with social-justice carping over how, for example, British Victorian urban environments are presented to tourists, and very much more concerned with providing a satisfying tourist experience which will reduce pressure on the Peak District or Dartmoor National Parks. But such an environmentalist argument would also be concerned with moderating the pressure on tourist-historic 'gem' cities such as York. There is surely a compelling case for strategic tourist-historic development to relieve peak pressure on both open land and existing tourist-historic resources, even though the new centres promoted will sometimes form part of a larger tourist circuit including these; the tourist simply cannot be in two places at the same time.

In summary, we suggest that the further development of the tourist-historic city merits interdisciplinary encouragement that is geographically discriminating, as to what it should include (on social and cultural grounds) and where it should occur (on economic and environmental grounds).

Conclusions for conservation

Tourism provides much of the economic rationale and consequently the financial wherewithal for conservation of the built environment, even when due allowance is made for the fact that some jurisdictions are more willing to subsidise conservation activity than are others. There is, however, a price to be paid in using the historic city as a resource for tourism. The tourist city, as we have shown, includes both service facilities and attractions which usually extend beyond the historic city and must be accommodated in competition with other land, labour and capital users. While they are typically supportive of the historic city and its conservation, non-historic tourist attractions could distract attention and business from it and, worse, both services and non-historic attractions can encroach upon and erode a historic fabric which is too restrictive to contain them (Ashworth, 1990a). However, the tourist-historic city may be extremely selective in its use of conserved artefacts, areas and images of the city; an overdependence on tourism may thus create the problem of how to manage the rest of the historic city. More generally, within the historic city the environment may be sufficiently strained by tourism that its liveability, hence long-term conservation, is called into question (Dalibard, 1988).

Clearly an optimum benefit/cost formula must be found, specific in detail to each city, for tourism to constitute an unequivocal net advantage for conservation. On the benefit side, it should consider that primacy of the tourist economy can motivate conservation of heritage otherwise perceived as culturally marginal or alien.

Conclusions for tourism

We witness on an everyday basis the implications of the tourist-historic city for tourism. Travel publicity, though often regionally-based, heavily emphasises urban attractions; these include artistic-cultural performances, retail opportunities and various non-historic elements, but almost invariably focus upon the historic city from which the fundamentally attractive and distinctive sense of place is primarily derived.

We have drawn attention to the opportunity and the need for tourism to be constructively channelled, to maximise this urban orientation selectively, simultaneously easing pressure on open land recreation areas and manipulating the flow to match more equitably the carrying capacity of cities. This would be a very positive contribution to a more sensitive 'alternative tourism', the attainability of which is otherwise in question (Butler, 1990).

In the final analysis, however, historic urban tourism is typically organised either in a network of historic cities or as the centre-piece of regional tourism, and it is usually in the interests of local authorities and tourist associations to continue to promote it in these contexts. Both the concept of the circuit of cities, and the city in its region, require promotion and management which operates at appropriate spatial scales, which may or may not correspond to existing jurisdictional partitions. One example, from many such situations, is the three neighbouring historic cities of Liège (Belgium), Aachen (West Germany) and Maastricht (Netherlands), which although in separate countries are jointly promoted as a single package of related tourism experiences.

While the characteristic geographical 'package' is the nodal city-centred region, there is an interesting tendency to develop regional packages in which several small cities form an integral but less central part of what amounts to a uniform region, in traditional geographical terminology.

Such regional packaging attempts to promote an established geographical identity in which culture plays a central role; it is, in effect, an applied regional geography addressed specifically to tourist marketing. The selling of the distinct identities of European regions from Wales to the Tyrol, or Friesland to Catalonia, as a commodified *'couleur locale'*, is as old as tourism itself. Following a French concept, Heritage Canada is currently promoting the idea of 'ecomuseums', in which such regional identities are sold to tourists with the active participation of the local inhabitants, whose activities and lifestyles are perceived as a vital part of a living museum (Carter, 1988). This approach is already being applied to the Beauce region of Quebec, Lanark County (west of Ottawa) in Ontario and an area of Vancouver Island, BC; a *de facto* British equivalent is the Ironbridge Gorge area in Shropshire (Chapter 9). Some observers will be disturbed by the socio-economic implications of a regional package identified as a museum; the student of the tourist-historic city will not be surprised, however, to see a variety of small cities being marketed within this framework, already implicit in much existing tourist marketing.

Conclusions for the city

At the outset, we asserted that this is first and foremost a book about cities and not a study of either conservation or tourism, or even an account of the rise or significance of a 'tourist-historic society'. Many conclusions about aspects of the city have already been drawn in terms of the implications of the historic and tourist cities respectively, and it remains only to comment on the tourist-historic city as a whole. In particular, the interest of the authors in this topic was aroused by a single but central aspect of the tourist-historic city, namely that it has a critical role to play in the solution of important urban problems.

In the last quarter of the twentieth-century cities throughout the world, to varying extents, are facing serious and fundamental problems arising from structural economic change, social polarisation, increasing difficulties of government, physically deteriorating infrastructure and increasingly unfavourable images as places to live, work or invest. While the tourist-historic city is far from being a magic panacea for all the many contemporary ills of the city wherever these may arise, it does offer one of the few real possibilities for finding distinctly urban solutions to these chronically urban problems.

The tourist-historic city offers the possibility of obtaining a new economic stimulus in the inner areas of cities by using existing urban structures and services, and even turns to advantage the relict features abandoned in the economic collapse of other industries. It offers the chance of generating a new set of amenity values again based principally in the inner city, and upon the essentially urban features of a dense and varied physical form and a varied intermixed set of functions. Finally, it involves focusing attention upon the history, beauty and entertainment qualities of the city. The promotion of these attributes to visitors can also provide a new source of identity and civic pride among residents, city managers and entrepreneurs. In short, the tourist-historic city implies a revaluation of the qualities of cities.

These possibilities are not in themselves solutions to specific urban problems: they do, however, outline the directions in which solutions can be found. The potential benefits are neither automatic nor likely to be endowed universally on all cities. Nor can they be obtained without considerable costs, some skills and a modicum of good fortune. Nevertheless, they offer hope in a situation sometimes bereft of other practical possibilities. The ultimate answer to almost all the objections, difficulties and misgivings about the tourist-historic city that have been aired throughout the book is quite simply 'what other set of activities uses the existing resources of the city, to satisfy such a large and growing market, with such a set of possible benefits?'; in some of the cities discussed above the question 'what else?' could only be answered by 'nothing'.

If the city has a future, and that question has been increasingly posed, then such a future must substantially lie in the satisfaction of those demands of a post-industrial society that can be met by cities. The tourist-historic city fulfils this criterion and therefore is likely to play a central role in securing a viable future for urban civilisation.

References

Abu–Lughod, J. (1980), *Rabat: Urban apartheid in Morocco* (Princeton University Press, Princeton, N.J.).

Advisory Council on Historic Preservation (1979), *The contribution of historic preservation to urban revitalisation* (U.S. Government Printing Office, Washington).

Aldous, T. (1979), *Book of London's villages* (Secker and Warburg, London).

Anderson, J.S. (1987), 'Integration of old and new in historical cities: U.K. examples of planning policies', (Proceedings Conference: International Federation of Housing and Planning, Seville), 105–15.

Ashworth, G.J. (1984a), 'The management of change: conservation policy in Groningen', *Cities*, 605–16.

—— (1984b), 'Urban conservation and urban renewal: partners or opponents in the West European city' in E. Lichtenberger and G. Heinritz (eds), *Crisis in the city* (Steiner Verlag, Wiesbaden).

—— (1985), 'The evaluation of urban tourism resources' in G.J. Ashworth and B. Goodall (eds), *The impact of tourism development on disadvantaged regions* (GIRUG, Groningen), 37–44.

—— (1987), 'Marketing the historic city: the selling of Norwich' in R.C. Riley, (ed.), *Urban conservation: international contrasts* (Department of Geography, Portsmouth Polytechnic), Occasional paper No.7, 51–67.

—— (1988), 'Swords into ploughshares: the peaceful uses of thè artefacts of war' (Proceedings: First Global Conference on Tourism in the Service of Peace, Vancouver).

—— (1989), 'Urban Tourism: an imbalance in attention' in C.P. Cooper (ed.), *Progress in tourism, recreation and hospitality management* (Belhaven Press, London).

—— (1990a), 'Tourism accommodation and the historic city', *Built Environment* 15(2), 92–100.

—— (1990b), 'The historic cities of Groningen: which is sold to whom?' in G.J. Ashworth and B. Goodall (eds), *Marketing tourism places* (Routledge, London).

Ashworth, G.J. and de Haan, T.Z. (1985), 'The tourist-historic city: a model and initial application in Norwich, U.K.', *Field Studies Series 6* (GIRUG, Groningen).

—— (1986), Uses and users of the tourist-historic city: an evolutionary model in Norwich, *Field Studies Series 10* (GIRUG, Groningen/Norwich).

—— (1987), Regionalising the resort system: tourist regions on the Languedoc Coast, *Field Studies Series 12* (GIRUG, Groningen).

Ashworth, G.J. and Jansen–Verbeke, M.C. (1989), 'Functional association and spatial clustering: preconditions for the use of leisure in urban economic revitalisation', *Proceedings* (World Leisure and Recreation Association, Rotterdam).

Ashworth, G.J. and Sijtsma P. (1987), 'Stedelijk conserviering en wonen: een goede combinatie?' *Planologische diskussiedagen Bijdragen*, 33–42, Almere

Ashworth, G.J. and Voogd H. (1986a), 'Marketing van het Europese erfgoed: een ondergewaarderde stedelijk-economisch hulpbron', *Plan*, 9, 28–34.

—— (1986b), 'Naar een aktief stedelijk konserveringsbeleid voor kleinere gemeenten'. *Planologische diskussiedagen Bijdragen*, 1, 11–18.

—— (1988), 'Marketing the city: concepts, processes and Dutch applications', *Town Planning Review*, 59(1), 65–80.

—— (1989), 'Can places be sold for tourism?', in G.J. Ashworth and B. Goodall (eds), *Marketing Tourism Places* (Routledge, London).

Ashworth, G.J., and de Vries, J. (1984), 'Methodes pour délimiter le centre-ville de Colmar', *Sbornik Praci*, 4, 85–111.

Ashworth, G.J. White P.E. and Winchester H., (1988), 'The redlight district of the West European city: a neglected aspect of the urban landscape', *Geoforum*, 19, 201–12.

Aysan, Y. (1982), 'Some aspects of conservation in Turkey', in R.W. Zetter (ed.), *Conservation of buildings in developing countries*, Working paper 60 (Oxford Polytechnic, Oxford).

Barrett, J.A. (1958), *The seaside resort towns of England and Wales*, unpublished Ph.D. (University of London).

Barrineau, P.S. and Sullivan, M.A. (1985), 'Charleston report', *Pace* (Fisher–Harrison, Greensboro, N.C).

Berkers, M., de Boer, G., v. Doorn, G., Glas, R, Jense, H., Koopman, K., Oost, L. and Renkema, J. (1986), 'Norwich; policy in a tourist-historic city', *Field Studies Series 9* (GIRUG, Groningen).

Berry, B.J.L. (1985) 'Islands of renewal in seas of decay' in P. Peterson (ed.), *The new urban reality* (Brookings Institution, Washington).

Binnenstad Amsterdam (1987), *Periodieke rapportage* (Dienst Ruimtelijk Ordening, Amsterdam).

Binney, M. and Hanna, M. (1978), *Preservation Pays* (SAVE, London).

Bond, C.C.J. (1961), *City on the Ottawa* (Queen's Printer, Ottawa).

Bonnain–Moerdijk, R. (1975), 'L'espace gastronomique', *L'espace Géographique*, 4 (2), 113–26.

Boorstin, D.J. (1963), *The image or what happened to the American dream*, (Penguin, Harmondsworth).

—— (1964), *The Image: a guide to pseudo-events in America* (Harper Row, New York).

Boston Redevelopment Authority (1984), *Harborpark: a framework for planning discussion* (Boston Redevelopment Authority, Boston).

Bradbeer, J.B. and Moon G. (1987), 'Defence town in crisis: the paradox of the tourism strategy', in M. Bateman and R.C. Riley (eds), *Geography of defence* (Croom Helm, London).

Brady, P. (1978), *The city of Boston: history, planning and development* (Boston Redevelopment Authority, Boston).

Brown, R. (1986), 'More than a business', *Canadian Heritage*, 12 (4), 15–20.

Burke, G. (1976), *Townscapes* (Penguin, Harmondsworth).

Burtenshaw, D., Bateman, M. and Ashworth, G.J. (1981), *The City in West Europe* (Wiley, Chichester).

Busson, A. and Evrard, Y. (1987), *Portraits économiques de la culture* (Notes et études documentaires 4846, Paris).

Butler, R.W. (1980), 'The concept of a tourist area cycle of evolution and implications for management', *Canadian Geographer*, 24, 5–12.

Butler, R.W., 1990, Alternative tourism: pious hope or Trojan horse?, *Journal of Travel Research*.

Carpenter, E.K. (1977), 'Savannah waterfront', *Urban Design*, 8 (4), 40–1.

Carter, F.W. (1972), *Dubrovnik (Ragusa)—a classic city state* (Seminar Press, London/New York).

—— (1981), *Conservation problems of historic cities in Eastern Europe*, Occasional Paper 39 (Department of Geography, University College, London).

Carter, H. (1965), *The towns of Wales: a study in urban geography* (University of Wales Press, Cardiff).

—— (1989), 'Whose city? A view from the periphery', *Transactions* (Institute of British Geographers), 14, 4–23.

Carter, K. (1988), 'Visiting the valley', *Canadian Heritage*, 14(3), 24.

Castells, M. (1978), *City, class and power* (Macmillan, London).

Cervellati, P. and Scannarini, R. (1973), *Bologna; politica e metodologia del restaurone i centro storico* (Bologna).

Charleston County, Park, Recreation and Tourist Commission (1978), *Tourism impact and management study: Charleston, South Carolina* (Barton–Aschman Associates, Washington).

Charleston Gateway, Inc. (1987), *Gateway to historic Charleston* (Charleston) May.

Chaudefaud, M. (1981), *Lourdes: un pèlerinage, une ville* (Edisud, Aix-en-Provence).

Church, A. (1988), 'Demand-led planning, the inner-city crisis and the labour market: London Docklands evaluated' in B.S. Hoyle, D.A. Pinder and M.S. Husain (eds), *Revitalising the waterfront: international dimensions of dockland redevelopment* (Belhaven, London).

City of Norwich (1969), *Conservation in Norwich* (City Planning Department, Norwich).

City of Pietermaritzburg (1986), *Pietermaritzburg 2000* (Pietermaritzburg).

Clary, D. (1977), *La façade littoral de Paris: le tourism sur la côte Normande. Étude géographique* (Ed. Ophrys, Paris).

Clawson, M. and Knetch, J.L. (1966), *Economics of outdoor recreation* (John Hopkins Press, Baltimore).

Cohen, E. (1979a), 'A phenomenology of tourist experiences', *Sociology*, 13, 179–201.

—— (1979b), 'Rethinking the sociology of tourism', *Annals of Tourism Research*, 6, 18–35.

Cohen, S.B. (1977), *Jerusalem, bridging the four walls: a geographical perspective* (Herzl, New York).

Coopersmith, P. (1976), *Heritage by design* (Ministry of State for Urban Affairs, MacMillan of Canada, Ottawa).

Court, Y. (1987), 'Planning urban conservation: the case of Ribe, Denmark' in R.C. Riley (ed.), *Urban conservation: international contrasts* (Department of Geography, Portsmouth Polytechnic, Portsmouth).

Crush, J. (1983), 'Third world tourism', *Area*, 15(3), 183–4.

Dale, A. (1982), *Historical preservation in foreign countries* (ICOMOS).

Dalibard, J. (1988), 'Can tourist towns be livable?' *Canadian Heritage*, 14(3), 3–4.

—— (1988/9), 'In old Quebec: a love story in four acts', *Canadian Heritage*, 14(4), 27.

Daniel, I., and Brusse, R. (eds) (1977), *Pietermaritzburg* (Tatham Art Gallery and Natal Provincial Institute of Architects, Pietermaritzburg).

Datel, R.E. (1985), 'Preservation and a sense of orientation for American cities', *Geographical Review*, 75, 125–41.

—— (1990), 'Southern regionalism and historic preservation in Charleston, South Carolina 1920–40', *Journal of Historical Geography* (forthcoming).

Davidson–Peterson Associates, Inc. (1988), *1987 market study and analysis for the Savannah Area Convention and Visitors Bureau* (Savannah).

Davies, G. (1987), 'Potted history', *Marxism Today*, 47.

Defert, P. (1966), *La localisation touristique, problèmes théoretique et practique* (Berne).

Department of Planning and Urban Development (1987), City of Charleston, S.C (Charleston).

Dilley, R.S. (1986), 'Tourist brochures and tourist images', *Canadian Geographer*, 30, 59–65.

Dobby, A. (1978), *Conservation and planning* (Hutchinson, London).

Duchesne, V. (1975) 'Quebec: no precise conservation policy', *Heritage Canada*, 1(6), 22.

Dumas, D. (1982), Le commerce de détail dans une grande station touristique balnéaire Espagnole: Benidorm', *Annales de Géographie*, 506, 480–9.

Dunning, J.H. and Norman, G. (1987), 'Locational choice of offices of international companies', *Environment and Planning*, A (19), 613–31.

English Tourist Board (1981), *Planning for tourism in England* (London).

Fay, S. and Knightly, P. (1976), *The death of Venice* (Andre Deutsch, London).

Firey, W. (1945), 'Sentiment and symbolism as ecological variables', *American Sociological Review*, 10, 40–8.

Fleming, R.L. (1981) 'Recapturing history: a plan for gritty cities', *Landscape*, 25 (1), 20–7.

Ford, L.R. (1978), 'Continuity and change in historic cities: Bath, Chester and Norwich, *Geographical Review*, 68(3), 253–73.

—— (1979), 'Urban preservation and the geography of the city in the U.S.A.', *Progress in Human Geography*, 211–38.

—— (1985), 'Urban morphology and preservation in Spain', *Geographical Review*, 75, 265–99.

—— (1986), 'The enduring romantic cottage: rethinking historic preservation', *Landscape*, 29 (2), 17–23.

Freeman, M. (1989), 'Urban impacts of current retailing trends', *Newsletter* (Urban Geography Study Group, Institute of British Geographers),[1]

Galt, G. (1976), 'Heritage and tourism', *Heritage Canada*, 2 (2), 18–21.

Garay, M. (1980), 'Le Tourisme culturel en France', *Notes et études documentaires* (Direction de documentation française, Paris).

Gazillo, S. (1981), 'The evolution of restaurants and bars in Vieux Québec since 1900', *Cahiers de Géographie du Québec*, 25 (64), 101–18.

Gemeente Groningen (1988), *Aanpak voor het Binnenstad* (Ruimtelijk Ordening, Groningen).

Gilmore, A. (1984), 'The Rideau Area Project: changing the face of the nation's capital', *Habitat*, 27 (2), 31–7.

Goldberg, M.A. and Mercer, J. (1986), *The myth of the North American city* (University of British Columbia Press, Vancouver).

Goodey, B. and Opher, P. (1982), 'Conservation—the necessary myth' in R. Zetter (ed.) *Conservation of buildings in developing countries*, Working paper 60 (Department of Town Planning, Oxford Polytechnic, Oxford).

Greater London Council (1978), *Tourism: a paper for discussion* (London).

Groote, P. de (1987), *De Belgische Hotelsector: een economisch-geografische analyse* (Universitaire Pers, Leuven).

Gutirrez, R.S. (1977), 'Localizacion actual de la hosteleria Madrilena', *Bol. de la Real Sociadad Geografica*, 2, 347–57.

Haan, T.Z. de (1982), 'Kuuroord: een onderzoek naar groei en funktie van de Kurort Bad Bevensen', *Field Studies Series 5* (GIRUG, Groningen).

Haan, T.Z. de and Ashworth, G.J. (1985a), 'Residents reactions to tourism in Norwich and Great Yarmouth', *Onderzoekverslagen 4* (GIRUG, Groningen).

—— (1985b), 'Modelling the seaside resort: Great Yarmouth (UK)', *Field Studies 7* (GIRUG, Groningen).

Hall, T. (1986), *Planung Europaischer Haupstaedte* (Almquist and Wiksell, Stockholm).

Hardy, D. (1988), 'Historical geography and heritage studies', *Area*, 20, 333–8.

Haswell, R.F. (1984), *An historic townscapes conservation scheme for Natal*, Natal Town and Regional Planning Commission Report, Vol. 61, (Pietermaritzburg).

Heritage Canada (1985), 'The malling of Canada', *Canadian Heritage*, 11 (3), 52.

Heritage Canada (1987), 'Founders Square project retains historic streetscape', *Canadian Heritage*, 13 (2), 12.

Hewison, R. (1987), *The heritage industry: Britain in a climate of decline* (Methuen, London).

Hindley, G. (1983), *Tourists, travellers and pilgrims* (Hutchinson, London).

Historic Savannah Foundation (1988), *Historic District Action Plan* (Savannah).

Holzner, L. (1967), 'World regions in urban geography', *Annals of Association of American Geographers*, 57, 704–12.

Horne, D. (1984), *The great museum: the re-presentation of history* (Pluto Press, London).

Hosmer, C.B. (1981), *Preservation comes of age: from Williamsburg to the National Trust 1926–1949* (University Press of Virginia/National Trust for Historic Preservation, Charlottesville, Va.).

Hoyle, B.S., Pinder, D.A. and Husain, M.S. (eds), (1988), *Revitalising the waterfront: international dimensions of dockland redevelopment* (Belhaven, London).

Husbands, W.C. (1986), 'Leisure activity resources and activity space formation in periphery resorts: the response of tourists and residents in Barbados', *Canadian Geographer*, 30 (3), 243–9.

Jansen, A.C.M. (1989), 'Fun shopping as a geographical notion or the attitudes of the inner city of Amsterdam as a shopping area', *Tijdschrift voor Economische en Sociale Geografie*, 80 (3), 171–83.

Jansen–Verbeke, M.C. (1986), 'Inner city tourism: resources, tourists, promoters', *Annals of Tourism Research*, 13, 79–100.

—— (1988), 'Leisure, recreation and tourism in inner cities: explorative case studies', *Netherlands Geographical Studies*, 58 (Utrecht/Nijmegen).

—— (1990), 'Fun shopping: a challenge to planning' in G. J. Ashworth and B. Goodall (eds), *Marketing tourism places* (Routledge, London).

Jones, A.R. (1988), *A strategy for tourism marketing and development* (Pietermaritzburg Publicity Association, Pietermaritzburg).

Jones, K.G. (1984), *Specialty retailing in the inner city: a geographic perspective* (York University Press, Toronto).

Kain, R. (1975), 'Urban conservation in France', *Town and Country Planning Review*, 43, 428–33.

Kain, R. (1981), *Planning for conservation: an international perspective* (Mansell, London).

Kain, R. (1984), 'Conservations du patrimoine architectural et des villes historiques en Grande Bretagne', *Norois*, 31 (123), 379–92.

Kamerling, J. (ed.) (1987), *Burger en Overheid in de Monumentenzorg* (Heemschut, Amsterdam).

Karabatsos, L.T. (1980), 'Lowell reborn', *National Parks and Conservation Magazine*, January.

Kay, F.G., and Smout, M. (1977), *Salisbury: a geographical survey of the capital of Rhodesia* (Hodder, London).

Kearns, K.C. (1982), 'Preservation and transformation of Georgian Dublin', *Geographical Review*, 72, 270–90.

Kotler, P. (1972), 'A generic concept of marketing', *Journal of Marketing*, 10–15.

—— (1975), *Marketing for non-profit organisations* (Prentice Hall, Englewood Cliffs).

—— (1987), *Principles of marketing* (Prentice Hall, Englewood Cliffs).

Kosters, M. (1981), *Focus op Toerisme* (VUGA, Amsterdam).

Kuhn, W. (1979), 'Geschaftsstrassen als Freizeitsraum', *Muenchner geographie*, Hefte 42 (Regensburg).

Labasse, J. (1984), Les congrès activités tertiaire de villes privilèges *Annales de Géographie*, 520, 687–703.

Lavery, P. (ed.) (1971) *Recreational geography* (David and Charles, Newton Abbott).

Law, C. (1988), 'Congress tourism', *Built Environment*, 13(2), 85–95.

Lawson, F. and Baud–Bovy, M. (1977), *Tourism and recreational development* (Architectural Press, London).

Leahy, G.W. (1986/7), 'Quebec: our city of world heritage renown', *Canadian Geographic*, 106, 8–21.

Lemoine, R. (1987), *Les promoteurs de la protection du patrimoine, Cap-aux-diamants*, édition spéciale, Québec fleuron du patrimoine mondial, 53–6.

Lengkeek, J. (1981), 'Het stedelijk recreatiemilieu en de stadsvernieuwing', *Recreatie*, 19, 2–8.

Ley, D. (1986), 'Alternative explanations for inner city gentrification: a Canadian assessment', *Annals Association of American Geographers*, 76, 521–35.

—— (1988), 'Social upgrading in six Canadian inner cities', *Canadian Geographer*, 32 (1), 31–45.

Ley, D and Olds, K. (1988), 'Landscape as spectacle: world's fairs and the culture of heroic consumption', *Environment and Planning*, D (6), 191–212.

Lindgren, E. (1984), 'Mixed use: rebuilding a waterfront', *Canadian Architect*, June, 20–9.

Lipton, S.G. (1977), 'Evidence of central city revival', *Journal of the American Institute of Planners*, 43 (2), 136.

Lloyd, N. (1989), 'When the houses are put to bed', *National Trust Magazine* 58, 25–7.

Lowenthal, D. (1975), 'Past time, present time: landscapes and meaning', *Geographical Review*, 65, 1–36.

—— (1985), *The past is a foreign country* Cambridge University Press, Cambridge

Lowenthal, D. and Binney, M. (1981), *Our past before us. Why do we save it?* (Temple Smith, London).

Lozato, J.P. (1985), *Géographie du tourisme* (Masson, Paris).

Lumley, R. (ed.) (1988), *The museum time-machine* (Routledge, London).

Lundgren, J.O.J. (1974), 'On access to recreational lands in dynamic metropolitan hinterlands', *Tourist Review*, 29 (4), 124–31.

Lynch, K. (1960), *Image of the city* (M.I.T. Press, Cambridge, Mass.)

MacCannell, D. (1973), 'Staged authenticity', *American Journal of Sociology*, 79 (3), 589–603.

—— (1976), *The tourist: a new theory of the leisure class* (Schocken Books, New York).

McGinn, F. (1986), 'Ersatz place', *Canadian Heritage*, 12 (1), 25–9.

McQuillan, D.A. (1985), *Urban redevelopment and conservation in China* (Dept. of Geography, University of Toronto, Discussion Paper 32), 33pp.

McQuillan, D.A. and Laurier, R. (1984), 'Urban upgrading and historic presentation: an integrated development plan for Zanzibar's old stone town', *Habitat International*, 8, 2, 43–59.

MacRae, P. (1988/9), 'In old Quebec: on the Plains of Abraham', *Canadian Heritage*, 14(4), 29.

Matthew, R., Reid, J. and Lindsay, M. (eds) (1972), *The Conservation of Georgian Edinburgh* (Scottish Civic Trust, University of Edinburgh Press, Edinburgh).

Mathieson, A. and Wall, G. (1982), *Tourism: economic, physical and social impacts* (Longman, London).

Mendel, D. (1988/9), 'In old Quebec: our lady of the snows', *Canadian Heritage*, 14 (4), 22–6.

Mennell, S. (1976), *Cultural policy in towns* (Council of Europe, Strasbourg).

Ministry of Citizenship and Culture, Ontario (1987), *Heritage: giving our past a future* (Ministry of Culture/Ontario Heritage Foundation, Toronto).

Miossec, J.M. (1976), 'Une modèle de l'espace touristique', *L'Espace géographique*, 6, 41–8.

Moindrot, C. (1984), 'La conservation du patrimoine nationale', *Norois*, 31 (124), 609–15.

Moore, C. (1984/5), 'The treasures of Louisbourg', *Canadian Heritage*, 10 (5), 18–23.

Moreschi, E.C. (1985), 'Le Tourisme à Padove' in F. Vetter (ed.), *Big city tourism* (Reimer Verlag, Berlin).

Murphy, R.E., Vance J.E. and Epstein, B.J. (1955), 'Internal structure of the CBD', *Economic Geography*, 31, 21–46.

Nader, G. (1976), *Cities of Canada: profiles of fifteen metropolitan centres*, Vol.2 (MacMillan of Canada, Toronto).

Naeyer, A. de (1975), *Monumentenzorg* (De Nederlandsche Boekhandel, Antwerp).

Nairn, I. (1958), *Outrage* Architectural Press, London.

N.B.T. (1987), *Toerism produkt, Nederland* (National Bureau voor Toerism, The Hague).

National Commissie Monumentenzorg (1989), *Wonen met monumenten* (The Hague).

National Trust (1988), 'Ironbridge Gorge', *National Trust Magazine*, 54, 27.

Nelissen, N.J.M (1975), *Monument en Samenleving* (Council of European Communities, Maastricht).

Newcomb, R.M. (1979), *Planning the Past* (Dawson, Folkestone).

—— (1983), 'A business and a charity: conservation in transition', *Geographical Papers*, 83 (Department of Geography, University of Reading).

Newton, M. (1980), 'The search for heritage in Ottawa's Lower Town', *Urban History Review*, 9 (2), 21–37.

NIROV (1981), *Zorgen om Monumenten* (Werkgroep Monumentenzorg, The Hague).

—— (1986), *Ruimtelijk Ordening en Monumentenzorg* (Staatsuitgeverij, The Hague).

Page, S. (1989), 'IGU Commission on Tourism and Leisure', *Area*, 1, 98–9.

Pearce, D.G. (1978), 'Form and function of French resorts', *Annals of Tourism Research*, 5, 142–56.

—— (1987a), 'Motel location and choice in Christchurch', *New Zealand Geographer* 43 (1), 10–17.

—— (1987b), *Tourism today* (Longmans, London).

Pietermaritzburg Publicity Association (1988), *Heritage Herald*, April, 1–3.

Pigram, J.J. (1977), 'Beach resort morphology', *Habitat International*, 2, 525–41.

Pred, A. (1984), 'Place as a historically contingent process: structuration and the time geography of becoming places', *Annals of American Association of Geographers*, 74 (2), 279–97.

Proudfoot, P.R. (1982), 'Development of Botany Bay as a second seaport for Sydney', *Australian Geographer*, 15 (3), 159–69.

Quasten, H. and Soyez, D. (1987), 'Zur Pflege des industriekulturellen Erbes im Saar-Lor-Lux Raum. Problematik und Perspektiven' in W. Bruecher, and

P.R. Franke (eds), *Probleme von Grenzregionen: das Beispiel Saar-Lor-Lux Raum, Beitraege zum Forschungsschwerpunkt der Philosophischen Fakultaet* (Universitaet des Saarlandes).

Riley, R.C. (1987), Urban conservation or private museum? Historic architecture in Portsmouth Dockyard, in R.C. Riley, (ed.), *Urban conservation: international contrasts* (Portsmouth Polytechnic, Department of Geography), Occasional Paper 7, 4–7.

Riley, R.C. and Shurmer-Smith, J.L. (1988), 'Global imperatives, local forces and waterfront redevelopment' in B.S. Hoyle, D.A. Pinder and M.S. Husain (eds), *Revitalising the waterfront: international dimensions of dockland redevelopment* (Belhaven, London).

Ritter, W. (1985), 'Hotel location in big cities' in F. Vetter (ed.), *Big city tourism* (Reimer Verlag, Berlin).

Rosenberg, M.W. (1984), 'Physician's location behaviour in metropolitan Toronto, *Canadian Geographer*, 28(2), 156–170.

Ross, K. (1984), 'Where the river has walls', *Canadian Heritage*, 10(3), 18–23.

Roussel, F.X. (1987), 'Urban conservation and renovation in Nancy', *Proceedings* (International Federation of Housing and Planning, Managing the Historic City, Seville).

Satoh, S. (1986), 'Innovations in town planning policies and methods in old Japanese castle towns since the Meiji restoration (1968)', *Proceedings* (World Planning and Housing Conference, Adelaide).

Schelleris, J. (1978), 'Kosten en baten van monumentenzorg', *Bouw*, 12, 364–5.

Segers, Y. (1989), 'Fes: de parel van Marokko: een verslag van een reddingsoperatie', *Eurostad*, 2(11), 5–12.

Sim, D. (1982), *Change in the city centre* (Gower, Aldershot).

Skovgaard, J. (1979), 'Conservation planning in Denmark', *Urban Studies*, 519–39.

Slater, T.R. (1988), 'Lower Silesia', *Urban Morphology Newsletter* (Urban Morphology Research Group, University of Birmingham), 3,5.

Slater, T.R. and Shaw, G. (1988) 'Historical geography and conservation planning in British towns', in D. Denecke and G. Shaw (eds) *Urban historical geography: progress in Britain and Germany* (Cambridge University Press, Cambridge).

Smith, S.L.H. (1983), 'Restaurants and dining out: a geography of a tourism business', *Annals of Tourism Research*, 10, 515–49.

Snedcof, H. (1985), 'Cultural facilities in multi-use developments, *Urban Land*, (Washington).

Solesbury, W. (1975), *Tourism and Conservation in historic towns* (ECE Symposium, Planning and Development in the Tourism Industry).

Soyez, D. (1986), 'Industrietourismus', *Erdkunde*, 40, 105–11.

Squire, S.J. (1988), *Tourist development and a literary landscape: L.M. Montgomery's Prince Edward Island* (Department of Geography, Carleton University, Ottawa), Discussion paper 6.

Stallibrass, C. (1980), 'Seaside resorts and the holiday accommodation industry: a case study of Scarborough', *Progress in planning*, 13 (3).

Stansfield, C.A. and Rickert, E.J (1970), 'The recreational business district', *Journal of Leisure Research*, 2(4), 213–25.

Stough, R.R. (1988), *A comparative analysis of visitors: Charleston area, South Carolina. 1983 and 1987* (Charleston Trident Convention and Visitors Bureau, Charleston).

Sutcliffe, A. (1970), *The autumn of Central Paris* (Arnold, London).

Sydney Cove Redevelopment Authority (1984), *The Rocks* (Sydney).

—— (1989), *Annual report* (Sydney).

Taafe, E.J., Morrill, R.L. and Gould, P.R. (1963), 'Transport expansion in underdeveloped countries', *Geographical Review*, 53, 503–29.

Taylor, J.H. (1986), *Ottawa: an illustrated history* (James Lorimer/Canadian Museum of Civilisation, Toronto).

—— (1989), 'City form and capital culture: remaking Ottawa', *Planning perspectives*, 4, 79–105.

Taylor, V. (1975), 'The recreational business district: a component of the East London urban morphology', *South African Geographer*, 2, 139–44.

Tournier, R.E. (1980), 'Historic preservation as a force in urban change; Charleston' in S.B. Laska and D. Spain, (eds), *Back to the City* (Pergamon, New York), 173–86.

Tunbridge, J.E. (1981), 'Conservation trusts as geographic agents: their impact upon landscape, townscape and land use, *Transactions* (Institute of British Geographers, N.S.), 6, 103–25.

—— (1984), 'Whose heritage to conserve? Cross-cultural reflections upon political dominance and urban heritage conservation', *Canadian Geographer*, 28, 171–80.

—— (1986a), 'Warehouse functions, insurance plans and inner-city revitalisation', *Canadian Geographer*, 30(2), 146–54.

—— (1986b), 'Clarence Street, Ottawa: contemporary change in an inner-city "zone of discard"', *Urban History Review*, 14(3), 247–57.

—— (1987a), *Of heritage and many other things: merchants' location decisions in Ottawa's Lower Town West* (Carleton University, Department of Geography), Discussion paper 5.

—— (1987b), 'Conserving the naval heritage: its role in the revitalisation of North American urban waterfronts' in R.C. Riley (ed.), *Urban conservation: international contrasts* (Department of Geography, Portsmouth Polytechnic), Occasional Paper 7, 14–24.

—— (1988), 'Policy convergence on the waterfront? A comparative assessment of North American revitalisation strategies' in B.S. Hoyle, D.A. Pinder and M.S. Husain (eds), *Revitalising the waterfront: international dimensions of dockland redevelopment* (Belhaven, London).

—— (1989), 'Geography, historical geography and heritage studies: some further reflections', *Area*, 21 (3), 316–7.

Turnbull, C.M. (1977), *A history of Singapore 1819–1975* (Oxford University Press, Oxford).

Turner, L.J. and Ash, J. (1976), *The Golden Horde: international tourism and the pleasure periphery* (Constable, London).

Turner, M., 1988, *The Jerusalem papers*, 1/2 Jerusalem Centre for Planning in Historic cities, Jerusalem.

Tuynte, J.C.M. ten and Dietvorst, A.G.J. (1988), *Musea anders bekeken: vier Nijmegse musea bezien naar uitstralingseffecten en complexvorming* (K.U. Nijmegen).

Urban Morphology Research Group (1988), *Urban Morphology Newsletter* (University of Birmingham, Birmingham), Autumn 3,4.

Vance, J.E (1977), *This scene of man: the role and structure of the city in the geography of Western civilisation* (Harper and Row, New York).

Vetter, F. (ed.), (1985) *Big city tourism*, Reimer Verlag, Berlin.

Ville de Québec (1988), *Une ville sur mesure: plan directeur d'aménagment et de développement de la ville de Québec*, (Quebec City).

Vlaeminck, S. (1987), Holland–Vlaanderen, 5:1; Zorg om monumentenzorg. *Europolis*, 5, 15–21.

Vries–Reilingh, H.D. de (1968), 'Het monumentkarakter van onze binnenstad' in W.F. Heinemeyer, *Het centrum van Amsterdam* (Amsterdam).

VVV Amsterdam (1987), *Middelangetermijn plan Toeristmarkt beleid 1987–1990* (Amsterdam).

VVV Delft (1970), *Vreemdelingenverkeer in Delft* (Delft).

Walker, J. (1988/9), 'In old Quebec: cockscombs on the tables', *Canadian Heritage*, 14 (4), 30–2.

Wall, G. and Sinnott, J. (1980), 'Urban recreational and cultural facilities', *Canadian Geographer*, 24, 50–9.

Ward, P. (ed.) (1968), *Conservation and development in historic towns and cities* (Oriel Press, Newcastle).

Weier, E. (1986), 'Whose house is home?', *Canadian Heritage*, 12 (3), 29–35.

Weiler, J. (1984), 'Reusing our working past for recreation and tourism', *Recreation Canada*, 42(2), 136–41.

Werkgroep Jongere Bouwkunst (1983), *Jongere bouwkunst en monumentenzorg in Groningen* (Gemeente Groningen, Groningen).

Werner, E. (1974), 'Die Fremdenverkehrsgebiete des Westlichen Hampshire–Beckens', *Regensburg Geografisches Schriften*, 4.

West, B. (1988), 'The making of the English working past: a critical view of the Ironbridge Gorge Museum' in R. Lumley (ed.), *The museum time-machine* (Routledge, London).

Western, J. (1981), *Outcast Cape Town* (University of Minnesota Press, Minneapolis).

—— (1985), 'Undoing the colonial city?', *Geographical Review*, 75, 335–57.

Whitt, J.A (1987), 'Mozart in the metropolis', *Urban Affairs, Quarterly*, 15–36.

Williams, N., Kellogg, E.H. and Gilbert, F.B. (1983), *Readings in historic preservation: Why, what, how?* (Rutgers University Centre for Urban Policy Research, New Jersey).

Wills, T.M., Haswell, R.F. and Davies, D.H. (1987), 'The probable consequences of the repeal of the Group Areas Act for Pietermaritzburg', *Pietermaritzburg 2000* (City of Pietermaritzburg/Department of Geography, University of Natal, Pietermaritzburg).

Windle, R. (1981), *Records of the Corporation 1966–1974* (Portsmouth City Council, Portsmouth).

Wright, P. (1985), *On living in an old country* (Routledge, London).

Young, G. (1973), *Tourism: blessing or blight* (Penguin, Harmondsworth).

—— (1977), *Conservation scene* (Penguin, Harmondsworth).

Yu Qingkang (1987), 'Urban conservation and development in Peoples Republic of China', *Proceedings* (International Federation of Housing and Planning, Managing the Historic City, Seville).

Zetter, R. (ed.) (1982), 'Conservation of buildings in developing countries', *Working Paper 60* (Department of Town Plannning, Oxford Polytechnic, Oxford).

Zywiecka, D. (1985), 'Historical values in tourism' in F. Vetter (ed.), *Big city tourism* (Reiner Verlag, Berlin).

Subject Index

Place index